RULES FOR THE WORLD

RULES FOR THE WORLD

International Organizations in Global Politics

Michael Barnett
Martha Finnemore

CORNELL UNIVERSITY PRESS

ATLANTIC®
PUBLISHERS & DISTRIBUTORS

ATLANTIC®
PUBLISHERS & DISTRIBUTORS
7/22, Ansari Road, Darya Ganj
New Delhi – 110 002
Tel: 2327 3880, 2327 5880, 2328 0451
Fax: 91-11-2328 5873
E-mail: info@atlanticbooks.com
Website: www.atlanticbooks.com

Published in India by
Atlantic Publishers and Distributors, New Delhi
in association with
Cornell University Press
Sage House, 512 East State Street,
Ithaca, New York 14850

First published 2004 by Cornell University Press
First Indian Reprint 2006

ISBN 81-269-0568-9

Printed in India by
Nice Printing Press, Delhi

CONTENTS

PREFACE

This book grew out of a series of conversations that began in 1994 when one of us (Barnett) was working at the UN and the other (Finnemore) was doing research on the World Bank. On occasion we would get together and exchange observations, almost always concluding our conversations with humorous musings about why our graduate school training had not prepared us for what international organizations were *really* like. These quips, in fact, expressed a real frustration on our part: we were seeing things on the ground in these organizations that were rarely discussed in the academic literature.

Our situation reflected the state of American scholarship at that time. Both of us received our graduate training in the 1980s, a time when the Cold War defined international politics and Kenneth Waltz's neorealism dominated international relations theory. Our home departments offered no courses on international organizations, which made them representative of a discipline that had lost interest in these organizations. International relations, in the 1980s, had become the study of states and what states did. All our theories were theories of states. Other actors, such as international organizations, were understood to be byproducts of state action, if, indeed, they were considered at all.

Perhaps more surprising, though, was that scholars interested in international governance also slighted the study of international organizations. By the late 1970s, the study of international organizations had been eclipsed by the study of interdependence and the emergent literature on international regimes. These students of international governance showed that there was more to international life than Great Power realpolitik and that enduring cooperation was possible with a little help from international institutions. These were important and enduring insights, but scholars couched their arguments within a statist framework borrowed from neorealists that gave short shrift to international organizations as independent actors. These scholars were interested in the "principles, norms, rules, and decision-making procedures" that governed *state* action. Treated as parts of regimes, international organizations were only arenas through which others, mostly states, acted. They were not actors in their own right and had no independent ontological status. For these scholars, the interesting theoretical question was why states would cooperate to set up an international organization in the first place. What these organizations did after creation, and whether their behavior conformed to what states wanted, apparently provoked very little curiosity. This shared disinterest among both neorealists and regimes scholars conspired to make international organizations, as Susan Strange wryly observed, a "great yawn."[1]

To understand how international organizations work, we found ourselves turning to theories of organization rather than theories of international politics. We were not the first to do this. Many international relations scholars have used microeconomic theories of organization to understand international cooperation generally and, occasionally, international organizations. In this view, international organizations are welfare-improving solutions to problems of incomplete information and high transaction costs. However, these approaches have at least two serious shortcomings, one theoretical and the other normative.[2] Theoretically, these approaches are better at explaining why organizations exist than what they do after creation. They provide no substantive preferences, capabilities, or character for international organizations. To explain the behavior of international organizations, we needed different tools, and we found them in sociology. Sociologists have developed a rich body of theory on organizations and bureaucracies. In their arguments, bureaucracy is a distinctive social form with its own internal logic that generates certain behavioral tendencies; we apply these insights to the international realm. This approach helped us solve some important problems. It provided a basis for treating international organizations as ontologically independent actors and for theorizing about their nature and behavioral proclivities. We found that the "logic of bureaucracy" offered distinctive claims regarding the sources of IO autonomy, the nature and effects of their power, the reasons international organizations fail, and the ways they evolve and expand. By thinking about international organizations as social creatures, we could better understand their authority, their power, their goals, and their behavior.

This approach also helped us address some normative concerns. Most scholarly approaches treat international organizations as a good thing.

There is a normative bias in favor of international organizations. They help states cooperate. They help peoples overcome oppressive governments. They spread good norms. They articulate a spirit of progress and enlightenment. This emphasis on the good things international organizations do is not simply a selection bias but also reflects a theoretical disposition. Microeconomic and liberal-inspired theories of international organizations almost always cast these organizations in a positive role. Within these microeconomic theories, no international organization should exist that is not serving valued goals since, by theoretical axiom, states will abandon any such organization that does not perform. Within liberal theories, international organizations have been viewed not only as facilitators of cooperation but also as carriers of progress, the embodiments of triumphant democracy and purveyors of liberal values, including human rights, democracy, and the rule of law.

If, however, we start from the premise that international organizations are bureaucracies and will behave as such, we generate different expectations. We see a world in which international organizations can act as good servants but can also produce undesirable and self-defeating outcomes. Indeed, the celebration of bureaucracy at the international level is unusual. Bureaucracy is generally derided in social life—it is notorious for red tape, stupidity, unresponsive behavior. Our approach allows us to identify a range of behaviors, which might be good or bad.

International bureaucracies are double-edged swords, and this feature has important historical analogues that we keep in mind. When Max Weber was formulating his seminal statements about bureaucracy and its potential as an "iron cage," he was wrestling on the national level with the same phenomenon that intrigues us now at the international level. Bureaucracies were proliferating in the Prussian state of the late nineteenth century in much the same way that formal organizations are spreading at the international level today. His questions were similar to ours. He wanted to know both why this was happening and what its implications were for social and political life. Weber's answers to these questions flow from his analysis of what, exactly, bureaucracies *are* as a social form, how they are supported by Western culture, and what work they do in the modern world. So do ours.

In this book we attempt to construct an approach to the study of international organizations. We are not the first to do so, but we are hardly in a crowded field. There has been an important revival of interest in international organizations, but remarkably little empirical research gets inside these organizations to see how they work. In many respects, we see ourselves involved in a process not unlike the advent of research on the state. Pluralist and class views of the state that dominated scholarship in the 1960s and 1970s treated it as a passive structure in which dominant classes ruled or societal interests competed, much the way realist and regimes scholars have treated international organizations. These views failed to examine the state itself in any meaningful way. Beginning in the early 1980s an impressive literature on the relative autonomy of the state developed. We write, in many respects, at a similar moment in scholarship on international organizations. Scholars are only now beginning to treat seriously the internal workings of these organizations and ask hard questions about how to approach them analytically.

It has taken us a long time to get here. We began exchanging views in 1994 and wrote our first statement in 1997. That argument formed the basis of an article in *International Organization.* We knew that there was much more to do, and were lucky to secure funding from the MacArthur Foundation, the Smith Richardson Foundation, the United States Institute of Peace, the University of Wisconsin Alumni Research Foundation, and the George Washington University Facilitating Fund. Although we expected to finish by the time the money ran out, our ambitions exhausted the money by several years. We thank these foundations not only for their initial support but also for their patience.

We have accumulated many debts over the years, and one of the real pleasures of finishing the book is acknowledging the many people who have provided their critiques and support. Howard Adelman, Emanuel Adler, Tom Callaghy, Jeff Crisp, Michael Doyle, Raymond Duvall, Barry Eichengreen, Peter Evans, Orfeo Fioretos, Guy Goodwin-Gill, Erica Gould, Jo-Marie Griesgraber, Robert Keohane, Gil Loescher, Chris Mackintosh, Aziz Ali Mohammed, Andy Moravcsik, Craig Murphy, Louis Pauly, Jon Pevehouse, Jacques Polack, Mark Pollack, Duncan Snidal, Jack Snyder, Barry Stein, Michael Tierney, Erik Voeten, Kate Weaver, Steve Weber, Tom Weiss, Alexander Wendt, Ngaire Woods, and an anonymous reviewer for Cornell University Press all provided extremely helpful suggestions. A special thanks goes to Jeff Legro, who read the manuscript on two occasions and gave us invaluable feedback and redirection. Individually, we have given talks on the specific cases and the broader argument at many locations, including the European University Institute, University of Chicago, University of Colorado, University of Minnesota, University of Toronto, University of Washington, Yale University, Duke University, Stanford University, the University of California–Berkeley, University of Maryland, and University of Pennsylvania. Staff of various nongovernmental organizations also provided important information regarding activities that were taking place in the field. We thank them and respect their request for confidentiality. Perhaps most of all, our deep appreciation goes to the staff of the organizations we have studied, who often gave generously of their time and patiently answered our many questions.

Thanks, of course, to Roger Haydon. Once again, he has done everything one can ask of an editor—and more. We distinctly remember his reaction to our news that we wanted to write a book together: he laughed out loud. He tried to recover by saying that he just could not imagine how two scholars with such different styles could ever collaborate on a full-scale book. At the time we thought he was being a little too honest and skeptical. We now realize that he was being a master motivator: we refused to quit because we refused to prove him right. Thanks, truly, Roger. Louise E. Robbins at the Press also provided invaluable advice. The book would have been better if she had been a coauthor.

Our deepest debts are personal. Our spouses and children have been much more involved in this book than they wanted to be. Their patience with endless phone calls made the book possible. Their demands that we do something besides this book kept us sane.

Michael Barnett dedicates this book to Judith and Martin Shampaine, the best parents a son-in-law ever had. Martha Finnemore dedicates this book, like all her work, to her family.

M. B.
M. F.

Madison, Wisconsin, and Washington, D.C.

RULES FOR THE WORLD

1

BUREAUCRATIZING WORLD POLITICS

International organizations have never been more central to world politics than they are today. At least 238 international organizations (IOs) are currently at work on every imaginable global issue.[1] Investigate almost any violent conflict, environmental concern, financial meltdown, or humanitarian crisis and you will find international organizations involved, probably in a leading role. These organizations do much more than simply execute international agreements between states. They make authoritative decisions that reach every corner of the globe and affect areas as public as governmental spending and as private as reproductive rights. They now work extensively in domestic governance issues, overseeing matters that once used to be the prerogatives of states. One IO, the European Central Bank, is now overseeing monetary policy for some of the most powerful states of the world. Different branches of the UN and NATO have become deeply involved in national military organizations of member states. A whole variety of IOs are busily defining human rights, refugee rights, children's rights, and women's rights, shaping how these rights are understood at both the international and the domestic level. The World Health Organization issues travel advisories and investigates and sanctions those countries that, in its judgment, have failed to take proper action in reporting and combating disease. When the international community engages in nation-building and postconflict transition assistance it is IOs that do much, even most, of the work. Organizations such as the UN, the International Monetary Fund (IMF), and the Organization for Security and Co-operation in Europe are entrusted with drafting new constitutions and judicial arrangements, re-creating financial institutions, and creating civilian police—in essence remaking entire states.[2]

Our goal in writing this book is to understand better why IOs behave as they do. Most international relations theory provides surprisingly little help in this regard. For all the ubiquitousness and importance of IOs, international relations (IR) scholars have not given systematic consideration to how IOs actually behave. Most of our theories are theories of states and state behavior. International organizations are treated as structures of rules, principles, norms, and decision-making procedures through which others, usually states, act.[3] IOs have no agency and cannot act in any meaningful way under most theoretical constructs in the field. To the extent that they allow IOs to "behave" at all, most theories simply assume that IOs do what states want. They offer functional accounts in which IOs are created and continue to exist because of the (usually desirable) functions they perform. States create IOs to solve problems of incomplete information, transaction costs, and other barriers to welfare improvement for their members. This functionalism is only an assumption of these theories, though, and tends to focus scholars' attention on why states create IOs to fulfill certain functions rather than on whether, in fact, subsequent IO behavior is as functional as assumed. The assumptions of these theories—their statism and functionalism—deserve scrutiny, and the preoccupation with creation at the expense of behavior needs correction. The notion that IOs simply do what states want quickly runs afoul of the many instances in which IOs develop their own ideas and pursue their own agendas. Similarly, the functionalist assumption runs into a sea of empirical anomalies. IOs often produce inefficient, self-defeating outcomes and turn their backs on those whom they are supposed to serve. We want to know why.

Scholarship on organizations generally (not just IOs) has made it abundantly clear that organizations routinely behave in ways unanticipated by their creators and not formally sanctioned by their members. Organizations that start with one mission routinely acquire others. Organizations adapt to changing circumstances in unanticipated ways and adopt new routines and functions without getting approval from their "stakeholders." Organizations are notoriously resistant to reform or redirection because change threatens entrenched organizational culture and interests. International organizations evidence all these familiar traits. They exhibit mission creep. They wander far from their original mandate and into new terrains and territories. They develop new rules and routines in response to new problems that they identify. They formulate rules that are politically safe and comfortably routine rather than efficient or effective. We want to understand these behaviors in IOs.

In this book we develop a constructivist approach to understanding IO behavior that provides a theoretical basis for treating IOs as autonomous actors and helps explain the power they exercise in world politics, their propensity toward dysfunctional, even pathological, behavior, and the way they change over time. We ground our analysis on the fact that IOs are bureaucracies. Bureaucracy is a distinctive social form of authority with its own internal logic and behavioral proclivities. It is because of their authority that bureaucracies have autonomy and the ability to change the world around them. Bureaucracies exercise power in the world through their ability to make impersonal rules. They then use these rules not only to regulate but also to constitute and construct the social world. IOs, through their rules, create new categories of actors, form new interests for actors, define new shared international tasks, and disseminate new models of social organization around the globe. However, the same impersonal rules that define bureaucracies and make them effective in modern life can also cause problems. Bureaucracies can become obsessed with their own rules at the expense of their primary missions in ways that produce inefficient and self-defeating outcomes. Thus, while bureaucracies can be forces of progress and good, they can also fail, sometimes in spectacular ways. Whether they meet success or failure, international organizations change and evolve over time. Bureaucracies adapt to new circumstances and challenges, drawing from experience that has become encoded in rules and embedded in the organizational culture. They also expand, taking on new missions, mandates, and responsibilities in ways not imagined by their founders.

We examine these themes both theoretically and empirically. After presenting a theoretical framework in chapter 2, we provide detailed empirical examinations of three IOs working in three different areas of world politics. We examine the IMF and the way its economic expertise made ever-increasing intervention in domestic economies seem logical and even necessary to states that had explicitly barred such action in the organization's Articles of Agreement. We then examine how the United Nations High Commissioner for Refugees (UNHCR) used its authority to expand the concept of refugee and later developed a repatriation culture that led to violations of refugee rights. Finally, we look at the UN Secretariat, the bureaucratization of peacekeeping, and the development of a peacekeeping culture that led to an institutional ideology of impartiality that made it legitimate to ignore crimes against humanity in Rwanda. In all three cases, IOs were not simply following the demands issued by states but instead acting like the bureaucracies that they are.

UNDERSTANDING IO BEHAVIOR

Treating IOs as bureaucracies allows us to provide insights into four aspects of IO behavior that have sparked debate among scholars of international relations: autonomy, power, dysfunction, and change.

First, we can address from a different angle the question, Can IOs act autonomously from states and if so, how? This connection of autonomy to authority requires some discussion. State-centric theoretical approaches provide no reason to expect, much less understand, autonomous IO behavior. Despite all their attention to international institutions, most international relations scholars treat IOs the way pluralists treat the state. For them, IOs are mechanisms or structures through which others (usually states) act; they are not purposive actors. There are, in fact, good reasons why scholars have been skeptical about IO autonomy. Large public IOs are almost always the creations of states and are almost always designed to give states, particularly powerful ones, a great deal of control. States often provide the money for these organizations, usually dominate their top decision-making bodies, and determine who becomes the chief executive. Thus, it has been difficult for many analysts to imagine IOs as anything more than tools in the controlling hands of states.

More recently, scholars have used principal-agent analysis to explore the question of IO autonomy. Treating IOs as agents of states (principals), these scholars recognized that states purposefully design IOs with some autonomy since otherwise IOs would not be able to carry out their assigned tasks. In these analyses, IOs may act autonomously within a "zone of discretion" to advance state interests or to make policy where state interests are unclear or weak, and at times may even advance policies contrary to the interests of some states.[4] Missing from these analyses, however, is a clear a priori specification of what IOs want in these interactions with states. Why would IOs ever want anything other than what their state principals want? These agents, after all, are created by their state principals. States write their mission statements and design their structure precisely to ensure they will be responsive tools. We need to understand how and why IO preferences diverge from state preferences, not just empirically but also theoretically.

Principal-agent dynamics are fueled by the disjuncture between what agents want and what principals want. To produce any insights, those two sets of interests cannot be identical. IR theory provides us with interests only for states, and since IOs are created by states and their mission statements are written by states, it is not at all clear how an independent set of IO preferences might be derived. Analysts could proceed on the assumption that IOs want an expanded budget or mandate, but this hardly begins to exhaust the range of interests that motivate IO behavior. Just as IR theorists now recognize that there is variation in state interests and that to understand that variation requires unpacking the state, so, too, scholars of IOs need to recognize that there is variation in IO interests and that to understand that variation requires unpacking the international organization.[5] If scholars want to understand when IOs exhibit autonomy, then they will have to be attentive not only to state interests but also to IO interests. Our approach, as we argue below, provides help.

Understanding IOs as bureaucracies opens up an alternative view regarding the sources of their autonomy and what they do with that autonomy. Bureaucracies are not just servants to whom states delegate. Bureaucracies are also authorities in their own right, and that authority gives them autonomy vis-à-vis states, individuals, and other international actors. By "authority" we mean the ability of one actor to use institutional and discursive resources to induce deference from others. Our claim that IOs possess authority puts us at odds with much of IR theory, which presumes that only states can possess authority because sovereignty is the only basis of authority.[6] We suggest otherwise. When societies confer authority on the state, they do not do so exclusively. Domestic societies contain an array of authorities, differing in degree and kind. The state is an authority, but academics, professionals and experts, heads of nongovernmental organizations, and religious and business leaders can also be conferred authority. So, too, in international life authority is conferred in differing degrees and kinds on actors other than states. Prominent among these are IOs.

What makes IOs authorities? As we discuss in chapter 2, IOs can have authority both because of the missions they pursue and because of the ways they pursue them. IOs act to promote socially valued goals such as protecting human rights, providing development assistance, and brokering peace agreements. IOs use their credibility as promoters of "progress" toward these valued goals to command deference, that is, exercise authority, in these arenas of action. In addition, because they are bureaucracies, IOs carry out their missions by means that are mostly rational, technocratic, impartial, and nonviolent. This often makes IOs appear more legitimate to more actors than self-serving states that employ coercive tactics in pursuit of their particularistic goals. Their means, like their missions, give IOs authority to act where individual states may not.[7]

What do IOs do with that authority? Often they do much more than the states that are their creators intend. IOs do not simply pursue the mandates handed to them. Indeed, they probably could not do so, even if they wanted to. The mission statements of most large public IOs are ambiguous and require interpretation. IO staff must transform these broad mandates into workable doctrines, procedures, and ways of acting in the world. Understanding how they do this is a major concern of our case studies. States may actually want autonomous action from IO staff. Indeed, they often create an IO and invest it with considerable autonomy precisely because they are neither able nor willing to perform the IO's mission themselves. Once in place, the staff of IOs take their missions seriously and often develop their own views and organizational cultures to promote what they see as "good policy" or to protect it from states that have competing interests. And, of course, neither states nor IO staff can predict new challenges, crises, and exigencies that force IO staff to change their missions and their existing policies.

Understanding the nature of bureaucracy as a social form allows us to reconsider a second important topic, namely, the power of IOs and the kinds of effects they create in the world. This question—whether IOs "matter," or have independent effects—has been at the core of the neorealist-neoliberal debate in international relations theory for almost two decades now.[8] Our approach provides strong reasons to expect IOs to have resources at their disposal overlooked by both these approaches—resources that make them far more powerful and consequential than even neoliberals would propose.

In their debate, neorealists and neoliberals have focused on only two tools of power—material coercion (or inducements) and information. Further, they have focused only on the ability of IOs to shape state behavior, which does not begin to capture the full range of ways IOs shape the world around them. Sometimes IOs do have material resources. They often have money, even guns, and can use these to influence the behavior of others. Refugees and poor farmers often do what UNHCR and World Bank officials want because of the material resources of those organizations. States, even sizable ones, may be coerced by the IMF into adopting policies they would not otherwise adopt because of the Fund's financial resources. But in this kind of power sweepstakes, IOs are usually dwarfed by large states. The IMF may be able to tell Zambia, Bolivia, or even Argentina what to do, but the most economically powerful states have a fair bit to say about what the IMF proposes. Because IOs can rarely coerce large states to do their bidding, IR scholars have tended to think they are not powerful.

Similarly, IOs do influence outcomes by manipulating information—creating transparency, monitoring compliance, and enforcing rules in ways that change incentives for state action. Having UN peacekeepers verify a cease-fire can cause parties to the agreement to abide by the agreement for fear of being caught if they do not. WHO reports about the HIV/AIDS pandemic and SARS can help states understand the transnational dynamics of the diseases and better devise policies to slow their spread. Clearer rules about what is (or is not) "fair" trade, coupled with an IO like the World Trade Organization (WTO) to arbitrate disputes, can provide incentives for greater liberalization worldwide. The Organization for Security and Co-operation's Office of High Commissioner for Minorities has encouraged respect for human rights by articulating what the standards are and broadcasting how countries might be falling short of them. IOs can collect, publicize, and strategically deploy information in order to try to shape behavior. But in this kind of informational sweepstakes, IOs rarely have an advantage over states. IOs seldom have private information, unavailable to interested powerful states. States, not IOs, tend to enjoy superior access to information.[9]

IOs are powerful not so much because they possess material and informational resources but, more fundamentally, because they use their authority to orient action and create social reality.[10] IOs do more than just manipulate information; they analyze and interpret it, investing information with meaning that orients and prompts action, thereby transforming information into knowledge. The World Bank does not only collect data and produce descriptive statistics on national economies. It also takes those raw data and couples them to particular policy problems, often of the Bank's own creation. The Bank defines development, telling us what data measure it. It tells us what constitutes poverty and what data are necessary to act on that policy problem. As discussed in chapter 2, transforming information into knowledge by giving it meaning, value, and purpose is one of the major activities of authorities in social life.

As authorities, IOs can use their knowledge to exercise power in two ways. First, they can regulate the social world, altering the behavior of states and nonstate actors by changing incentives for their decisions. Frequently they do this in order to get actors to conform with existing rules and norms of behavior. The UN Human Rights Commission publishes information about states' torture practices, thus creating incentives for states to comply with human rights norms. IOs have a range of tools to regulate state and nonstate behavior.

Second, we can better understand the power IOs wield by viewing them as bureaucracies. IOs exercise power as they use their knowledge and authority not only to regulate what currently exists but also to constitute the world, creating new interests, actors, and social activities. This can be understood as "social construction power" because IOs use their knowledge to help create social reality.[11] IOs are often the actors to whom we defer when it comes to defining meanings, norms of good behavior, the nature of social actors, and categories of legitimate social action in the world. IOs are often the actors empowered to decide if there is a problem at all, what kind of problem it is, and whose responsibility it is to solve it. IOs thus help determine the kind of world that is to be governed and set the agenda for global governance. UNHCR helps to determine not only who is a refugee but also what a refugee is and what should be done about their plight. The IMF, World Bank, and other IOs have been involved not only in assessing good economic performance but also in defining what are "best practices" and "good governance" for national economies and in determining whose responsibility it is to create and manage economic reform. IOs have helped determine not only who is in violation of human rights but also what human rights are and what should be done to promote or protect them. In this fundamental respect, IOs shape both how the world is constituted and our agendas for acting in it.

Treating IOs as bureaucracies also gives us insights into a third set of issues, those connected with the propensity of IOs for undesirable and self-defeating behavior. Surprisingly, this has received relatively little attention.[12] The reason for this neglect, we suspect, is that the theoretical apparatus many scholars use provides few grounds for expecting undesirable IO behavior. State-centric utility-maximizing frameworks borrowed from economics simply assume that IOs are reasonably responsive to state interests (or, at least, more responsive than alternative policy tools); otherwise states would withdraw from them. This, however, is a logical implication of these frameworks; it is rarely treated as a hypothesis subject to empirical investigation.[13] With little theoretical reason to expect counterproductive or self-defeating behavior in IOs, these scholars do not look for it and have had little to say about it.

Sometimes the reasons why IOs fail are obvious. IO staff are often the first to point out that they are frequently given mandates without funding and assigned tasks that others cannot or will not do. Further, large public bureaucracies are often designed to satisfy political rather than performance criteria and are, in this sense, designed to fail.[14] Staff are frequently selected according to national background and not merit, and the redundancy and inefficiency in staff structure can derive from the need to satisfy political requirements of regional or ideological representation.

Yet not all undesirable IO behavior can be blamed on states. IOs often generate their own mistakes, perversities, even disasters. In fact, it is often the very features that make bureaucracies authoritative and effective that can encourage bureaucratic dysfunction. Bureaucracies divide labor, create standardized rules of action, and deploy relevant social knowledge to solve problems in an orderly, rational way. These are virtues. It is precisely because bureaucracies act this way that they can effectively carry out the complex social tasks we give them. However, each of these capabilities also carries with it liabilities. Division of labor and specialization can create tunnel vision among staff. Standardized rules of action can make it difficult to respond to unique situations. Expert knowledge may solve some problems but inevitably carries biases and limitations that can create new problems. Bureaucracies can thus become obsessed with their own rules and captives of parochial outlooks and internal culture. We call "pathologies" those dysfunctions that are attributable to bureaucratic culture and internal bureaucratic processes and that lead the IO to act in a manner that subverts its self-professed goals. There are many ways in which a bureaucratic culture can create pathologies. One of our aims is to identify several possibilities and then explore in detail a few of those.

Finally, our approach provides insight into change in international organizations. Conventional IR approaches assume that change in IOs must be the result of changing demands of strong states, but as policymakers are well aware, getting any large bureaucracy, including international bureaucracies, to reform or respond to demands for change can be an exercise in frustration. U.S. efforts to reform the World Bank and the UN did eventually spur some change, but change was slow and very incomplete. These efforts encountered huge resistance and probably were more successful at altering the formal structures than at changing everyday practices and routines. Conversely, these organizations often change in ways that states do not ask for or anticipate. IOs continually formulate new tasks and new procedures for doing their work in response to changing world situations, changing expertise, and other factors. States can usually stop these changes if they want to (although often only after tremendous exertion), but they do not generally initiate them. We need to better understand both what prompts unsolicited change and what sparks resistance to demands for change, as well as what types of change are likely to succeed (or fail).

There are many possible causes of change in IOs, and we discuss a variety of these in chapter 2. However, the constitutive arguments we develop about IOs suggest several important observations about IO dynamics. One is that IOs are not black boxes that respond to external stimuli (state demands for change, policy shocks) in an obvious or unproblematic way. Over time these organizations develop strong bureaucratic cultures that profoundly shape the way external demands or shocks are interpreted and the kinds of responses the organization will entertain and, eventually, implement. Second, because of these cultures, change in IOs is almost always highly path dependent. Bureaucracies encode experience into their governing rules and standard operating procedures, which strongly discourage some types of change and make others more likely. Any attempts at change must be filtered through that accretion. Finally, our constitutive argument provides insights into the often remarked, often derided, and generally pervasive phenomenon of mission creep in bureaucracies, including IOs. IO missions may expand simply because states give them more tasks, but, as the term "mission creep" suggests, there is an unintended internal logic at work here as well. As IOs go about their business of defining tasks and implementing mandates, they tend to do so in ways that permit, or even require, more intervention by more IOs. This is not bureaucratic imperialism so much as it is a logical outgrowth of the nature of their authority. As rational-legal authorities, bureaucracies tend to value the technocratic impartiality that legitimates them and so tend to construct problems and solutions in ways that reflect those preferences. They define problems and appropriate solutions in ways that favor more technocratic impartial action, which, of course, they are uniquely able to supply.

In sum, we can better understand what IOs *do* if we better understand what IOs *are*. International organizations are bureaucracies, and bureaucracies are a distinctive social form that exercises authority in particular ways. Perhaps most influential and least noticed are the ways in which IOs use their authority to both regulate and constitute the world. By opening up the black box of international organizations and examining how they are constituted and use their authority, we can begin to understand their power, their capacity for pathological behavior, and the way they evolve.

The claims we make in this book thus flow from an analysis of the "social stuff" of which bureaucracy is made. We are asking a standard constructivist question about what makes the world hang together. As Alexander Wendt puts it, "How are things in the world put together so that they have the properties they do?"[15] In this sense, our explanation of IO behavior is constitutive and differs from most other international relations approaches. This approach does not make our explanation mere description, since understanding the constitution of things is essential to explaining how those things behave and what causes outcomes. Understanding how bureaucracies are constituted socially allows us to hypothesize about the behavior of IOs and the effects this social form might have in world politics. This type of constitutive explanation does not allow us to offer law-like statements such as "if X happens, then Y must follow." Rather, by providing a more complete understanding of what bureaucracy is, we can provide explanations of how certain kinds of bureaucratic behavior are possible, or even probable, and why.

CASE DESIGN

Chapter 2 explores what IOs are. In it we develop a constitutive argument about the nature of bureaucracy and theorize about the implications of that social form for IO behavior. This framework provides guidance for structuring our case studies. Each case study begins by treating the statist approach and our framework as competing arguments. Statist arguments claim that IO behavior follows directly from state demands, ergo IOs exhibit little autonomy of any consequence. We assess the statist hypothesis by examining the kinds of pressures states put on organizations and the way IOs respond. Tracing these interactions, we show that, while state demands are extremely important, state action by no means determines all, or even most, IO behavior.[16]

This suggests that IOs can act autonomously, but clear demonstration requires that we be specific about what counts as autonomy. If autonomy exists only when IOs are able to coerce powerful states, forcing them to act contrary to their expressed interests, then we would have to agree with the statists that there are, indeed, few instances of IO autonomy. This criterion seems unnecessarily restrictive, however, since it excludes a wide variety of IO activity that might be independent of states but not actively opposed by the powerful. If, by contrast, we understand autonomy to exist when IOs are able to act in ways not dictated by states, we capture the range of activity not well explained by statist arguments and can provide a fuller argument. We look in our cases for precisely such instances.

To identify this autonomy empirically in the three cases, we look for consistent patterns of IO action that cannot be traced to state pressures. Certainly these IOs paid close attention to what states, especially strong states, wanted, but in all three cases we found these organizations pursuing important, often defining, policies that were not demanded by state members. Even where the IO did adopt policies favored by states, however, we must remember that correlation is not causation. IOs and states can arrive at similar policies but for very different reasons, as we see in the Rwanda case. In other cases, for example that of UNHCR, IOs can be the policy leaders, setting the agenda in their domain of action and cajoling states to adopt it. At times, IOs may actually shape the policy preferences of states by changing what states want. It matters who initiates policy and why. By investigating IO interests and determining both where they came from and whether they differ from those of states, we are better able to identify potentially autonomous actions.

Autonomy is not simply present or absent in IO behavior, however. It varies in both degree and kind, and in each case we assess the degree and kind of autonomy we see. In chapter 2 we identify five different kinds of autonomous behavior that IOs might exhibit with respect to states. IOs might act independently from, but consistently with, state interests, interpreting mandates and implementing policy in ways that are perhaps unanticipated but are agreeable to states. They also might operate in areas to which states are indifferent. They might fail to carry out state interests, oppose state interests, or change state interests. IOs thus have complicated relationships of both autonomy and dependence with a variety of other actors, including states. While state demands matter, they leave much unexplained.

We then attempt to explain the autonomous IO behavior we see. Here, too, our framework provides guidance. We deduce from general principles of bureaucracy a set of expectations about how IOs might behave and the kinds of effects they might have in the world. Using these insights, elaborated in chapter 2, we look inside the IOs at the way they are put together socially and culturally, at their authority, and at their rules and show how these organizational characteristics can explain the behavior we see.[17] The framework suggests that IOs will formulate goals for action that reflect the sources of their authority—their rational-legal character, their mandate from states, and the expertise and moral claims that legitimate them in the broader political scene. It suggests that as bureaucracies and rational-legal entities, IOs will exercise power and further their goals through impersonal rules. In each case we examine the use of rules and their effects, both intended and otherwise, on those inside as well as on those on whom the organization acts. In addition, the framework suggests that the specific sources of authority for an organization will shape its work, and we examine these connections.

Understanding how IOs work demands both historical and interpretive analysis. Understanding the historical experience encoded in these organizations is crucial. It is not enough to open up the black box and take a snapshot of the organizational culture at one moment in time. Instead, it is critical to follow the sequence of events as they unfolded in an organizational and historical context and were subsequently encoded in the organizational culture. Our historical analysis, therefore, involves detailed reconstructions. Just as an investigator analyzing an airplane crash must pay attention to a sequence of contributing factors, not just the pilot's final words, so, too, do we insist that any examination of IO decisions, and especially of pathologies, go beyond the immediate to consider how environmental forces shaped the rules that IO staff use to see the world and make decisions.[18]

We also undertake interpretive analysis. We are interested in how IO staff come to create and interpret the bureaucratic rules that shape both how they classify and see the world and how they act in it.[19] It is never enough to stand outside the organization and impose a set of meanings or interpretations of what the rules are. Instead, it is absolutely critical that we ask how and why IO staff interpreted the rules the way they did. To do this, we supplement archival and textual analysis with interviews of many of the key participants in the events we analyze.

Proceeding in this manner allows us to determine how, when, and why IOs are able to act in ways that are not demanded by states and thus to exhibit different kinds of autonomy. It also has an additional advantage: it advances a more complete understanding of IO-state interactions. As should be clear, the approach we develop in no way denies a role for states. On the contrary, the case studies illustrate that states are a central fact of life for each of these IOs. State support is a crucial component of IO authority, states significantly constrain IO behavior, and IOs are keenly conscious of state demands as they formulate policy. We do not want to create a mythical world of IO omnipotence to replace a mythical world of IO obsequiousness. But state demands are only one component of IO behavior. IOs are not simply passive servants of states. They are political actors in their own right, having their own particular resources for shaping political action, and both shaping and being shaped by others. One decided advantage of our approach is that it puts the interactive relationship between states and IOs at the center of analysis rather than presuming that the relationship is a one-way street in which states simply dictate to IOs.

We apply our approach in three case studies. Chapter 3 examines the International Monetary Fund and highlights the authority and autonomy that come from professional expertise. Deploying specialized knowledge to carry out tasks is a hallmark of bureaucracy—one of the rational-legal behaviors that legitimate it—yet it is not clear that we understand this process well. Political scientists have tended to think of expertise as information that exists independently of organizations and creates organizational power by giving an advantage to those who have it. Our examination of the IMF suggests that neither of these is true. IMF staff had to create the "intellectual technologies" and economic models that made balance-of-payments problems tractable for policymakers. These models were influential, however, not because the IMF kept this knowledge inside the organization but because the Fund disseminated it widely, reducing rather than exploiting information asymmetries. Only by understanding the economic models could states and others be persuaded to follow their prescriptions.

We then consider the relationship between the IMF's expertise, its power, and its growing role in Third World states. The models used by the Fund led it to recommend policies that were designed not only to regulate member states' domestic economies but also, ultimately, to (re)constitute them. The IMF faced the challenge of getting deficit governments to accept its recommendations. Toward that end it began to set conditions on use of its resources. Conditionality, however, often did not produce the desired results. When programs failed to solve members' payments problems, the Fund's assessment usually concluded that the original models were too narrow and that new variables had to be included. Policy failure justified expansion, not retrenchment. Over time, the Fund moved from a limited focus on balance-of-payments lending to ever more sweeping structural interventions in members' economies and societies in an attempt to control activities that might contribute to stabilization. Alongside conditionality, the IMF established technical assistance programs that were designed to help develop new economic institutions and enable the country to absorb the knowledge and recommendations imparted by the agency. The IMF thus uses its expert authority both to regulate the economy of Third World societies and to help reconstitute those societies in the process.

Chapter 4 examines the United Nations High Commissioner for Refugees and the way it used its moral authority to expand the category of refugee and its scope of action. It then explores the emergence of a repatriation culture and rules governing repatriation that led to the violation of refugee rights, that is, pathological behavior. When states created UNHCR in 1951, they gave it a three-year life span, almost no autonomy, and a very circumscribed mandate. UNHCR was to provide legal, not material, assistance only to people who had been displaced by events in Europe prior to 1951. Yet the agency was able to capitalize on refugee-producing events and use its institutional position and moral authority to expand the concept of refugee, to widen its assistance and protection activities, and to significantly extend its sphere of operations. By the late 1970s it was no longer a small European refugee agency but a global humanitarian organization.

UNHCR was established to help find "permanent solutions" to refugee circumstances and to do so in accord with the refugee regime's foundational principle of nonrefoulement: refugees cannot be returned against their will to a situation that continues to represent a threat to their existence. In the early decades of its life, the organization's favored solution involved resettling refugees in some new country. Over time, however, the organization has increasingly favored "voluntary repatriation" as a solution for refugees that satisfies political dilemmas and still respects refugee law principles. In fact, voluntary repatriation has become so ingrained in the organization's culture that beginning in the late 1980s there was growing evidence that the organization was sponsoring repatriation exercises that were hardly voluntary and clearly violated refugee rights. To illustrate this repatriation culture at work, we detail UNHCR's handling of the Rohingyan refugee flight in 1994, one of the largest refugee flights of this or any period. In response, UNHCR authorized the repatriation of the Rohingyas from Bangladesh to Burma in ways that violated the principle of voluntary repatriation.

Chapter 5 considers the case of UN peacekeeping and the theme of pathology in the UN Secretariat's policy toward Rwanda through late April 1994. Before 1989 the UN operated with clear peacekeeping rules involving consent of parties, impartiality, and neutrality in any mission. The spate of missions authorized in the early 1990s involving humanitarian emergencies, domestic conflict, and nation-building suddenly made those rules unworkable and led the organization to use much more assertive rules to carry out these new, more ambitious missions. Failure of these missions, particularly the one in Somalia that departed from consent-based rules and used force, made UN officials fear that these new missions and the departure from the rules of classical peacekeeping threatened the survival of peacekeeping as an enterprise. As a consequence, they reasserted old rules emphasizing neutrality and impartiality in autumn 1993 and directed that peacekeeping be used under very restrictive conditions. These rules, in force by the time of the outbreak of the Rwandan genocide on April 6, 1994, guided UN officials to see the genocide as a civil war and to conclude that there was no basis for intervention to stop the killing of eight hundred thousand people.

This array of cases has several advantages for our purposes. First, choosing IOs working in security (UN Security Council), finance (IMF), and humanitarian affairs (UNHCR) helps us demonstrate the utility of this approach across many issue areas. Second, selecting cases where there are obvious and often widely accepted statist explanations of the behavior of IOs makes these good test cases for our argument. The Secretariat did not push the Security Council to authorize intervention to stop killings in Rwanda because powerful states who opposed intervention (particularly the United States) pressured it into silence. IMF staff advocate particular economic models and intrusively apply them around the world because those are the models of powerful states, home to powerful capitalists. UNHCR made repatriation the durable solution to refugee plights and engaged in acts of involuntary repatriation because states wanted to repatriate refugees and were willing to violate refugee rights over the objections of UNHCR staff in places like Burma. The existence of robust counterexplanations rooted in state demands makes these cases hard ones for our autonomy hypothesis. Third, these cases offer some variation in the sorts of controls that states place on IOs and the ways in which IOs are dependent on states. Financial dependence varies. The IMF is largely self-financed, paying for its operating budget with money returned on the funds it manages. The UN levies annual dues but has no sure way to collect them should states decide to withhold payment. UNHCR, by contrast, must pass the hat for voluntary contributions. Similarly, voting structure and governance arrangements vary. The IMF and the Secretariat are both under very immediate direction by state representatives who are constantly present in the building when business is conducted. Although UNHCR's Executive Committee helps to set broad policy directions, it is much less involved in daily operations. Finally, we selected cases that provide variation in one of the key elements of bureaucracy identified in chapter 2—authority. Each of these IOs traffics in a different mix of authority claims. The IMF relies heavily on expert authority, the Secretariat on moral authority, and UNHCR on a mix of moral and expert authority. While such a limited number of cases permits only provisional generalizations, variation in authority types helps us to begin to understand how different types of authority have different consequences for organizational behavior.

In the concluding chapter we explore both empirical and normative implications of our argument. Empirically, one consistent finding is that IOs tend to expand. Our framework provides reasons why this should be true, and our case studies illustrate how these theoretical mechanisms play out on the ground. Consistent expansion of IOs raises questions about the future shape of politics, however. It raises the prospect of an ever more bureaucratized world, with international organizations becoming steadily more involved in more aspects of our daily lives. This, in turn, raises questions about whether such increasing bureaucratization, which we suspect is inevitable, is a good thing. On the one hand, a strong thread running through the ever-expanding world of IOs is their substantively liberal character. Most IOs were founded by Western liberal states and are designed to promote liberal values. To the extent that one likes political liberalism, IO expansion is, indeed, good. However, the liberal norms embodied and promoted by these organizations are generally not matched with the accountability or participation procedures that liberalism favors. These are emphatically not democratic organizations. This raises the possibility that at the global level we face an undemocratic liberalism, and we explore this possibility at the end of the book.

2

INTERNATIONAL ORGANIZATIONS AS BUREAUCRACIES

In this chapter we develop a framework for understanding IOs as active participants in world affairs. We do this by theorizing about their nature and form. IOs are constituted as bureaucracies, and that bureaucratic character profoundly shapes the way they behave. The first section examines the nature of the bureaucratic form, focusing on its organizing principles and the centrality of rules and rule-making processes to bureaucratic authority and behavior. Section II explores in detail the connection between bureaucracy and authority in order to identify several sources of IO authority. As bureaucracies, IOs are conferred rational-legal authority, yet they also derive authority from delegation processes, moral claims, and expertise. Together, these sources give IOs authority to act and provide the foundation for their autonomy. Determining the bases for IO autonomy is crucial for our project since unless IOs can be understood as autonomous to at least some degree, a theory of IO behavior such as ours is unnecessary.

The remainder of the chapter uses the insight that IOs are bureaucracies to derive propositions about how IOs exercise power, the ways they may fail, and the ways they evolve. Section III examines how IOs use their authority to exercise power in two ways, both regulating and constituting the world. IOs regulate the behavior of states and nonstate actors in consequential ways by manipulating incentives for these actors. Some aspects of IO regulative power have been amply explored by neoliberal scholars, for example, the ability to use information to encourage (or prevent) coordinated action. Other aspects will be more familiar to constructivists, such as the ability to frame problems, set agendas, and shame actors into compliance with agreed-upon rules. However, IO power goes beyond regulation. IOs can also constitute the world as they define new categories of problems to be governed and create new norms, interests, actors, and shared social tasks. This constitutive power of IOs has not been explored or well understood by IR scholars but has profound consequences, among them a consistent tendency of IOs to create a world that subsequently licenses yet more intervention by IOs.

Section IV considers the issue of IO pathology. We construct a typology that maps theories of dysfunction and show that the same internally generated cultural forces that give IOs their authority and power also can be a source of dysfunction. We label as pathologies those dysfunctions that originate from the bureaucratic culture, and we elaborate five mechanisms by which an IO's organizational culture can generate pathologies. We conclude by considering the issue of organizational change. Like pathology, organizational change has been theorized to flow from several sources, and we map these onto the same typological grid we applied to dysfunction. As with power and pathology, we then show how the bureaucratic form and internal characteristics of bureaucratic culture of IOs cause them to change and shape their evolution.

I. BUREAUCRACIES

Bureaucracy is a ubiquitous feature of modern life. Whenever there are complex tasks to be done, we set up a bureaucracy to do them, yet our attitudes toward bureaucracy are decidedly ambivalent. While we view bureaucracies as necessary to organize an increasingly complex world, we routinely deride them in public discourse, complaining about bureaucratic red tape and incompetence. This ambivalence is nothing new. The term "bureaucracy" was coined by Vincent de Gournay in 1745. Marrying the French word *bureau,* which means both a table and an office, to the Greek verb *kratein,* "to rule," he attempted to convey how government officials were gathering more power and developing an "illness called bureaumania."[1] Although he and many others since have come to equate bureaucracy with all that has gone wrong with modern society, bureaucracy continues to be the mechanism of choice for organizing and regulating much of an increasingly complex world. Indeed, it is hard to imagine any alternative. More and more of the world is bureaucratized. We may (or may not) live in a globalized world, but we certainly live in a bureaucratized world.

The modern bureaucracy is defined by four central features.[2] Modern bureaucracies exhibit *hierarchy,* in that each official has a clearly defined sphere of competence within a division of labor and is answerable to superiors; *continuity,* in that the office constitutes a full-time salary structure that offers the prospect of regular advancement; *impersonality,* in that the work is conducted according to prescribed rules and operating procedures that eliminate arbitrary and politicized influences; and *expertise,* in that officials are selected according to merit, are trained for their function, and control access to knowledge stored in files. Bureaucracy breaks down problems into manageable and repetitive tasks that are assigned to particular offices and then coordinated under a hierarchical command. These are the qualities and traits that led Max Weber to characterize modern bureaucracies as more efficient than other systems of administration or organization and reflective of the rationalization processes that were unfolding in the modern world.[3]

Impersonal rules are the building blocks of a bureaucracy and figure prominently in any explanation of bureaucratic behavior. "Theories of organizations—both traditionally and currently—are often theories of rules, rule making and rule following."[4] Rules are explicit or implicit norms, regulations, and expectations that define and order the social world and the behavior of actors in it. Bureaucracies are both composed of and producers of rules. Bureaucracies are collections of rules that define complex social tasks and establish a division of labor to accomplish them. At the same time, bureaucracy's preferred (and often prescribed) job is to create more rules that structure social action for others in ways perceived to accomplish tasks.

Bureaucratic rules can thus have a variety of effects, four of which interest us. First, bureaucratic rules prescribe action for actors both inside and outside the organization. Internally, bureaucratic rules are the standard operating procedures that allow the organization to respond more efficiently and predictably to environmental demands. However, bureaucracies often make rules that prescribe the behavior of others—indebted countries, refugee host countries, parties in conflict. Rules of this kind are widely recognized as an essential part of IO behavior and have been much studied by IR scholars of many orientations.[5] Second, rules can shape how bureaucrats see the world and perceive the problems they face. Rules define, categorize, and classify the world.[6] They provide criteria for distinguishing between a civil war and a genocide, between a refugee and an economic migrant, between a short-term balance-of-payments shortfall and chronic disequilibrium. Third, bureaucrats use their rules to help create or constitute the social world and tend to so do in ways that make the world amenable to intervention by bureaucrats themselves. The IMF creates rules governing how best to solve balance-of-payments deficits through economic restructuring, rules that in turn often require greater levels of intervention by the organization. UNHCR creates rules governing how to solve and prevent refugee flows which, in turn, legitimate intervention by the organization in host and refugee-producing states. Finally, rules can be constitutive of identity, particularly of the identity of the organization. For instance, rules about consent are integral in the practice of UN peacekeeping in part because they differentiate the UN from other actors using coercive means of dispute resolution and help define the UN's special role in world politics.

Bureaucratic rules thus shape the activities, understandings, identity, and practices of the bureaucracy and consequently help to define the bureaucratic culture.[7] By bureaucratic culture we mean "the solutions that are produced by groups of people to meet specific problems they face in common. These solutions become institutionalized, remembered and passed on as the rules, rituals, and values of the group."[8] Bureaucracies such as the IOs we study are established to accomplish certain tasks. To do this, they develop general consensus around their understandings of their core mission and the functions of their organization; goals to be pursued; basic means to pursue those goals; and some way to measure results. Thus organizations create a shared discourse, symbols, and values for their staff. These shared elements, in turn, generate a group identity for the organization and structure interactions among those within it. They also create a boundary between the organization and the external world and supply the organization with ways to explain that world.[9] While bureaucratic cultures always draw on cultural elements from the environment, notably professional norms and legitimacy requirements imposed by the larger society, all bureaucracies develop cultures that are distinct from the environment in which they are embedded.[10] These cultures, in themselves, are neither good nor bad. They may be valued and actively promoted by heads of the organizations as a source of improved performance, as many business executives do, or they may be a source of dysfunction.

Bureaucratic culture guides action but does not determine it.[11] The rules and routines of a bureaucracy shape bureaucrats' view of the world, define their social tasks, shape their interests, and orient them in similar ways toward the world. They do more than just bound rationality; actors' rationality itself, the very means and ends that they value, are shaped by the bureaucratic culture.[12] We illustrate this in our case studies, identifying in each the formal and informal meanings of the rules within the organization, how these rules shaped what was considered to be appropriate action, how these rules structured social reality for staff, and how these rules helped to define the very ends of the organization. However, rules do not determine action. Bureaucrats are often uncertain whether the existing rules will solve new problems or which of several rules are most appropriate. In such circumstances, bureaucrats will act creatively as they rearrange old organizational notions and import or invent new ones to solve pressing policy problems. Further, the same rules will not necessarily hold the same meaning or be interpreted in the same way by everyone within the bureaucracy. Bureaucracies are organized according to specialization and a division of labor and consequently develop divisions and subunits that are likely to have subcultures that generate their own interpretation of rules.[13] Also, bureaucrats can use rules strategically, pushing one interpretation in order to pursue alternative agendas or to avoid work. Rules and their interpretation can also change. As bureaucrats assess past performance and deal with changes in their environment—new resource constraints or demands imposed by powerful actors—they will adapt and reinterpret existing rules. Thus, while rule-driven bureaucratic culture figures centrally in our understanding, the relationship between bureaucrats and rules is mutually constitutive and dynamic. Bureaucracies create rules that shape future action, but action, in turn, shapes the evolution and content of rules.

II. THE AUTHORITY AND AUTONOMY OF IOS

Bureaucracies are, by definition, authorities—they are rational-legal authorities in their domain of action. IOs enjoy this rational-legal authority but also draw authority from other sources, notably from their moral standing, their expertise, and their delegated tasks. With this authority they are able to use discursive and institutional resources in order to get other actors to defer to them.[14]

Authority is a social construction. It cannot be understood and, indeed, does not exist apart from the social relations that constitute and legitimate it. One of authority's most prominent features is that it requires some level of consent from other actors. Authority is conferred. When actors confer authority and defer to the authority's judgment, they grant a right to speak and to have those statements conferred credibility.[15] There are always a range of opinions about any contentious political problem, but not all views receive equal weight or equal hearing. Authority helps an actor's voice be heard, recognized, and believed. This right to speak credibly is central to the way authority produces effects. Because individuals defer to those in authority, they are likely to alter their behavior in ways that are consistent with the directions laid out by that authority.

Authority involves more than the ability to get people to do what they otherwise would not; authority often consists of telling people what is the right thing to do. Compliance is not automatic, though. Actors might recognize an authority's judgment as legitimate but still follow an alternative course of action for some other set of reasons. Sometimes there are alternative authoritative voices giving different judgments and instructions to actors, who must choose among them. Crises of authority may also develop, when actors that were once conferred authority no longer are given the same deference. Consequently, we should not assume that authority is fixed, singular, or always obeyed.

Authority does two kinds of work in making IOs what they are and shaping their behavior. It provides the social form and behavioral vocabulary of

IOs as social actors, and it supplies the social purposes these actors pursue. Authority provides the substance of which IOs are made. At the most basic level, IOs are bureaucracies, and bureaucracy is the embodiment of rational-legal authority. As we know from Max Weber, this is a form of authority that modernity views as particularly legitimate and good. In contrast to earlier forms of authority that were invested in a leader, legitimate modern authority is invested in legalities, procedures, and rules and thus rendered impersonal.[16] Investing authority in bureaucracies has important consequences since bureaucracies make general, impersonal rules that order and classify the world. Their rules define shared tasks (like "development"), create and define new categories of actors (like "refugees"), and create new interests for actors (like "promoting human rights"). Rational-legal authority thus constitutes IOs in the sense that it gives them a specific form (bureaucracy) and empowers them to act in specific ways (general, impersonal rule making).

In modern bureaucracies this form is connected with a distinctive behavioral vocabulary centered on self-effacement. Bureaucracy is powerful and commands deference, not in its own right, but because of the values it claims to embody and the people it claims to serve. IOs cannot simply say, "we are bureaucracies; do what we say." To be authoritative, ergo powerful, they must be seen to serve some valued and legitimate social purpose, and, further, they must be seen to serve that purpose in an impartial and technocratic way using their impersonal rules. The authority of IOs, and bureaucracies generally, therefore, lies in their ability to present themselves as impersonal and neutral—as not exercising power but instead serving others.[17] The acceptance of these claims is critical to their authority. As we will see in the case studies, IOs work hard to preserve this appearance of neutrality and service to others. The need to be seen as impartial servants of state members is crucial in the UN Secretariat's behavior. Similarly, being perceived as apolitical technocrats is essential to the IMF's credibility with both member states and the larger public and drives its behavior in important ways.

Yet IOs confront the recurring problem that neutrality is often, probably always, impossible. Bureaucracies always serve some social purpose or set of cultural values, even when they are shrouded in myths of impartiality or value-neutral technocracy. Further, there often is no neutral stance one could take in many of the situations IOs confront, yet IOs need to find one in order to maintain the claim that they are impartial and are acting in a depoliticized manner. The fact that they are legitimated by a myth of depoliticization is a source of stress for IOs when impartial action is impossible. For example, if one side in a conflict is committing far more and more serious human rights violations, it may be difficult for peacekeepers to look impartial on the ground. Similarly, protecting refugees and enforcing nonrefoulement may be inherently political if one party's war aim is ethnic cleansing.

This instrumental character of bureaucracy—its need to serve others—means that rational-legal authority alone is not sufficient to constitute it. Rational-legal authority gives IOs their basic form and behavioral vocabulary, but the form requires some substantive content. Bureaucracy must serve some social purpose. It is the values and the people they serve that make bureaucracies, including IOs, respected and authoritative. We see three broad categories of authority that undergird IOs—delegation, morality, and expertise.

Delegated Authority

At a rudimentary level IO authority is delegated authority from states.[18] IOs are authorities because states have put them in charge of certain tasks. The UN's authority to do peacekeeping comes from the mandate given to it by member states through the Security Council. UNHCR's authority derives from its statute created by member states. Member states delegate to the IMF the authority to act in certain domains regarding international financial matters. IOs are thus authoritative because they represent the collective will of their members, who themselves have the authority to delegate tasks to IOs.

At first glance, this type of authority would not appear to provide any autonomy for IOs. After all, if the only type of authority IOs have is what states give them, then IOs can do only what states tell them. State-centric analysis would suffice, and no theory of IO action would be necessary. However, the delegation process is not so simple, nor is the kind of authority delegation confers.[19] States often delegate to IOs tasks which they cannot perform themselves and about which they have limited knowledge. Mandates to IOs are often vague, broad, or conflicting. Consequently, delegation rarely results in unproblematic service of state interests. Mandates need to be interpreted, and even with oversight the agenda, interests, experience, values, and expertise of IO staff heavily color any organization's response to delegated tasks. Indeed, IOs *must* be autonomous actors in some ways simply to fulfill their delegated tasks.[20] One important reason states delegate to IOs in the first place is precisely that they want some other actor to take charge of a problem and sort it out. At some level, delegation creates autonomy precisely because being autonomous *is* the mandate.

As in the case of rational-legal authority, though, delegation authorizes IOs to act autonomously only to the extent that they appear to be serving others, in this case the delegators. Delegated authority is always authority on loan. To use it, IOs must maintain the perception that they are faithful servants to their mandates and masters. However, serving their mandates may often conflict with serving the desires of particular (often powerful) state masters, and balancing these tensions can be a major activity for many IOs. Moreover, member states might have very different interpretations of existing rules and procedures and how they should be extended to confront new challenges. Under such circumstances, IO staff are likely to try to adjudicate between different interpretations held by members. They can use the autonomy generated by these divisions to offer an authoritative response and are likely to present their own response as impartial. Although the very act of delegation and the use of rational-legal means to implement policies generate some autonomy, IOs work hard to present themselves as acting not autonomously but at the behest of their principals.

Moral Authority

IOs are often created to embody, serve, or protect some widely shared set of principles and often use this status as a basis of authoritative action.[21] They frequently claim to be the representative of the community's interests or the defender of the values of the international community, and such a presentational stance helps to generate some autonomy. The UN secretary-general, for example, often uses the organization's status as protector of international peace and security and of human rights to create autonomy from member states and to induce deference from governments and citizens. UNHCR similarly uses its moral duty to protect refugees as a basis for autonomous action on their behalf. In no small measure, the moral authority of IOs is dependent on a contrary discourse of states protecting their own national and particularistic interests. In this discourse, states promote their national interests and IOs represent the community's interests. Indeed, IOs frequently emphasize their neutrality, impartiality, and objectivity in ways that are intended to contrast their universal concerns with the self-serving claims of states. Thus, heads of IOs expend considerable energy attempting to demonstrate that they are not doing the bidding of the Great Powers but instead represent the "international community." The moral valence here is clear: IOs are supposed to be more moral (ergo more authoritative) in battles with governments because they represent the community against self-seekers.[22]

This aspect of moral authority also allows IOs to present themselves as depoliticized and impartial. Obviously, defending moral claims is almost always political and partisan because one set of moral claims is invariably being advanced over another set, but to the extent that IOs present themselves as champions of the shared values of the community against particularistic interests, they can appear to be above politics and draw support for their actions. In 1993 UN Secretary-General Boutros Boutros-Ghali argued effectively that the Security Council was privileging the humanitarian crisis in Bosnia because it was in the (white) West and neglecting the humanitarian crisis in Somalia because it was in (black) Africa, and that the criteria used to justify intervention in Europe could also be used, and should be used, to demand action in Somalia.

Expert Authority

IOs are often authoritative because of their expertise. One reason we create bureaucracies is that we want important social tasks to be done by people with detailed, specialized knowledge about those tasks.[23] We want nuclear proliferation to be monitored by physicists and engineers who know about nuclear weapons, and we want the HIV / AIDS pandemic to be handled by doctors and public health specialists who know about disease prevention. Specialized knowledge derived from training or experience persuades us to confer on experts, and the bureaucracies that house them, the authority to make judgments and solve problems. Deployment of specialized knowledge is central to the very rational-legal authority that constitutes bureaucracy in the first place because what makes such authority rational is, at least in part, the use of socially recognized relevant knowledge to carry out tasks.

There is also a moral dimension to claims to expertise based on technical knowledge and professional training. Professionals and experts believe that as repositories of socially valued knowledge they can and should be trusted. They value technical knowledge because of their awareness that such knowledge could benefit society. As guardians of this knowledge, professionals perceive themselves to be acting in the name of the public good. In this respect, they are, according to Steven Brint, "social trustee professionals," believing that their duty is to ply their knowledge in ways that would improve society.[24] IO officials similarly believe that their expertise and professional training make them well suited to advancing the community's goals and aspirations.

Expertise not only makes IOs authoritative but also shapes the way these organizations behave. Just as IOs authorized by a moral principle must serve that principle and make their actions consistent with it to remain legitimate and authoritative, so too must IOs authorized by expertise serve that specialized knowledge and make their actions consistent with it. The IMF cannot propose any policies it chooses. It can offer only policies that are supported by the economic knowledge it deploys. In fact, the organization will not readily entertain policy options not supported by its expertise. Professional training, norms, and occupational cultures strongly shape the way experts view the world. They influence what problems are visible to staff and what range of solutions are entertained.[25]

Like delegated and moral authority, expert authority also enables IOs to be powerful by creating the appearance of depoliticization. By emphasizing the "objective" nature of their knowledge, staff of IOs are able to present themselves as technocrats whose advice is unaffected by partisan squabbles. Some kinds of expertise make this presentation easier than others. As we shall see in the chapter on the IMF, quantification vastly enhances the power of these claims of objectivity and impartiality. Ironically, the more successful experts are at making numbers appear to speak for themselves and yield clear policy prescriptions without interpretation from bureaucrats, the more powerful those policy prescriptions are. The greater the appearance of depoliticization, the greater the authority associated with the expertise.

These four types of authority—rational-legal, delegated, moral, and expert—all contribute in different ways to making IOs authoritative and, by virtue of their authority, autonomous to at least some degree. They make IOs authoritative in at least two ways: by putting them "in authority" or by making them "an authority" or some mix of the two.[26] Actors whose authority derives from the institutional roles they occupy can be said to be "in authority." The person in authority is the person occupying the role or position society recognizes as legitimate to exercise power. Thus, the president is the person in authority when it comes to deploying troops. When he or she ceases to be president, that authority will be transferred to someone else. A person who is "an authority" derives standing from expertise demonstrated by credentials, education, training, and experience. Authority of this kind inheres in the individual who has it, regardless of changes in social position or institutional role. Rational-legal authority and delegation are central to putting an IO in authority; expertise tends to be central for making it an authority. Moral claims can contribute to both kinds of authoritative status in ways that show how easily these lines are blurred. IOs often use the fact that they are "in authority," in particular institutional roles, to make moral claims that they understand to represent the wishes of the international community against the claims of self-serving states—claims to be "an authority." For example, UN secretaries-general routinely use their position to make this sort of moral claim in order to generate deference to and compliance with UN policies. At the same time IOs may parlay the moral principles they are mandated to protect (human rights, world peace) into a moral claim to be an authority on those matters. For example, UNHCR may use its institutional position as assistant to refugees and promoter of refugee law as a basis for claiming that it speaks for refugees and is uniquely able to act on their behalf.

The distinction between being "an authority" and being "in authority" provides analytic leverage over the ways in which expertise, moral claims, delegation, and bureaucratic capabilities interact. IO authority is intensified to the extent that others perceive the IO as being both an authority and in authority. Often the perception is correct. IOs tend to promote people into positions of authority who have credentials, training, and experience that make them an authority. However, the two types of authority do not always go together. IOs frequently are given jobs about which there simply is not much relevant knowledge to be had, often because these are brand-new tasks that have never before been attempted. UNHCR was created at the same time as the refugee law it was supposed to promote and protect; there was no large group of refugee experts on which to draw. Similarly, when the IMF was created, there was not a lot of economic knowledge about how to solve balance-of-payments problems because under the gold standard such problems were not solved by the coordinated actions of governments. Peacekeeping, too, was an invention of the Secretariat, and there was no expertise about how to run these operations at the time. In all three cases, IO staff were compelled or able to use their status as being in authority to define or create the knowledge relevant for carrying out these tasks, that is, to create the knowledge that makes them an authority. Sometimes this intermingling of knowledge and position is a product of circumstances and is forced upon the IOs. Other times, IOs may strategically manipulate this relationship. IO staff are aware that their authority is dependent on being perceived as both in and an authority, and they can be expected to present themselves as the expert by virtue of the fact that they occupy the position. In these ways, being in authority may allow a staff member to become an authority in the field.

Although the interconnected nature of being "in authority" and "an authority" can enhance the overall authority of an IO and its ability to execute tasks, the two also can run at cross-purposes and create tensions, complications, and even a crisis of authority for the IO. IO staff occupying positions of authority may be delegated tasks for which they lack proper training or knowledge or, in fact, tasks for which little formal knowledge or expertise exists. Although IOs often succeed at creating knowledge necessary to carry out new tasks, they do not always do so. States may also demand that IOs take on tasks that staff believe are inappropriate either because they are inconsistent with their expert knowledge or require action that staff believe is highly political and partial. Economists at the IMF are often uncomfortable when they are asked to make political or value decisions that they feel fall outside their economic expertise. UNHCR protection officers, who frequently have background in legal fields, may determine that protection standards are not adequate and that a repatriation exercise is not warranted, but be forced to adopt a compromise or pragmatic position because of political pressures from states.

IO staff often find themselves under pressure to reconcile these different bases of their authority. Authority rarely comes only from delegation, or rational-legal principles, or moral claims, or expertise; instead, these different bases mingle to generate the authority of the IO. UNHCR, for example, is conferred authority because of its statute (delegation), its claim to represent humanitarian principles and the interests of the voiceless (morality), and its expertise acquired through years of refugee relief work (expertise). Sometimes these sources of authority are complementary, but at times they conflict and generate competing demands, tugging and pulling IO staff in different directions. This is most obvious where states determine a course of action that IO officials believe runs counter to the behavior demanded by their expertise or moral claims. This strain can also exist when IO officials believe that the bases of their authority pull them in different directions. For example, as chapter 5 demonstrates, UN officials who cling to principles of impartiality and consent as the basis of their authority may find themselves forced to turn a blind eye to human rights abuses and even crimes against humanity, thus undermining their moral authority.

In sum, bureaucracies are constituted by rules that are intended to rationalize, depoliticize, systematize, and automatize how staff respond to problems and pursue ends. It is because bureaucracies are rational, impartial, and technical that they are valued and viewed as a superior way of organizing and coordinating activities. Yet standing behind these seemingly technical rules are cultural values—shared goals, moral understandings, and collectively recognized knowledge—each conferring authority on bureaucracies that serve or invoke them. Different organizations will be constituted by a different mix of these types of authority and will be guided by this mix in carrying out their tasks. Although this mix can be mutually reinforcing, quite often IOs are forced to navigate conflicting imperatives that come from different sources of authority.

The authority of IOs creates a basis for their autonomous action. It provides a basis for conceptualizing IO action as not merely epiphenomenal of the behavior of their state creators. If IR scholars have tended to overlook evidence of IO autonomy, it is partly because they have assumed that the only autonomous action that counts is behavior that overcomes opposition from powerful states. Although we agree that this would provide impressive demonstration of autonomy, it is not the only evidence of autonomous behavior. After all, states create IOs because they believe that IOs will be helpful to them, and IOs are frequently invested with autonomy to help states achieve their interests. IOs, then, are expected to exercise some discretion. States presumably hope that IOs use that discretion within a zone that is demarcated by state interests. Yet sometimes IOs also can act outside that zone in ways that work against state interests or even transform those interests. For example, sometimes IOs try to convince states that it is in their interest to allow them to expand their zone.[27] IO autonomy from states may thus come in different degrees, but also in different kinds, and scholars should look for variation in both dimensions. Loosely, we can imagine IOs' autonomous relations with states as falling into one of the following types (arranged roughly in order of increasing conflict with state interests):

1. IOs may exercise autonomy to further state interests. IOs may interpret policy and develop rules and guidelines that do not follow directly from explicit

state demands but that nevertheless help states realize their self-perceived interests.[28] This might be called autonomy by design. States know that if IOs were not autonomous then they would not be able to help states further their interests. Consequently they deliberately design some autonomy for the IOs, and IOs use their autonomy to advance mandates that are directly connected to state interests. The analytically interesting questions here revolve around how, among the possible ways they could advance state interests, IOs decide what those interests are and how best to serve them.

2. IOs may act where states are indifferent. There are a range of policy issues on which state preferences are weak either because states have little knowledge about the matter and so do not know what policy to prefer or because the matter is not perceived to be particularly important. On such issues, IOs may have wide latitude for autonomous action.

3. IOs may fail to act and therefore fail to carry out state demands. This inactivity can take a variety of forms. Sometimes it can come from standard bureaucratic slowness and barriers to nimble action. Bureaucracies often promise and in good faith intend action that they do not or cannot deliver. Other times, a strategically minded IO may consent to state demands and then proceed, by design or default, to pursue its own distinctive interests. Policy directives often look quite different after they have been filtered through bureaucratic procedures, and what gets implemented on the ground is often not what was intended by states at the outset. At still other times IOs may explicitly refuse to carry out new demands on the grounds that such demands contradict existing routines, mandates, and their expert knowledge.

4. IOs may act in ways that run against state interests.[29] We see a range of possibilities here. IOs often act contrary to the preferences of weak states, as chapter 3 shows, and often frustrate the will of strong states. IOs may build alliances with publics, nongovernmental organizations, other IOs, and other states to protect policies from powerful states that oppose them. They may initiate policies or establish agendas that garner support from these allies and that become difficult for even the most powerful states to ignore or overturn. Often these moves are oblique. IOs less frequently challenge the core interests of dominant states directly.[30]

5. IOs may change the broader normative environment and states' perceptions of their own preferences so that they are consistent with IO preferences.[31] Often IOs have principled agendas and act as missionaries that encourage others to adopt new practices and identities consistent with their missions and aspirations. International organizations such as UNHCR and the United Nations High Commissioner for Human Rights (UNHCHR) are given mandates to try to lobby states to change their behavior in ways that are consistent with existing international humanitarian and human rights law.

These five types of relationships suggest that we need to expand our thinking about how states and IOs interact and how IOs use their autonomy.

Rationalist approaches typically look for correlation between what states want and what IOs do. If IOs do what states want, they conclude that state demands drive IO behavior. This list suggests additional possibilities. IOs may set agendas for states and create policy situations that drag states along, perhaps using publics and NGOs as allies. IOs can even transform state preferences, teaching states to value new policy outcomes that they previously opposed. Recognizing the range of ways in which IOs can exhibit autonomous behavior also prepares us for the possibility that IOs can exercise power, a point we now consider.

III. THE POWER OF INTERNATIONAL ORGANIZATIONS

The power of IOs is produced by the authority that constitutes them. As bureaucracies, IOs are conferred authority, and this authority enables them to use discursive and institutional resources to induce others to defer to their judgment. Sometimes deference is a sign of acceptance, that is, conviction of the IO's rightness. At other times such deference is better understood as acquiescence or even submission because the individuals feel neither the authority to credibly voice their opposition nor the ability to act otherwise because of possible sanctions. Here, such deference more nearly justifies Weber's claim that authority is domination legitimated. It is because the exercise of authority often contains elements of consent and coercion that the concept of authority is part of the conceptual family of social control, just as is the concept of power. As expressions of social control, both concepts are intimately concerned with steering, guiding, regulating, and imposing. Consequently, the distinction between power and authority is almost always blurry, frequently intentionally so.[32] For our purposes, we define power as the "production, in and through social relations, of effects that shape the capacities of actors to determine their own circumstances and fate."[33] Because authority is produced through social relations and gives its bearer the capacity to get others to defer, it can be an exercise of power even as it contains some element of consent.[34]

The heart of bureaucratic power, as Weber argued, is control based on knowledge.[35] Sometimes this is nothing more than control over information. Neoliberal institutionalists have recognized this phenomenon and written extensively about it.[36] It is because bureaucrats have information and others do not, or because they can dictate what information other actors must collect and reveal, that they can increase their control over outcomes. But bureaucratic power involves more than just control over information as the neoliberal institutionalists conceive of it. Bureaucratic power also includes the ability to transform information into knowledge, that is, to construct information in ways that give it meaning.[37] Creating knowledge by giving meaning to information shapes social reality and prompts action. It is only because of the meaning information has to us that we act in response. The information that millions of Africans live on less that two dollars per day might have been unremarkable eighty years ago but today is understood as a "development problem" and a "poverty crisis." Thus, information or raw data may stay the same, but the way we interpret them (and act as a consequence) changes as meanings change. The information that a regime is hunting down and killing dissidents might have been understood as a prerogative of state law enforcement eighty years ago but now is understood as a major human rights violation that is subject to international scrutiny. Those meanings are socially constructed and often are constructed by bureaucracies. Bureaucracies are often the authorities that classify, label, and invest meaning in information. Indeed, they are often the authorities that decide what information should be collected in the first place. Bureaucracies map social reality as they collect and store files and data, create divisions of labor and specialized units, and construct rules that define, categorize, and classify the world.[38] In this way, bureaucratic knowledge not only reflects the social reality as defined by the bureaucracy but also constructs that reality.[39]

The distinction between regulation and constitution helps to clarify the different effects of IO power.[40] By regulative effects, we mean the ability of an actor to manipulate incentives to shape the behavior of another actor. Occasionally IO staff can deploy material resources to induce or compel actors to comply with existing rules. The IMF and other international financial institutions have very concrete and material ways to encourage compliance. However, IO power also comes from the ability to use rules and deploy knowledge in order to change incentives and regulate behavior. Neoliberal institutionalist scholars have emphasized how IOs collect information on the activities that are to be regulated and then publicize that information in ways that are intended to keep states honest and punish defectors. Classical UN monitoring of cease-fires, International Atomic Energy Agency monitoring of fissile material diversion, and IMF transparency requirements are all efforts at "regulation by revelation," by which IOs rely on simple publicity of behavior to prompt remedial action.[41] IOs can use their positions of authority in other ways to regulate behavior. They can collect some data and information, but not others. They can use their institutional authority to set the agenda so that some items are discussed and not others. They can invite some actors to participate in the decision-making process and exclude others.[42] In these and other ways, IO staff can use their institutional and expert authority to regulate behavior, guiding it in a direction that is consistent with their preferences and with existing rules and mandates.

By constitutive effects, we mean the ability to create, define, and map social reality.[43] International relations scholars have examined this kind of power in other contexts. They have investigated the ability of actors to define a problem or a moral good, to identify the legitimate means to pursue collectively generated ends, and to establish the rules of the social situation that limits the scope of action.[44] IOs, too, exhibit this sort of power and these sorts of effects. They constitute social kinds, tasks, and rules and so help generate the world in which we live. They do not accomplish these outcomes on their own. They often act in concert with states, both at the moment of creation when states define the mandate and at various moments afterward. Nongovernmental organizations also have conspicuously attempted to help create new international fields of action, norms, and law, often working with and through international organizations.[45] Yet because of their multiple sources of authority, IOs have decided advantages for helping to constitute social reality.

IOs are able to use their authority, knowledge, and rules to regulate and constitute the world that subsequently requires regulation. We identify three related mechanisms by which they do this. IOs (1) classify the world, creating categories of problems, actors, and action; (2) fix meanings in the social world; and (3) articulate and diffuse new norms and rules. All these mechanisms can have both regulative and constitutive effects. Sometimes the classification of the world, the fixing of meanings, and the diffusion of norms alter the incentives for particular policies or types of behavior, and thus serve to regulate action. At other times such mechanisms help to define social reality itself and thus provide the constitutional foundations for subsequent action that needs to be regulated.

Classification of the World

An elementary feature of bureaucracies is that they classify and organize information and knowledge. This classification process is a form of power. "Bureaucracies," writes Don Handelman, "are ways of making, ordering, and knowing social worlds." They perform these tasks by "moving persons among social categories or by inventing and applying such categories."[46] The ability to classify objects, to shift their very definition and identity, is one of bureaucracy's greatest sources of power.

International organizations are not only established by states to solve problems and pursue collective interests but also help to define these problems and pursuits. The world is littered with problems that cause harm or block considerations of practices that generate benefit to populations, but only some of these problems become a matter of political concern.[47] Problems have to be constructed. Human rights was not always defined as a problem. Lack of good governance is not necessarily and objectively a problem. Instead, IOs and others have been actively involved in defining human rights and global governance as problems that require solutions. Problems are not part of objective reality but are subjectively defined and constituted within social experience. Authorities help to create that subjective reality and to define what are the problems that require solutions.[48]

Classification schemes shape not only how IOs see the world but also how they act on the world in ways that can directly affect the behavior of others. The IMF has a particular way of categorizing economies and determining whether they are on the right track, defined in terms of their capital accounts, balance of payments, budget deficits, and reserves. To be categorized as not on track can affect the ability of a state to get external financing at reasonable rates, to get access to IMF funds, or to escape the IMF's conditionality demands. Similarly, a great many individuals in the world have either been forced or chosen to flee their homes, and UNHCR operates a classification scheme that distinguishes between refugees, migrants, internally displaced peoples, and others. UNHCR's very unwillingness to extend refugee status to groups or individuals can leave them on the margin or physically vulnerable.[49] In chapter 4, we examine how UNHCR's expansion of the category of refugees to include new groups of individuals constitutes an act of power, and how its refusal to extend refugee status to groups constitutes a life-threatening act. Similarly, classification of a conflict as a civil war triggers one set of responses by international actors, including international organizations, while classification as genocide triggers another, as we show in chapter 5.

The Fixing of Meanings

While classification focuses on naming and labeling the social context and on grouping similar social kinds, IOs also exercise power by virtue of their ability to help fix the meanings of those social kinds.[50] Because actors are oriented toward objects and objectives on the basis of the meaning that they attribute to them, the ability to invest situations with a particular meaning constitutes an important source of power.[51]

IOs can fix meanings in ways that orient action and establish boundaries for acceptable action. IOs often play a central role in establishing meanings for a broad range of international actors. For example, in the development field IOs have been at the center of efforts to define (and redefine) what development is, who gets to do the developing (usually states or IOs), and who is to be developed (usually local groups).[52] Similarly, in post–Cold War security politics, IOs have been at the forefront of efforts to shift the definition of "security" from state security against invading armies toward human security against a much wider range of economic, environmental, and political as well as military threats.[53] In chapter 3, we see the IMF defining and redefining "conditionality" on its loans and, in the process, defining (and redefining) what a good economy is for members. In chapter 4 we see UNHCR defining and redefining "durable" and "permanent" solutions to refugee problems. In chapter 5 we see the UN Security Council defining the meaning and applicability of "peacekeeping" in ways that are hugely consequential for millions of people.

IOs (and other actors) are often able to do this sort of work through framing. Frames "are specific metaphors, symbolic representations, and cognitive cues used to render or cast behavior and events in an evaluative mode and to suggest alternative modes of action."[54] Actors use frames to situate events and to interpret problems, to fashion a shared understanding of the world, to galvanize sentiments as a way to mobilize and guide social action, and to suggest possible resolutions to current plights. Events, in short, do not have an objective meaning but must be made meaningful by actors, and actors compete to affix meaning to these events because doing so creates boundaries of acceptable action. For example, IOs and NGOs recently were able to reframe the meaning of landmines for other actors. With appeals to the laws of war (to emphasize the indiscriminate nature of landmines and their lack of military effectiveness) and skillful use of media to mobilize public opinion (with pictures of victims), these groups were able to transform landmines from a pedestrian piece of military hardware into an illegal source of large-scale human rights violations.[55]

Diffusion of Norms

Having established rules and norms, IOs are eager to spread the benefits of their expertise and often act as conveyor belts for the transmission of norms and models of good political behavior.[56] There is nothing accidental or unintended about this role. Officials in IOs often insist that part of their mission is to spread, inculcate, and enforce global values and norms. They are the missionaries of our time. Armed with a notion of progress, an idea of how to create the better life, and some understanding of the conversion process, many IO staff have as their stated purpose to shape state action by establishing best practices and by articulating and transmitting norms that define what constitutes acceptable and legitimate state behavior. The IMF, for example, is hard at work persuading members to reconfigure domestic financial institutions and practices in ways that harmonize with international standards. Promoting awareness of and adherence to international refugee law among states and other actors is an explicit part of the UNHCR mandate.

As IOs classify the world, promote and fix meanings, and diffuse norms, they frequently legitimate and facilitate their own expansion and intervention in the affairs of states and nonstate actors. As they constitute social tasks and frame problems, IOs also assign responsibility for solving or addressing them. Often there are a great many ways in which a problem might be addressed. They could be addressed by states, by NGOs, by decentralized markets, or by international organizations. As authorities, IOs are frequently the ones to determine what is the suitable solution to a problem and who gets to (or has to) solve it. Because of their rational-legal character, IOs tend to craft rational-legal solutions and favor rational-legal authorities (like themselves) to carry them out. Solutions that involve regulation, arbitration, and intervention by rational-legal authorities (themselves or other organizations) appear sensible, rational, and good to IOs and so disproportionately emerge from IO activity. For instance, international organizations have undertaken a range of peacebuilding operations as a way of trying to develop stable, legitimate states in the aftermath of violent conflicts. Establishing a civilian police force has become a routine part of these efforts. But a professional police establishment assumes a professional judiciary and a penal system where criminals can be tried and jailed. A professional judiciary, in turn, presupposes lawyers who can come to court and law schools to train them. Trained lawyers presuppose a code of law. The result is that what began as a relatively narrow technical intervention (training police) expands to a package of reforms aimed at transforming non-Western societies (where most peacebuilding takes place) into Western societies.[57] Many, if not most, of these activities are undertaken by IOs.

By establishing categories, fixing meanings, and diffusing norms, IOs use their authority to exercise power and influence the world. The power of IOs is broader than their ability to use material resources to get states and nonstate actors to do what they otherwise would not do. Their authority allows them to persuade and induce compliance with existing rules, and it also gives them the ability to help constitute the world that then requires regulation. IOs define problems for other actors (by classifying them as such), specify which actors have responsibility for solving those problems, and use their authority to identify the right or appropriate kind of solution for the particular problem under consideration. IOs do not carry out these activities alone. States and nonstate actors are often involved. But IO authority and the powers it creates are crucial components of this process. It is through their authority to regulate and constitute that IOs are able not only to exercise power but also to authorize their own expansion.

IV. PATHOLOGIES OF INTERNATIONAL ORGANIZATIONS

Bureaucracies are created, propagated, and valued in modern society because of their supposed rationality and effectiveness in carrying out social tasks. Yet bureaucracies are infamous for creating and implementing policies that defy rational logic, for acting in ways that are at odds with their stated mission, and for refusing requests of and turning their backs on those to whom they are officially responsible.[58] Scholars of U.S. bureaucracy have recognized this problem and have devoted considerable energy to understanding a wide range of undesirable and inefficient bureaucratic behaviors caused by bureaucratic capture by special interests, slack in control by principals, usually Congress, and other conditions that give rise to suboptimal equilibria in organizational structures. Similarly, scholars researching foreign policy decision making have investigated organizational dynamics that produce self-defeating and inefficient behavior in those contexts.[59]

International organizations, too, are prone to dysfunctional behaviors, but IR scholars have rarely investigated this, in part, we suspect, because the theoretical apparatus they use provides few grounds for expecting undesirable IO behavior.[60] The state-centric utility-maximizing frameworks most IR scholars have borrowed from economics simply assume that IOs are reasonably responsive to state interests (or, at least, more responsive than other policy tools would be); otherwise states would withdraw from them. This, however, is a necessary theoretical axiom of these frameworks; it is rarely treated as a hypothesis subject to empirical investigation.[61] With little theoretical reason to expect suboptimal or self-defeating behavior in IOs, these scholars do not look for it and have had little to say about it. Policymakers, however, have been quicker to perceive and address these problems and are putting them on the political agenda. It is time for scholars, too, to explore these issues more fully.

Analysis of dysfunction requires that we develop criteria so that we can identify it when we see it. Dysfunction is always a matter of *degree, perspective,* and *kind.*[62] The degree issue is the most straightforward. Few IO policies serve any end perfectly. There is always noise in the system, and some amount of stupidity, inefficiency, and especially compromise is inherent in all social life. In this sense, some dysfunction is inevitable. What we care about here, though, are those occasions when behavior significantly exceeds the inevitable minimum of noise and leads the organization to act in ways that are inconsistent with its social purpose. Thus, we study a UN Secretariat that presents itself as a guardian of human rights but nevertheless turns a blind eye to crimes against humanity. We study financial stabilization programs that produce one failure after another. We study a UNHCR that violates refugee rights. These failures are not merely technical miscues. They create a crisis of conscience for those in the organization and raise questions about the organization's efficacy and legitimacy among both staff and outsiders.

The perspective issue is thornier. The problem here is that most IOs have multiple audiences, multiple principals, and multiple missions. Consequently, it is difficult analytically to label a behavior "bad" or even "undesirable," since most behaviors serve someone's interest. A UNHCR that fails to challenge states every time they violate refugee rights might be functional for interested governments and even for the organization, which must pick its battles wisely to preserve state support. IMF policies may create widespread misery in deficit countries but be extremely functional for global capitalism. The decision by the UN Secretariat not to intervene in the Rwandan genocide might have been completely dysfunctional from a human rights perspective but extremely functional for strong states that wanted to stay out of the conflict and for a Secretariat that believed that the likely failure of the operation would fatally damage the organization. At a minimum, dysfunction's referent must always be made clear. Behavior is dysfunctional only *for* something or someone; behavior by itself is neither functional nor dysfunctional.

Our approach to this problem has been to employ a multi-sited analysis. We do not try to obliterate the referent-dependent nature of dysfunction and pathology. Rather, we analyze potential pathologies from several different angles, showing how behaviors that seem self-defeating or undesirable from one perspective might make perfect sense from another.[63] We begin each case by searching for behavior that departs from the mission statement and publicly proclaimed goals of the organization. We thus look for financial policies that do not produce financial stability, refugee policies that do not protect refugees, peacekeeping operations that undermine rather than promote peace and security. This helps identify problematic behavior for future inquiry. We then adopt a more interpretive lens. In each case, we asked the bureaucrats themselves how they understood their actions, how they reconciled apparent contradictions between actions and goals. The result is a nuanced account that shows how behavior that might seem completely dysfunctional, even horrific, from one perspective can seem completely reasonable, justifiable, even necessary from another. Thus, we attempt to do more than merely code events dichotomously as pathology or nonpathology. We show the mechanisms that generated the pathology and how pathologies grew from the internal understandings and rules of the organization.

In addition to issues of degree and perspective, our analysis alerts us to the many kinds or sources of IO dysfunction. Extant theories about dysfunction can be categorized in two dimensions: whether they locate the cause inside or outside the organization, and whether they trace the cause to material or cultural forces. Mapping theories on these dimensions creates the following typology:

	Internal	*External*
Material	bureaucratic politics	realism / neoliberal institutionalism
Cultural	bureaucratic culture	world polity model

Each cell identifies a representative body of theory familiar to most IR scholars.

Explanations of IO dysfunction that emphasize the pursuit of material interests within an organization typically examine how competition among subunits over material resources leads the organization to make decisions and engage in behaviors that are inefficient or undesirable as judged against some ideal policy that would allow the organization to achieve its stated goals. Bureaucratic politics is the best-known theory here, and while current scholars of international politics have not widely adopted this perspective to explain IO behavior, it is relatively well developed in the older IO literature.[64] Graham Allison's central argument is that the "name of the game is politics: bargaining along regularized circuits among players positioned hierarchically within the government. Government behavior can thus be understood as . . . results of these bargaining games."[65] In this view, decisions are made not after a rational decision process but rather through a competitive bargaining process over turf, budgets, and staff that may benefit parts of the organization at the expense of overall goals.

Another body of literature traces IO dysfunctional behavior to the material forces located outside the organization. Realist and neoliberal theories might posit that state preferences and constraints are responsible for producing dysfunctional behavior. In this view, IOs are not to blame for bad outcomes, states are. IOs do not have the luxury of choosing the optimal policy, but rather are frequently forced to choose between the bad and the awful because more desirable policies are denied to them by states that do not agree among themselves and/or do not wish to see the IO fulfill its mandate in some particular instance. The important point of these theories is that they trace IO dysfunctional behavior back to material factors outside the IO, usually to states.

Cultural theories also have internal and external variants.[66] For analytical clarity we divide cultural theories according to whether they see the primary causes of the IO's dysfunctional behavior as deriving from normative and cultural factors of the IO's environment (external) or the culture of the organization itself (internal). The world polity model exemplifies theories that look to external culture to understand an IO's dysfunctional behavior. There are two reasons to expect dysfunctional behavior here. First, because IO practices reflect a search for symbolic legitimacy rather than efficiency, IO behavior might be only remotely connected to the efficient implementation of its goals and more closely coupled to legitimacy criteria that come from the cultural environment.[67] Second, the world polity is full of contradictions. For instance, a liberal world polity has several defining principles, including human rights, markets, and democracy, that might conflict at any one moment. Thus, environments are often ambiguous about missions and contain varied and often conflicting functional, normative, and legitimacy imperatives.[68] Because they are embedded in that cultural environment, IOs can mirror and reproduce those contradictions, which, in turn, can lead to contradictory and ultimately dysfunctional behavior.

Finally, organizations frequently develop distinctive internal cultures that can promote dysfunctional behavior, behavior that we call "pathological."[69] We define pathological behavior as behavior generated by the internal organizational culture that violates the self-understood core goals of the organization. Dysfunctions of this type flow from constitutive features of bureaucracy as a social form.[70] Two features of the modern bureaucratic form are particularly important in creating pathology-producing cultures. The first is the simple fact that bureaucracies are organized around rules, routines, and standard operating procedures designed to trigger a predictable response to environmental stimuli. These rules can be formal or informal, but in either case they tell actors what action is appropriate in response to a specific event, request, or demand. In many ways, this kind of routinization is good. Routinization is precisely the behavior bureaucracies are supposed to exhibit—it is what makes them effective and competent in performing complex social tasks. However, the presence of such rules also compromises the extent to which means-ends rationality drives organizational behavior. Rules and routines may come to obscure overall missions and larger social goals. They may create ritualized behavior in bureaucrats and construct a very parochial normative environment within the organization whose connection to the larger social environment is tenuous at best.[71]

The second constitutive feature that can lead to pathology is that bureaucracies specialize and compartmentalize. They create a division of labor on the logic that because individuals have only so much time, knowledge, and expertise, specialization will allow the organization to emulate a rational decision-making process.[72] Again, this is one of the virtues of bureaucracy in that it provides a way of overcoming the limitations of individual rationality and knowledge by embedding those individuals in a structure that takes advantage of their competencies without having to rely on their weaknesses. However it, too, has some negative consequences. Just as rules can eclipse goals, concentrated expertise and specialization can (and perhaps must) limit bureaucrats' field of vision and create subcultures that are distinct from those of the larger environment. Professional training plays a particularly strong role here since this is one widespread way we disseminate specialized knowledge and credential experts. Such training often gives experts—indeed, is designed to give them—a distinctive worldview and normative commitments, which, when concentrated in a subunit of an organization, can have pronounced effects on behavior.[73]

Once in place, a bureaucracy's culture—"the solutions that are produced by groups of people to meet specific problems, and then how those solutions become institutionalized as rituals, values, and ultimately as rules"—has important consequences for the way individuals who inhabit that organization make sense of the world.[74] It provides interpretive frames that individuals use to generate meaning.[75] This is more than just bounded rationality; actors' rationality itself, the very means and ends that they value, are shaped by the organizational culture.[76] Divisions and subunits within the organization may develop their own cognitive frameworks that are consistent with but still distinct from those of the larger organization, further complicating this process.

Bureaucracy's emphasis on rules, specialization, and compartmentalization can combine to create pathologies in a variety of ways. We identify five such mechanisms: the irrationality of rationalization, universalism, normalization of deviance, organizational insulation, and cultural contestation. These all flow from defining features of bureaucracy itself. Consequently, we expect them to be present in any bureaucracy to a limited degree. Their severity may be increased, however, by specific empirical conditions of the organization, particularly if these mechanisms operate in conjunction with one another.[77]

1. *Irrationality of rationalization.* Max Weber recognized that the rationalization processes at which bureaucracies excel could be taken to extremes and ultimately become irrational if the rules and procedures that enabled bureaucracies to do their jobs became ends in themselves. Rather than designing the most appropriate and efficient rules and procedures to accomplish their missions, bureaucracies often tailor their missions to fit the existing, well-known, and comfortable rulebook.[78] Thus, means (rules and procedures) may become so embedded and powerful that they determine ends and the way the organization defines its goals.

2. *Bureaucratic universalism.* This mechanism derives from the fact that bureaucracies "orchestrate numerous local contexts at once."[79] Bureaucrats necessarily flatten diversity because they are supposed to generate universal rules and categories that are by design inattentive to contextual and particularistic concerns. Part of the justification for this, of course, is the bureaucratic view that technical knowledge is transferable across circumstances. Sometimes this is a good assumption, but not always; when particular circumstances are not appropriate to the generalized knowledge being applied, the results can be disastrous.[80]

3. *Normalization of deviance.* Over time, organizations sometimes allow exceptions to rules (deviance) to become routine and normal parts of procedures, and the normalization of what was once deviant can increase the probability that the organization will undertake actions that risk failure.[81] Bureaucracies establish rules to provide a predictable, safe, and successful response to environmental stimuli. At times, however, bureaucracies make small, calculated deviations from established rules because of new environmental or institutional developments, explicitly calculating that bending the rules in this instance does not create excessive risk of policy failure. Over time, these

exceptions can become the rule: they can become institutionalized to the point where deviance is normalized. The result of this process is that what at one time might be weighed seriously and debated as a potentially unacceptable risk or dangerous procedure comes to be treated as normal at a later time. Indeed, because of staff turnover, those making decisions at a later point in time might be unaware that the now-routine behavior was ever viewed as risky or dangerous.

4. *Insulation.* Organizations vary greatly in the degree to which they receive and process feedback from their environment about performance. Those insulated from such feedback often develop internal cultures and procedures that do not promote the goals of those who created the organization or those whom it serves. Lack of feedback can create the conditions for pathological behavior when parochial worldviews produce goals, procedures, and classification or categorization schemes that come to define the way bureaucrats see the world such that they routinely ignore information that is essential to the accomplishment of the organization's goals.[82]

   Two causes of insulation seem particularly applicable to IOs. The first is professionalism. Professional training does more than impart technical knowledge. It actively seeks to shape the normative orientation and worldviews of those who are trained. Doctors are trained to value life above all else, soldiers are trained to sacrifice life for certain strategic objectives, and economists are trained to value efficiency. Bureaucracies, by their nature, concentrate professionals inside organizations, and concentrations of people with the same expertise or professional training can create an organizational worldview distinct from the larger environment. Second, many organizations do not face strong external performance pressures, and successful performance may be difficult to measure. Many do not compete with others on the basis of output but are valued more for what they represent than for what they do. Inability to evaluate performance, either within the organization, so it can self-correct and learn in a rational fashion, or from outside, increases the potential for pathologies. Rules and procedures contributing to poor performance can go uncorrected and proliferate. Internal cultures and understandings of goals that do not contribute to effective action are allowed to persist.[83]

5. *Cultural contestation.* Organizational coherence is an accomplishment rather than a given. Organizational control within a putative hierarchy is always incomplete, creating pockets of autonomy and political battles within the bureaucracy.[84] Such contests occur partly because bureaucracies are organized around the principle of division of labor and different divisions tend to be staffed by individuals who are experts in their assigned tasks. These different divisions may battle over budgets or material resources and so follow the bureaucratic politics model, but they may also clash because of distinct internal cultures that grow up inside different parts of the organization. Different segments of the organization may develop different ways of making sense of the world, may experience different local environments and receive different stimuli from outside, and may be populated by different mixes of

professions or be shaped by different historical experiences. All of these contribute to the development of different local cultures within the organization and different ways of perceiving the environment and the organization's overall mission. Organizations may try to minimize complications from these divisions by arranging these demands hierarchically, but to the extent that hierarchy resolves conflict by squelching input from some subunits in favor of others, it causes the organization to lose the benefits of a division of labor that it was supposed to provide. More commonly, though, attempts to reconcile competing worldviews hierarchically are simply incomplete. Most organizations develop a set of overlapping and contradictory preferences among subgroups.[85] Consequently, different constituencies representing different normative views will suggest different tasks and goals for the organization, resulting in a clash of competing perspectives that generates pathological tendencies.

Every bureaucracy has the potential for pathology. The mechanisms outlined above are inherent in all bureaucracies, including international organizations. We examine two cases of pathologies in detail: UNHCR's repatriation culture and its sanctioning of involuntary repatriation of the Rohingyan refugees from Bangladesh to Burma in 1994; and the Secretariat's institutional ideology of impartiality and its preference not to intervene in the opening weeks of the Rwandan genocide. Although the ideal-typical mechanisms we traced above provide guidance, in practice any actual instance of pathology is likely to involve several of these types. In both case studies we see mixes of different bureaucratic sources of pathology that led IO staff to wonder in retrospect whether the organization had compromised its principles to the point that it had lost its way.

V. ORGANIZATIONAL CHANGE

International organizations, like all organizations, evolve in ways not intended by their creators.[86] Institutional and organizational theorists have developed a wealth of explanations for organizational change, but international relations theorists have rarely applied these arguments to IOs and, indeed, have not given much thought to how and why international organizations have evolved. Their (often implicit) assumption has been that IOs change because states want them to change and that states have demanded and directed changes in tasks or responsibilities. Although this is certainly one plausible explanation, it has not been empirically investigated in any systematic way or weighed against alternatives. Below we lay out an array of alternatives, including one that flows directly from our constitutive argument about bureaucracy. Our empirical studies both demonstrate the importance of this constitutive mechanism of change and suggest ways in which it combines with other sources of change to create the complex organizational dynamics we find in real-world politics.

We can map theories of organizational change on the same 2×2 matrix we used to understand theories of dysfunction. Theories of international organizational change can be distinguished according to whether they conceptualize the change as originating in internal or external forces, and coming from cultural or material variables. These distinctions can be characterized and mapped in the following ways:

	Internal	*External*
Material	resource conflict	statist / functionalist
Cultural	bureaucratic form and culture	world polity

Resource conflict arguments about organizational change come in two varieties. One is that organizations are constantly searching for ways to minimize their resource dependence and manage their dependence on other organizations.[87] In order to minimize dependence, organizational leaders will constantly develop rules and procedures to control the flow of their resources and to control the resources that sustain rival organizations. The other argument about change is that conflicts between different bureaucratic units within an organization often are driven by a struggle for power, prestige, and resources.[88] This struggle for power and prominence in the organization can lead to the adoption of new rules that might enable some units within the bureaucracy to gain a greater role in the formulation and implementation of the organization's mandate. Resource conflict models, then, hold that political struggles over resources within an organization and between organizations represent the primary source of organizational change and rule evolution.

Statist and functionalist arguments contend that states and their demand for power or desire for cooperation drive change in organizations and rules. Realist arguments claim that Great Power demands are the primary source of international organization change and rule evolution.[89] Functionalist arguments highlight how states attempt to design and modify international organizations so as to help the states achieve their goals in a pareto-superior way with efficient and effective rules.[90]

Also falling under the statist and functionalist heading are principal-agent approaches. There is a strong and a weak position here. The strong position is that any organizational change can be attributed largely to explicit decisions by states. Certainly there are cases when member states amend charters or formally delegate new tasks to IOs, but empirically, change without state intervention is common. The weak position, and the one that is arguably held by most principal-agent scholars, is that IOs are likely to use their autonomy and work within a zone of discretion to accumulate new tasks; the presumption is that if the IO bumps up against or crosses this zone, the states will sanction the IO or rewrite the contract so that the IO conforms more closely to state interests.[91]

Sociological-institutionalist approaches emphasize the way the rules and routines that define the organization come from the broader external culture or world polity. Accordingly, these scholars tend to view organizational change as a response to shifts in the regulatory and normative patterns in the environment.[92] Organizational survival and acceptance are dependent on demonstrating legitimacy, in this view, and organizations will change in response to new normative demands or requirements from outside. Although sociological institutionalists have varied ways of thinking about how the environment affects the organization, they share a common starting point with the claim that the environment plays a prominent role in the direction and content of organizational change.[93]

The internal/cultural box highlights bureaucratic culture. Here, shared understandings within an organization shape staff action and create change. The bureaucratic culture argument stands in stark contrast to the statist, functionalist, and world polity arguments about change. Their theoretical assumption is that organizations are empty vessels that channel external stimuli (from states, markets, or world culture) into functional or appropriate behavior in an unproblematic way. In contrast, bureaucratic culture arguments emphasize how the processes by which staff interpret and negotiate the meanings of their rules and actions and the ways staff understand their overall mission shape how they respond to external stimuli.[94]

Although bureaucratic culture arguments about change are highly contextual and organization specific, they offer two distinctive claims.[95] First, organizational change tends to be path dependent. Existing rules and culture inside an organization strongly shape decisions about the future, foreclosing some options and biasing outcomes toward others. Because much of organizational change consists of revising existing rules, it can often be understood as adaptation.[96] Following on our previous arguments about pathology, though, we make no presumption that such adaptation reflects any sort of functional logic or desire to be more efficient.

The second claim is that bureaucracies, by their nature, tend to expand in both size and scope of tasks. This is often not the result of some imperialist budget-maximizing impulse so much as a logical extension of the social constitution of bureaucracy. The courses of action likely to be preferred by rational-legal authorities are, not surprisingly, rational-legal ones. Left to their own devices, bureaucracies are likely to craft policies that promote rational (in the Weberian sense), impersonal, rule-governed, and technocratic approaches to social tasks. Who better to provide intervention of this type than a bureaucracy? Consequently, IOs tend to define both problems and solutions in ways that favor or even require expanded action for IOs. We saw this in the way IOs exercise power. IOs tend to define human rights, security, development, and other international goods along with methods for protecting or promoting them in ways that legitimate or even require expanded action by IOs. In addition, bureaucracy's effort to rationalize the world by dividing it into neat categories and mapping each category of problem or task onto a specified solution is fraught with tension and, at some level, doomed to failure. This can be especially true when bureaucracies are given huge, aspirational tasks like advancing development, protecting refugees, and promoting global health. As we will see in the case studies, a complex world defies the bureaucracy's tidy boxes and neatly circumscribed division of labor. In their efforts to protect human rights, provide security, and promote development, bureaucracies continually find that their definitions and standard operating procedures do not take into account features of reality that threaten their ability to accomplish these missions. Thus, the World Bank and IMF have repeatedly discovered that their models of development and economic stabilization have omitted variables and that these omissions have compromised success. Failure to attend to subsidies, incomes policies, good governance, and program ownership have led these IOs to expand their work into new sectors of the economy and society. Similarly, the failure of the UN's original procedures for peacekeeping has led to expanded missions involving police forces, judiciaries, and job creation—what we now call "nation-building." The result has been a steady expansion of tasks for all these organizations as they try to square their rationalized abstractions of reality with facts on the ground.

The steady expansion of international organizations and the bureaucratization of the world are among the most important developments of the last two centuries. This expansion did not happen by accident. It occurred because states and nonstate actors looked to international organizations to fulfill certain functions and purposes. Sometimes these functions were technical and involved coordination of already existing behavior. At other times organizations were expected to fulfill a more expressive purpose, to articulate and pursue a notion of progress, and to do work that promoted the desired values of the broader international community. IOs, then, were conferred authority because of the various functions they were expected to perform and their standing as experts and as moral agents. Once created, international organizations, acting like the bureaucracies they were, used their authority to expand their control over more and more of international life. Indeed, the majority of international organizations are now created by other international organizations.[97] To understand this impressive expansion requires understanding the constitution of international organizations. The social stuff of which they are made—specifically, their rules and the nature of their authority—yields insight into the ways that they exercise power and how their good intentions can sometimes lead to unfortunate and tragic outcomes. The following empirical chapters are designed to illuminate these connections.

3

EXPERTISE AND POWER AT THE INTERNATIONAL MONETARY FUND

Today's International Monetary Fund (IMF) is not the organization anticipated by states at its founding in 1944. The IMF does much more than monitor exchange rates and provide currency to help states through balance-of-payments difficulties. Through its technical advice and conditionality programs, it has become intimately involved in members' domestic economies in ways specifically rejected by its founders. The Fund now intervenes in members' monetary, fiscal, income, labor, industrial, and environmental policies. It has become very active in reconfiguring domestic political and business institutions of all kinds, advising countries on appropriate configurations of everything from their social spending to their stock markets and banking sectors. These changes cannot be understood simply as the result of new demands by states. While states initiated some of these changes, such as expansion into environmental affairs, they did not initiate most of these new activities. Instead, we find IMF staff driving many of these developments, and staff, in turn, are motivated by the content of their expertise. By tracing the history of these changes, we show how the IMF's expert authority prompted shifts in its mission in ways that have greatly expanded its ability to regulate domestic economic life and to constitute those very systems that need regulation. We also show how this expansion has been the result, not of organizational success, but of persistent failure to stabilize the economies of member states.

We begin by examining the birth of the IMF to understand the controls states initially placed on its operations and the different sources of autonomy they gave it. The Fund was explicitly designed to serve the interests of powerful states; staff have few obvious levers of power. The two structural features of the organization that do contribute to autonomy are the staff's ability to shape the agenda at meetings of the executive board and the fact that the organization's currencies generate revenue to fund its operations so that it does not rely on states for regular dues or contributions in the way the UN or UNHCR do. These factors are important, but we argue in this chapter that a far more crucial determinant of the IMF's autonomy and behavior is its expert authority, the specialized knowledge held by the organization. Expertise, after all, is what determines what staff put on the agenda and what they do with the slack created by relative financial autonomy.[1]

In section II we investigate how the IMF's expertise shaped its approach to solving balance-of-payments problems and how those solutions drove it deeper into domestic economic governance. When states established the IMF, there was little detailed knowledge about what policies would correct a payments deficit. In order to fulfill their mandate, IMF staff drew from their economic training to develop models that created new intellectual connections between domestic economic stability and balance-of-payments position. The basic model they developed, later elaborated in many ways, provided a relatively simple way of assessing financial flows that influence balance-of-payments positions on the basis of limited data. Further, it identified a single variable over which governments had some control—domestic credit creation—as the key to solving payments problems. The model was attractive within the Fund because it solved a number of organizational problems, notably limited data from these deficit countries and the need to provide some prescription for action to their governments, and it did so in an elegant, intellectually defensible way. The model also explicitly connected balance of payments with the workings of the domestic economy in ways that made intervention in domestic economic policymaking seem not just desirable but also necessary, if Fund staff were to accomplish their mission. Under the logic of this new "intellectual technology," the remedies for payments imbalances increasingly were perceived by Fund staff and other economists to lie in changes to what had previously been thought of as domestic economic policies.

These models thus led the Fund to recommend policies that would not only regulate member states' domestic economies but also, ultimately, (re)constitute them. The challenge was to get deficit governments to accept its recommendations. The Fund has two principal tools to accomplish this, conditionality and technical assistance, and we discuss these in section III. Both tools aimed at (re)constructing domestic economies in ways Fund staff believed would not only improve balance-of-payments position but also promote better overall economic health. Beginning in the 1950s, members were allowed to borrow funds from the IMF only on the condition that they implement certain policy measures designed by the Fund to improve the borrower's financial health. At the same time, Fund staff began offering technical advice, teaching officials in national governments how to configure central banks and do the IMF-style "financial programming" that would guide good policies. Conditionality and technical assistance, however, often did not produce the desired results. When programs failed to solve members' payments problems, the Fund's assessment usually concluded that their original models were too narrow and that some omitted variables—fiscal policies, domestic market structures, incomes policies, banking structure—were contributing to financial instability and must be remedied through additional conditionality. As a result, the Fund moved from a limited focus on balance-of-payments lending to ever more sweeping structural interventions in members' economies and societies in an attempt to control activities that might contribute to stabilization. These solutions were not, however, purely technical and value-neutral; they aimed to reconstitute these economies to conform with the market-dominated models that have become known as the Washington Consensus.

In section IV we consider how this expansion has moved the Fund further and further away from some of the core macroeconomic competencies and the technical expertise that originally justified its work. Much of the current debate over the Fund's future centers on whether it is competent in these new areas and whether growing conflicts among goals have hurt the IMF's primary mission. "Goal congestion" of this kind is common in large IOs and is a frequent source of dysfunction.[2] Although states, especially the powerful ones, sanctioned these developments, they did not devise them or push them on staff. Rather, the creation of most (and the most effective) forms of conditionality can be traced to the IMF staff and the intellectual equipment they use to understand their job and the economic world. To the extent that goal congestion and poor performance result from shared knowledge inside the organization, the Fund's behavior has pathological elements, as we define that term. However, not all new goals are generated internally. Some come from states, NGOs, and private financial actors, and we show that new goals are treated differently by the organization depending on their source.

We conclude by considering three features of the IMF's expert authority that bear on our general argument about IOs. First, we discuss how the Fund's expertise shapes its understanding and categorization of the world. The content of the IMF's expertise shapes its understanding of what constitutes a problem and how these problems are best solved. It matters, for instance, that the IMF is staffed by economists and not anthropologists or political scientists. We then consider why others defer to the IMF. Authority, as we argued in chapter 1, contains elements of coercion and consent. There is little doubt that the IMF frequently uses its institutional authority to coerce—to compel others to make economic changes that they otherwise would not. But IMF staff believe that these policies are objectively warranted and attempt to convince states of this fact, thereby obtaining some measure of consent. IMF staff spend significant resources developing objective, quantitative tools—statistics and economic models—on which to base their policy prescriptions and use these to persuade others of the necessity of these policies. They also work hard to educate national officials in borrower countries about macroeconomic policymaking. Persuasion and education of this kind depend on reducing information asymmetries, not exploiting them, to exercise power. Last, we consider the relationship between expert authority and power, focusing on the IMF's ability to regulate and constitute an international and domestic economy that requires more regulation.

I. THE MISSION, STRUCTURE, AND AUTONOMY OF THE IMF

The Articles of Agreement under which the Fund was created list six purposes for the organization: promoting international monetary cooperation; facilitating the expansion and balanced growth of world trade; promoting exchange stability; assisting in the establishment of a multilateral system of payments and elimination of foreign exchange restrictions; making resources available, under adequate safeguards, for balance-of-payments adjustments; and shortening the duration and lessening the degree of balance-of-payments disequilibria.[3] From the beginning the Fund has operated on the understanding that the first four purposes, dealing with the general health and stability of the monetary system, are best served by pursuit of the last two. Overall monetary stability, cooperation, and economic health of the system are best achieved when the balance-of-payments positions of members are satisfactory.[4]

States designed the Fund to ensure that major policy decision-making power resided firmly with state members. Each member of the Fund appoints a governor who represents that state at the annual meetings in Washington. This large and unwieldy gathering is not equipped to carry out any real managerial or policy business, however. Day-to-day policy decisions are taken by a twenty-four-member executive board of state representatives who are resident in Washington and meet three times per week to make most of the policy decisions of the Fund. They approve all uses of Fund resources by members as well as staff reports on member countries, quota changes, and most other major actions by the Fund. The five largest shareholders (the United States, Japan, Germany, France, and the United Kingdom) appoint their own executive directors (EDs) on this board to cast their votes at the Fund, as do China, Russia, and Saudi Arabia. The other sixteen EDs represent groups of countries.[5] The managing director of the Fund chairs executive board meetings and also runs the Fund's staff of roughly 2,700. The managing director is chosen by the member states for a renewable five-year term and has traditionally been a European (complementing the tradition of an American head of the World Bank).[6]

The Fund is explicitly constructed to reflect not just the preferences of states but the preferences of the Fund's richest and most powerful members. Unlike the UN General Assembly and many other IOs founded after World War II, the Fund weights the voting power of its 184 members according to their contributions to the Fund's resources. The more money a country contributes to the Fund, the more votes it receives. Further, individual states cannot simply decide they would like more votes at the Fund and increase their contribution unilaterally. The Fund's executive board decides how much states will be allowed to contribute. The United States has long had slightly more than 17 percent of the total votes in the Fund. The next largest voteholders—Japan, Germany, France, and the United Kingdom—have 5.0–6.0 percent of the votes apiece. These five states alone control almost 40 percent of the voting power in the Fund. Note that contributions to the Fund and, consequently, the distribution of votes are based not on the size of a member's economy but on its wealth and prosperity. The Netherlands and Belgium both have more votes at the Fund than India or Brazil.[7]

The Fund is also directly dependent on states for its material resources, but not in the same manner as the UN Security Council, UNHCR, or even the Fund's sister institution, the World Bank. It is not dependent on states for annual payments of dues the way the UN is, nor does it have to solicit voluntary contributions from states as the UNHCR does; and unlike the World Bank, the Fund does not raise its money on private capital markets.[8] At bottom, the Fund is exactly what its name implies—a fund or pot of currencies. It functions roughly like a credit union. Countries contribute currency to the Fund when they join. Then, when they run into balance-of-payments problems, they can borrow currency back from the Fund to cover their short-term foreign exchange needs. Thus, once set up, the organization is largely self-sustaining. The operating budget of the Fund—the currency it lends to members—comes from the one-time standing contribution of currency ("quota") that members have made available to the organization upon joining. Quotas are occasionally increased by a vote of the executive board to keep pace with the growing world economy, but states do not pay money to the Fund every year as they would in many organizations. The administrative costs of running the organization—staff salaries, travel, overhead—are paid for by interest that members pay to borrow currencies from the Fund, as well as by interest the Fund earns by investing its stock of available currency.[9] The fact that the IMF does not have to raise its own funds helps to bolster the organization's autonomy because it does not have to negotiate on a regular basis with states and, more important, rely on nonexpert branches of government like the U.S. Congress, which would have to appropriate money.

The other important structural feature that gives the staff autonomy is its capacity to set agendas. When the executive board meets, it considers measures that staff have prepared and presented to it.[10] Thus, when the board meets to consider whether a member should be allowed to use Fund resources and, if so, under what conditions, it is considering a specific proposal constructed by the staff that suggests a level of resource use and specific conditions the borrower must meet. But staff do not have unlimited license. Since the executive directors are resident at the Fund and meet three times per week, staff are familiar with their concerns and dispositions. They rarely send proposals to the board that they believe it will reject. Concerned board members may also get involved in the drafting of these proposals, particularly when the package is for a constituent country or is a large one. But most programs for most borrowers are staff creations. EDs do not need to accept programs they do not like, and they may send comments back to staff about practices they would like changed, but they rarely reject a program proposed by staff.[11]

This delegation of agenda setting to staff is the result of both a straightforward bureaucratic division of labor and the staff's presumed expertise. The twenty-four executive directors do not have the time to construct detailed financial stabilization programs for each borrower and carry out the annual reviews of each member's economy. The Fund is staffed by people with strong macroeconomic credentials who have significant experience dealing with the financial difficulties of member states accumulated over many years.[12] Further, the staff proposals are supported by extensive data and econometric analyses of the country's economy. Fund staff are sometimes the best or only available source of data on a country. The fact that these have been gathered during a recent on-site mission to the country in question adds to the credibility of staff proposals.[13]

The ability to use expertise and knowledge is the Fund's most important source of autonomy.[14] The staff's technical knowledge, solid credentials in monetary policymaking, and experience in the field have made the organization "an authority" and a credible source of policy advice. Its delegated mandate to promote financial stability places it "in authority" in matters of macroeconomic policy, and in the next section we explore how the organization's expert knowledge shapes its policy actions. We also explore how the form of the Fund's knowledge contributes to its influence. The Fund's analyses are often mathematical, rooted in extensive statistics about national economies. While quantitative analyses of statistics are not all the Fund does in its assessments, they are the core of these assessments; they are the baseline from which stabilization programs are formulated and the basis upon which these programs are justified—to member states, the executive board, and the broader public. In the conclusion of this chapter we explore the ways quantification helps to create the perception that experts are impartial and that their analyses are objective. The numbers, after all, are there for all to see, and the Fund is only recommending policies suggested by the numbers.

II. EXPERTISE AND THE CREATION OF THE POLAK MODEL

When the IMF was established to help states manage their balance-of-payments problems, economists at the time, including those at the Fund, did not have the economic knowledge required to carry out this mission. Balance-of-payments adjustment was a new public policy problem in 1944.[15] Under the previous gold standard system, balance-of-payments adjustment occurred automatically, at least in theory, through what was called the price-specie flow mechanism. According to the quantity theory of money, then widely accepted by economists, the supply of money in a country determined general levels of income, output, and prices in that country. The size of the money supply, in turn, was set by legally fixing the relationship between money and the country's stock of gold. If a country's stock of gold changed, so would its money supply, domestic prices, output, and income. Balance-of-payments adjustments entailed precisely this kind of change. A country with overall current and capital account deficits had to settle them by payment in gold to trading partners with surpluses. Loss of gold stock reduced the money supply in the deficit country, which had a downward effect on prices, income, and output, causing it to export more and import less, which reduced external payments and restored equilibrium. The reverse took place in surplus countries. Importation of gold expanded the money supply, raising income, output, and prices, causing exports to fall and reducing the external surplus. Balance-of-payments adjustment occurred automatically as long as countries followed the rules. No complex policy decisions were required.[16]

In practice, of course, the gold standard did not work so smoothly or simply. Intellectually, it was a static equilibrium model that did not easily allow for major shocks to the system such as economic expansions, changes in the world gold supply, or world wars. World stocks of gold grew far too slowly to finance the economic expansion of major traders like the United States and the United Kingdom, making it difficult for them to follow the rules. Similarly, after World War I a number of countries set their exchange rates in gold at unrealistically high levels, and changing these relationships between gold and major currencies without undermining confidence turned out to be extraordinarily difficult. Politically, the system became unpopular because it imposed unacceptably high costs on domestic societies. The huge swings in prices, income, and employment resulting from the flows of gold needed to correct payments imbalances caused massive suffering and destabilized political systems. As a result of the experience of the 1920s and 1930s, the gold standard came to be identified with deflation and unemployment and was largely discredited.[17]

In creating the Fund, financial officials sought an alternative to domestic deflation as a way to correct balance-of-payments deficits. They wanted to pursue domestic policies designed to promote full employment and growth, minimizing constraints imposed by balance of payments. The system they devised used foreign currency reserves, in addition to gold, to settle payments and created an international buffer stock of reserves (the Fund) on which countries could draw to extend the time over which domestic adjustments had to be made and so smooth transitions. The Fund's reserves were to be used only to finance temporary disequilibria; fundamental disequilibria were to be corrected through par value changes (subject to approval by the Fund).

Operating this new system required a wide range of knowledge that economists at the time, including those at the Fund, simply did not have. How did one distinguish between temporary and fundamental disequilibria in payments positions? What was the relationship between the size of the par value change and the size of the balance-of-payments effect it would cause? Would a par value change always correct a balance-of-payments deficit, or only under some conditions? What other tools could be used to influence balance of payments short of par value change, for example what role should exchange restrictions and controls on capital movements have, and what might their impacts be? Detailed understandings of these relationships did not exist, yet they were essential for the Fund to act.[18]

Some academic economists did become interested in balance-of-payments issues, but much of the thinking about these topics was done by staff at the Fund, particularly in its research department. Often spurred by pressing practical problems, Fund staff made important contributions to and often created knowledge in fields of economics relevant to its work.[19] They had to create the insights, identify the relationships, and formulate the conceptual tools to analyze balance-of-payments problems and produce recommendations for policy. Two such creations were particularly important and illustrate this process: the absorption approach and the monetary approach to balance of payments.

Economists working on balance-of-payments and exchange rate issues now all use the absorption approach as an integral part of their analytic toolkit, but this framework for understanding balance-of-payments problems did not exist when the Fund was founded and was developed largely by Fund staff. Previously, analysis of the effects of an exchange rate change would have focused on its effect on the trade deficit and on devaluation's effect on supply and demand conditions, both in the devaluing country and in the rest of the world. It was presumed that devaluation would reduce prices for a country's exports, thus increasing foreign demand for those exports, which would eventually bid up their price at least partway to predevaluation levels. How much devaluation changed the balance of payments was therefore a function of the elasticity of foreign demand for a country's exports as well as the elasticity of their domestic supply. Similarly, on the imports side, the initial effect of the devaluation would be to raise the price of foreign imports in the devaluing country, presumably lowering demand for them and reducing their price. How much devaluation changed the balance of payments would depend on the elasticity of demand for imports as well as elasticity of world supply. Thus, four different elasticities had to be estimated in order to assess the probable impact of a devaluation. Further, the "elasticities approach" was a static equilibrium model that ignored changes a devaluation might create in the domestic economy, particularly on incomes and aggregate expenditure.

The absorption approach was both simpler technically and superior analytically to the elasticities approach. As Jacques Polak of the Fund's research department described it at the 1951 meetings of the American Economic Association:

> I submit that the analysis of exchange rate changes would become much more useful if it did not start out from two, four, or eight elasticities, but from a simple social accounting identity, viz., that the existence of a balance-of-payments deficit implies that the country absorbs more resources in consumption and investment than it produces. Therefore, if devaluation is to cure this deficit, it must either increase production with consumption and investment constant, or decrease consumption and investment with output constant, or achieve some combination of the two. This I think is a more useful starting point for a discussion of the effects of a change in an exchange rate.[20]

Polak developed the seeds of the approach in an unpublished internal analysis of Mexico's proposal for a currency devaluation in 1948.[21] In it, he opened the black box of domestic economies to speculate on different kinds of causes of balance-of-payments problems and on the responsiveness of each to devaluation. In Mexico's case, he argued that devaluation would be ineffective because the cause of the payments deficit was overinvestment and high demand for output in domestic markets (excess absorption), which were unlikely to be influenced by devaluation. The basic insights were elaborated in a subsequent IMF staff publication by Sidney Alexander in 1952. Writing about unexpected effects of the 1949 devaluations in Europe, he emphasized the effect of the devaluation on income levels.[22]

As a policy tool, the absorption approach was attractive because it required domestic incomes and expenditure data, which were just then appearing as part of the new national accounts data that states began to collect systematically after World War II, instead of import and export data, which were often fragmented and nonexistent. However, this approach also changed the focus of analytical thinking. It focused analysts' attention on the structure of domestic economies and linked these analytically to a country's payments position.[23] It thus provided a strong basis for concern about what had previously been domestic economic policy problems.

The monetary approach to balance of payments built on the absorption approach and was attractive for similar reasons. The absorption approach focused analysts' attention on the structural features of a country's domestic economy that might cause balance-of-payments problems (as opposed to focusing on import/export data). But Fund staff still lacked a way of modeling domestic economies, unpacking the different elements that might contribute to payments problems, and linking those problem features with policy tools for remedying imbalances. Thinking about these problems tended to be in terms of national accounts and fiscal policy tools, but econometric models to describe member state economies did not exist, and the national accounts data were being generated slowly and unevenly across members. Members most in need of Fund assistance were often the least effective at supplying accounts data—a situation that continues today.

In a 1957 paper, written again in response to events in Mexico, Jacques Polak developed an alternative framework.[24] Treating payments as essentially a monetary phenomenon, he constructed a balance sheet of assets and liabilities in the banking system and linked it to simple behavioral relationships involving income in such a way as to yield a unique relationship between domestic credit creation and foreign reserves. The advantages of this way of thinking were many. Analytically it was superior in several dimensions. It was a simple model, yet flexible and versatile. It could be extended in many ways without disturbing its basic insights. Further, it was dynamic; it linked changes in reserves to changes in income and credit creation. Practically, it was far more workable than anything else in the toolkit. It relied primarily on banking and trade data, which were usually more complete and more timely than just about any other data a country might have. Most important, it pointed to a clear set of policy prescriptions. It identified a unique relationship between domestic credit and international reserves, and domestic credit creation was a variable that national governments could control. The model thus gave governments, and the Fund, a focus for policy interventions.[25]

Like all theoretical constructs, this one had normative implications, and policy work based on these models was not value neutral. The monetary approach to balance of payments, by its structure and assumptions, framed the problem as one in which both the cause of and the solution to balance-of-payments problems lay in the deficit state. The cause of disequilibrium was understood to be excess aggregate demand relative to output (the state absorbed more resources than it produced). In this construction, solutions were either to decrease absorption or increase productivity. Since productivity increases are difficult to obtain in short time horizons (e.g., twelve months), the obvious place for staff to focus their attention was on the demand side—on budgets and credit constraint. None of these were unreasonable policy decisions. In fact, they were extremely sensible policy decisions from the perspective of the staff in the 1950s and 1960s. They fit well with the policy tools the Fund had been given and with the political conditions under which the Fund operated. They enabled the Fund to do useful work in the 1950s when its position was precarious and its relevance to policy was in doubt. But that should not obscure the fact that the Fund's analytic tools carry a clear set of normative judgments: imbalance is the fault of the deficit states. Imbalances appear because the economy of the deficit state is "mismanaged"; ergo it must adjust. Blame and burden of remedy are clearly assigned.

The understandings embodied in the monetary approach are certainly not wrong, but they are not the only understandings one could have of balance-of-payments problems.[26] There are other ways of conceptualizing balance-of-payments issues that locate cause and solution differently, and therefore create different foci for policy and different intellectual justification for assigning the burden of adjustment. For example, in theory every deficit has a mirror surplus somewhere in the system. Analysis of these relationships would entail construction of systemic models of payments rather than country-by-country models. Such a framework would suggest some different methods for managing payments imbalances, notably inducing adjustment in surplus states. In the Fund's intellectual and policy framework, adjustment is compulsory only for deficit countries; for surplus states it is voluntary. Theoretically, one obvious direction that the Fund's work could have taken would have been to expand Fund influence over surplus states in some way as a means of promoting systemic adjustment.[27]

Why did this not occur? State power certainly provides an important part of the explanation. Surpluses are a source of power for members. Deficits are an immediate problem for those who run them; surpluses are a problem for the system. Those who run surpluses can comfortably adopt mercantile policies and have no immediate need of the Fund. One might think, however, that as powerful states like the United States went into deficit, the Fund's attitude toward chronic surplus members might have changed. However, the Fund had no tools to induce adjustment in surplus states. Equally important, its staff requested none. The analytic framework of the Fund was not systemic and did not emphasize the policies of surplus states as causes of global disequilibria. Thus, it is not the case that Fund staff saw influence over surplus members as crucial, pushed for the ability to act, and were rebuffed by surplus members on the board. Instead, they did not see surplus states as pressing problems because surplus states were not apparent as pressing problems within the analytic frame staff used.

These normative issues are much clearer with hindsight than they were at the time. In the 1940s and 1950s, when the Polak model and the absorption approach were developed, they were embraced as vast improvements over previous intellectual tools, which they were. They solved local, practical problems for the organization and its members. They required data that were more widely available than those required by other intellectual constructions, and they suggested courses of action that governments might reasonably attempt to implement. Their content strongly shaped Fund action over the coming years. They shaped the contacts Fund officials had with member states. National officials who controlled the money supply—central bankers and finance ministers—became the chief interlocutors of Fund officials. They shaped the kinds of data the Fund collected and what Fund staff, as well as national bureaucrats, knew about member state economies.

Most important, though, these models directed the Fund's interventions in national economies in very particular ways. Whereas the old elasticities approach had focused attention on imports and exports, the monetary approach connected payments positions to credit expansion, fiscal policy, and a host of factors previously understood to be purely domestic policy matters.[28] Consequently, the model led Fund officials to become more concerned with the workings of domestic economies than the Bretton Woods founders would have anticipated because these new intellectual technologies told them that domestic economic changes were key to payments adjustment.[29]

III. CONSTRUCTING SOUND ECONOMIES

The intellectual connections created by Fund staff constructed balance-of-payments difficulties as a different type of problem requiring new types of solutions. In these new understandings, payments problems were not just about currency flows but were intimately linked with the workings of the domestic economy in deficit states. Solutions to payments problems logically demanded that the Fund intervene to regulate and reconstruct domestic economic arrangements in ways that would stabilize the country's payments position. Toward that end staff used their institutional positions and drew from their intellectual understandings embodied in the monetary approach to develop two new policy tools. They created "conditionality" in order to compel governments to adopt the desired economic policies. They also created technical assistance programs in order to train government officials in the tools of economic analysis so that they could better understand the IMF's policy recommendations and the need to create new institutional arrangements for the economy. These policies became more visible and prominent as the IMF shifted its attention in the late 1950s from the European economies recovering from World War II to the newly emerging Third World economies.

Conditionality

Much of what the Fund now does is construct policy programs that members must implement in order to use its resources. These often involve extensive intrusion into the domestic economies and societies of member states and have become extremely controversial. However, conditionality on lending, as such programs are called, is not discussed in the original Articles of Agreement.[30] The only mention of such activity in the articles is a directive that the Fund lend with "adequate safeguards," but the term is never defined. Certainly the delegates to the original Bretton Woods conference envisioned nothing like the current practices. Conditional lending had been tried by the League of Nations and judged counterproductive.[31] Many representatives at the Bretton Woods conference, particularly the Europeans, favored a relatively automatic disbursement of resources. Such a system was attractive in part because it was apolitical and avoided thorny questions about what kinds of conditions might be attached. Conditional lending put the Fund in the position of being "grandmotherly," in John Maynard Keynes's phrase.[32] Even the Americans, who supported the notion of conditions on lending, had a very limited view of this power for Fund staff. Restrictions on lending were to be used only where "misbehavior is flagrant," according to Bretton Woods architect Harry Dexter White. The Fund would be justified in intervening if a country were using Fund resources for rearmament, for example; it would not be justified in intervening in the more simple and common case of an unbalanced budget.[33] Yet this is precisely what the Fund was doing by the mid-1950s.

The principle that Fund staff had discretion to impose conditions on use of the Fund's own resources was not firmly established until the early 1950s. "Automaticity," or access to Fund resources on demand and without conditions, continued to have strong champions, particularly the British, and prevailed as the operating principle in the European Payments Union (EPU), established in 1950, to which the Fund was frequently compared. However, the EPU dealt in much smaller lines of credit over much shorter periods than the Fund. Further, it lacked the larger political objectives of the Bretton Woods institutions involving trade liberalization and convertibility.[34] Fund staff were able to use these differences to justify intervening in lending and conditioning loans on domestic policies. They made several proposals for increased Fund discretion over resource use in the first years of the Fund's operations and were usually supported by the United States but opposed by other members. Marshall Plan aid temporarily strengthened the hand of opponents of conditions, and by 1950 member unwillingness to submit to conditionality had brought the Fund to a standstill; there were no drawings at all that year.[35]

It was the second managing director, Ivar Rooth, who proposed a solution and persuaded member states to agree. Rooth proposed the now-familiar system of increased conditionality with increased borrowing. Drawing the first 25 percent of a member's quota (the "gold tranche") would be automatic, but for larger sums the staff could impose conditionality and surveillance over the member's use of these resources. Rooth first floated these ideas to board members in October 1951. Encouraged by general support from the board, he appointed a staff working party to draft specific recommendations. The staff's recommendations were approved by the board in 1952.[36] That same year, the board approved what became the principal vehicle for conditionality, the standby arrangement. Under these arrangements, members could negotiate access to higher tranches (to be drawn as needed) on the condition that certain policy measures were taken. Like the tranche system, standby arrangements are nowhere in the articles. While it was member state requests (notably from Belgium) that put the concept on the Fund's agenda, it was Fund staff who generalized the concept of standbys for the board and drafted the terms under which they were made.[37]

Promoting "Sound Economics"

These events established the ability of Fund staff to condition loans, and conditionality, in turn, allowed them to induce, if not compel, states to adopt economic policies preferred by the Fund. Borrowers have thus seen conditionality as an enormous source of power. From the perspective of IMF staff, however, conditionality is simply an economic necessity. Without substantial changes in their economies, many members will never be able to manage their payments or get on a path toward sustainable growth. These conclusions are the logical outgrowth of conceptual economic knowledge possessed by staff and lessons they draw from experience over the past fifty years.

Early conditions on lending flowed directly from the insights of the new analytical tools developed at the Fund. With the absorption and monetary frameworks in hand, Fund staff understood the financial health of a domestic economy to be a prerequisite for eliminating or reducing balance-of-payments deficits. Consequently, early lending very often required states to adopt a financial stabilization program containing specific guidelines for credit expansion, the variable emphasized by the monetary approach. Fiscal conditions, notably budgetary restraints, were added soon thereafter.

These tools seemed to work well among the industrialized members with whom the Fund did most of its early business during the 1950s.[38]

In the 1960s, however, the Fund's clientele shifted. Industrialized states had largely rebuilt their economies and had less need of Fund resources, but a very large number of newly independent states joined the Fund and needed them desperately. These states presented the Fund with new problems. They were often poor, their economies were incompletely marketized, their financial systems were rudimentary, and most had balance-of-payments problems. Initially, the Fund focused on the same variables central to its analytical model that had worked well in industrialized members—domestic credit and budget constraint. Programs manipulating these variables in developing states did not achieve the same results as in industrialized states, however. The Fund was set up for short-term borrowing to cover temporary disequilibria, but by the early 1970s it became clear that a sizable group of developing countries were in chronic balance-of-payments difficulties. Missions evaluating the reasons for this quickly found additional features of these domestic economies that contributed to payments problems and needed to be changed. Tax collection systems were found to be inefficient, and subsidies were found to distort markets and change import/export balances. Consequently, conditions regarding change in these domestic practices were added to IMF loans. Similarly, traditional fiscal and monetary conditions became increasingly detailed (containing not just targets but both ceilings and floors), and new macrocriteria on debt ceilings and arrears were added.

When the oil shocks hit in the 1970s, the Fund recognized external sources of balance-of-payments difficulties and set up a special fund to help these states offset the effects of rising prices on payments, but this was not enough to get many states out of their chronic difficulties. Further evaluation revealed structural features in these economies that contributed to poor payments performance. Having concluded that additional pressure on the demand side was not politically possible (and having resigned itself to long-term engagement with these members), the Fund began to tackle supply-side issues over what it called "the medium term."[39] These programs featured measures designed to increase export productivity in a variety of ways, including improving infrastructure, diversifying exports, liberalizing trade, eliminating price controls, enforcing wage restraint, and changing tax policy and government expenditure patterns.[40]

The Fund steadily increased both the number and variety of conditions on lending. In the 1970s the number of performance criteria in IMF stabilization programs averaged six. In the 1980s it averaged ten. By 1999 there were an average of twenty-five performance criteria attached to IMF stabilization programs required of borrowers for use of IMF resources.[41] As the number of criteria expanded, so did their substantive breadth and degree of intrusion into what were formerly national sovereign prerogatives. The Fund is now involved in reconstructing relations among domestic private actors as it reforms banking and financial sectors of these economies. It takes an active role in designing poverty alleviation programs. It is involved in labor policies beyond simple wage restraint. It advocates reorganizations of government agencies, promotes new forms of government-society relations (emphasizing participation of civil society groups), and oversees restructuring of important business sectors (e.g., banking and finance) and private institutions. The Fund has become so intimately involved in the policies of many members that it stations in-house advisors there. These staff live in the country and have offices there, usually in the Finance Ministry. In fact, members actively seek such on-site advisors (as of this writing there was a waiting list for them) because it reassures both the Fund and private investors that the government is following sound policies that will promote economic health and, consequently, a sustainable balance-of-payments position.

Technical Assistance

In addition to establishing conditionality and increasing the conditions on loans, the IMF vastly expanded technical assistance programs to member states in order to help them build sound economic institutions and to improve their governments' economic knowledge and statistical capabilities. Standing behind these technical programs, though, were particular values that were, ideally, to become institutionalized not only in state apparatus but also in the minds of government officials running national economies. The Fund has always seen the transmission of economic ideas and information as a major part of its mission. Publication of its *Staff Papers* series and dissemination of statistical data have been a central part of its activities since the beginning. With many of these newly independent states, however, the task was not simply keeping national officials up-to-date. These states needed to create national economies virtually from scratch, and the Fund's response was to provide technical assistance so that they could develop the proper economic institutions. For instance, many of the new African states in the 1960s had no central bank and no expertise with which to build one. The Fund's Central Banking Service was set up in 1963 to help with this task. Similarly, in 1969, the Fund's Bureau of Statistics began providing technical assistance to improve data collection efforts in member states.

Part of the Fund's mission was not only to help build institutions but also to help develop a cadre of trained professionals who could collect and analyze the relevant data and understand what sorts of macroeconomic solutions were required. The IMF Institute was launched in 1964 as a training institution to which national officials could come for seminars on financial topics and statistical techniques. Prominent in the curriculum were courses on "financial programming," which taught national officials how to use the Fund's analytic techniques in their own policymaking at the national level. In 1969 the Fund's Bureau of Statistics began assisting countries to improve data collection and establish or extend central bank bulletins.[42] Much of this teaching was intertwined with the now-regular cycle of Fund missions to member countries. Since the 1950s the Fund has been sending small teams (four to six people) to member states at least once per year, more often for those using Fund resources. This was a way of investigating the payments situation of members and establishing the conditions for any lending the Fund might do, but it was also a means by which the Fund could communicate its views to member states.[43] Mission teams demanded certain kinds of data for their analysis from members, thus shaping data collection inside states and determining what national governments knew (and wanted to know) about their own societies, particularly among these weaker new members.[44] Missions also offered strong suggestions about the kinds of technical changes needed for these governments to understand and manage their own economies.[45]

Since the 1950s the Fund has greatly expanded its conditionality requirements and technical assistance programs, but this expansion has not always produced the desired results. Indeed, by the 1990s, the word "intractable" was beginning to creep into the Fund's vocabulary in discussing some of its members' payments problems.[46] Evaluations of IMF program success suggested that members often had difficulty implementing programs but that, even where implemented, these programs did not reliably produce desired results.[47] These evaluations highlighted a variety of new variables that had thwarted previous programs and that would require attention in future lending. Responding to the finding that many programs were not implemented (or not fully implemented), the Fund launched efforts on two fronts.

First, it sought to increase the capabilities of members to implement their IMF programs. It launched efforts to reform public and financial institutions of member states in ways that would develop their capacities, improve their transparency, eliminate corruption, and generally promote "good governance."[48] Fund programs, backed by technical assistance from Fund staff, led to overhauls of entire sectors of some of these economies, notably banking and financial sectors, but also major export sectors and major infrastructure sectors such as transportation, power, and water.

Second, evaluations found that implementation of Fund programs was often blocked not just by lack of capacity but also by lack of will on the part of key actors in these member states. For example, the head of the central bank and the finance minister might persuade the government to agree to a stabilization program involving elimination of agricultural subsidies and wage restraint, but if the agriculture minister and the unions did not agree on the necessity of these measures, they were unlikely to be implemented. The Fund's remedy has been to enter the world of public relations and actively try to sell its programs to a broad base of constituencies in borrowing states. Staff on missions used to meet only with central bankers and finance ministers. Now, as one staffer put it, "I'll meet with almost anyone who wants to talk with me."[49] Mission staff meet with opposition politicians, labor unions, business leaders, church groups, NGOs, and a variety of civil society actors with the aim of explaining the program to them and persuading them that the recommended stabilization program is both necessary and prudent.

Staff understand that this need to persuade a broad spectrum of society to accept the Fund's program is the result of their expanded missions and conditionality tools. When the Fund's principal intervention was a one-time fix like a devaluation or a centralized policy change like domestic credit control, implementation was less complicated. The government did it or not; there was no ambiguity about whether the change had been implemented, and very few people had to agree in order to carry it out. As conditionality has expanded to include more goals across more areas of the government and society, more kinds of actors need to cooperate in order to make these programs happen. Democratization has exacerbated this phenomenon. Between broadened goals and broader political participation in borrower countries, Fund staff have concluded that their work will have little effect without a broad base of public support.[50]

"Participation" and "ownership" are current buzzwords within the Fund. Ownership has been particularly emphasized in the poverty reduction component of Fund programs. The concessionary financing facility, formerly called the Enhanced Structural Adjustment Facility, was renamed the Poverty Reduction and Growth Facility in 1999, and, as part of borrowing from that facility, members must submit a Poverty Reduction Strategy Paper. To promote ownership of these programs (and increase chances of implementation), borrower states are supposed to write these papers in consultation with the Fund, rather than the other way around.[51] Ownership is not just authorship, however. It involves commitment to the program. The idea is that the more stakeholders in the civil society get input into these papers, the more likely they will be to implement them.

This need to sell Fund programs and garner support for them illustrates the circumscribed and conditional nature of authority, in this case expert authority. As discussed in chapter 2, authority almost always contains elements of coercion and consent. Certainly member states that accepted the IMF's medicine did not always do so willingly or because they were convinced that it would improve their economic health. Instead, they often felt that they had few good choices and that medicine was better than the alternatives. Yet IMF staff worked hard to convince member states that their recommendations should be accepted not because borrowers had no good alternative but because they were the proper course of action. Staff also understood that a willing patient was more likely to follow the entire treatment plan. Toward this end they supplemented conditionality with technical assistance.

The need to sell IMF programs by explaining their underlying economic logic to noneconomists also underscores the ways in which expertise differs from information, as political scientists have understood it, and does not have the same political effects. IR scholars have extensively studied the role of information asymmetries as a source of power for IOs and other actors.[52] The fact that one actor has information unavailable to others is thought to empower and give an advantage to the informed. Fund staff, however, usually see expertise asymmetries as a source of weakness. Fund staff are often frustrated because nonexperts do not see the wisdom of their advice. They believe that people would be more willing to accept Fund advice if they understood the economic logic undergirding these stabilization programs. The expansion of contacts on missions to promote programs and, indeed, the entire technical assistance enterprise are an effort to increase Fund influence by reducing, not exploiting, asymmetries in expertise.

IV. GOAL PROLIFERATION AND ORGANIZATIONAL DYSFUNCTION

We have argued that the IMF's intellectual apparatus contains a logic that has led it to expand its involvement in domestic political economies. Staff are often the initial drafters of these policies, but powerful member states remain the arbiters of the Fund's overall policy direction, and executive directors who represent them on the board can and do exert important influence over the way staff apply conditions to lending. These interventions may reflect power politics on the board. For example, powerful states may be subjected to less onerous performance criteria than weak states. Developing states complained bitterly about the easy terms of a large loan to the United Kingdom in 1967.[53] More recently, the size and terms of loans to Mexico and Russia have been attributed to U.S. influence on the Fund's lending process. In addition to weighing in on particular loans, the board and its powerful members can influence the broad recommendations and the overall substance of conditionality. It can direct the staff to pursue additional goals via conditions on lending—goals that the staff would not have chosen. Fund conditionality related to the environment, military expenditures, and poverty has largely emanated from the board, from outside criticism, especially by NGOs, and from managing directors concerned about public opinion; it has generally not come from staff.[54]

Yet goal proliferation and conflict come not only from delegation or outside pressures but also from dynamics inherent in bureaucracies. When we create bureaucracies and assign them tasks, we are artificially compartmentalizing a very messy reality. Conscientious bureaucrats very quickly recognize that to accomplish a great many of the ambitious social tasks we set for them, they need to reach outside the narrow compartments in which we place them. On the one hand, this is good. We want our expert civil servants to take their jobs seriously and to use their autonomy to think creatively about how to accomplish their missions. On the other hand, this process can quickly come to resemble pulling on a loose thread. In the social world, everything is related to everything else, and the limits to the kinds of activities that could potentially contribute to realization of a sound economy or poverty alleviation or development are very distant indeed. In this way mission expansion eventually undermines the rationale for bureaucratizing in the first place. We bureaucratize so that we can divide social labor, focus people's efforts, and get something accomplished, yet the artificiality of the divisions limits bureaucrats' ability to accomplish their missions. In their attempts to succeed, bureaucrats interpret their mandate ever more broadly, disrupting the original division of labor.

Staff will be more receptive to new goals and more active in implementing them when they believe that these goals flow logically from the organization's own expert knowledge about how to achieve its primary mission. Teaching financial techniques (like financial programming analyses or setting up a treasury bill market), or teaching states how to build institutions that eliminate market imperfections (like reorganizing the banking sector to ensure adequate capitalization and accounting rules)—such work makes sense to Fund staff. It clearly contributes to improvement of economic performance in ways that logically should improve payments position and growth potential. Further, staff are fairly confident about what is needed to accomplish these tasks and know how to go about them. Consequently, such activities receive much attention and tend to be broadly integrated into the workings of different departments of the Fund. Some externally imposed conditions may also fit well with staff concerns. Macroeconomic conditions on lending demanded by private financial institutions that provide the supplementary private sector capital necessary for borrower success often make economic sense within the staff's intellectual framework and so receive extensive attention in formulation of programs.[55]

By contrast, when staff believe that new goals are only marginally related to the primary mission they are likely to be less responsive. Goals perceived to be tangential are most often generated outside the organization. Mandates like protecting the environment, controlling military expenditures, or alleviating poverty are often driven onto the Fund's agenda not by internal Fund assessments of economic performance but by political considerations in the wider organizational environment.[56] These receive somewhat less attention and are less well integrated into basic decision making. It is not that staff actively oppose such goals. Rather, they do not know how to pursue them within their intellectual framework and do not feel competent or expert in these areas. Unlike the World Bank, which has broadened its expertise considerably in the past fifteen years, the Fund is still staffed overwhelmingly by macroeconomists. They do not know a great deal about environmental engineering or military planning. As a consequence, the board's directive to consider the environmental implications of Fund programs was operationalized as a boilerplate paragraph in programs, and even this is beginning to disappear.[57] Poverty alleviation is a more mixed case. It is a very large part of the Fund's activities and prompts mixed reactions from staff. One interviewee whose work was research oriented and technical was eloquent about the inappropriateness of the Fund's work in poverty. "Don't misunderstand me: poverty alleviation is an important job. It's more important than what the Fund does. But it's not the Fund's job and we shouldn't be doing it." This staff member not surprisingly saw the poverty alleviation goals as largely imposed on the Fund by G-7 countries. Another interviewee who works regularly with some of the poorest borrowers, however, thought improving these countries' economic situations (and, presumably, their balance of payments) was probably impossible without making progress on poverty. Without attention to poverty, Fund programs would not be domestically legitimate in these very poor states and so would not be accepted or implemented.[58]

These assessments use similar reasoning processes but come to different conclusions. In each case, the degree to which poverty alleviation makes sense as a mission depends in some part on the degree to which staff understand it to be logically connected to the realization of more fundamental economic stability goals. Ironically, then, while the Fund has been trying to make member states take ownership of its programs, it turns out that ownership matters just as much inside the Fund itself. When the Fund has ownership of a goal, when it generates the goal internally and/or the goal "makes sense" internally, that goal is much more likely to be implemented than when it is dumped on the organization from outside.

Goal proliferation of this kind can have a range of effects within an organization, not all of which are bad. Goal proliferation may simply be a form of multitasking. That is usually what those generating the new goals intend—more productivity on more fronts for the organization. Moreover, often there are ways to reconcile conflicting goals. The Fund increasingly views some new goals as preconditions to others and works to phase in or sequence reforms. Banking sector reform is now understood to be a prerequisite to capital openness, for example. The Fund also views goals as conflicting only in the short term. Financial stabilization and poverty alleviation, for example, may conflict in the short term, as the poor suffer from smaller public budgets and higher prices, but over the medium term, the Fund understands that financial stabilization is essential for poverty alleviation since only a sound economy can produce the necessary wealth for its population.

Yet the IMF's expanding intervention and increasingly diverse goals can create the potential for dysfunction in at least two ways. First, each layer of new goals added to stabilization programs is increasingly distant from the Fund's core competencies. Conflict may be as simple as having too few resources to do too many jobs, but it may involve the more direct clash of task demands. Poverty alleviation is at least related to domains of economics, but it is not usually the focus of the kinds of macroeconomic talent hired by the Fund. Good governance and protecting the environment are even further removed. As the gap between the Fund's goals and its expertise grows, the organization's credibility becomes suspect and the possibilities for poor policy grow. NGOs have been quick to point out blunders.[59]

Second, as goals proliferate and become more disparate, the possibility of conflict among them increases. In financial crises, the Fund may need to act quickly to ensure global monetary stability, but the resulting policies are unlikely to be the product of broad-based participation or to be consistent with the goal of ownership. Similarly, the goal of openness to capital markets can conflict with stability when the institutional infrastructure is not in place to manage the potential volatility brought by openness. Fund policies pushing Asian "tiger" states to open themselves to capital markets without due attention to the domestic institutional ability to cope are a painful illustration. Tensions and value tradeoffs of this kind are endemic in social life and, again, need not constitute pathologies as we have defined them, as self-defeating behaviors flowing from bureaucratic culture. However, conflicting goals can be conducive to pathologies, and, at the least, they obviously make organizational success difficult to achieve and compromise an organization's effectiveness.[60]

V. EXPERTISE, QUANTIFICATION, AND POWER

The IMF's structure, mission, and place in the world economy have changed dramatically since its founding. Originally created to provide short-term funding for balance of payments, it now spends much of its effort doing precisely what its founders wanted to prevent—intervening in members' domestic economies, often in sweeping ways. Changes in the global economy, including deepening interdependence and shifts in the structure of national economies, certainly encouraged states to sanction a more expansive IMF that could help them achieve their interests. State power also played an important role. The fact that G-7 states do not need to borrow Fund resources or submit to Fund conditionality is an essential factor in the executive board's support for staff recommendations about interventions in weaker states. If G-7 countries believed they might ever have to submit to similar programs, the board's attitude would almost certainly be different.

Although both state interests and state power provide necessary conditions for the emergence of an authoritative Fund that can exercise power in these ways, they are not sufficient to explain either the scope of Fund authority or the specific forms of action the Fund has taken. To understand the Fund we now have, why it acts as it does, and why states accept those actions, we need to understand the nature of the expertise it deploys. Specifically, attention to both the form and the content of expertise helps us to understand three things: how international organizations like the IMF construct problems and develop appropriate solutions; how objective rules and quantification enhance their authority and increase deference to their actions; and why IMF interventions in member states expand ("mission creep").

Expertise and Construction of the World

The Fund's analytic tools shape what staff "see" and the kinds of policy measures that seem obvious to them. Expertise, in this fundamental sense, alerts individuals to the problems that exist in the world, the connections between these problems, and the appropriate solutions to these problems. The particular set of analytic tools the IMF developed in the early days of the organization shaped the way it understood both the cause of balance-of-payments problems and the kinds of policy measures that would remedy them. These tools were attractive, not because they were the only way to understand these problems, but because they allowed the Fund to act. They could be used with the limited data at hand, they provided policy solutions governments could hope to implement, and they were intellectually elegant. It was not until the connection between balance of payments and domestic credit creation was "understood" that policymakers inside and outside the Fund could imagine, much less undertake, intervention in domestic economies.

The Fund's intellectual tools have focused its attention on the domestic economy as the location of the problem of payments imbalance and have led it to prescribe policies that place the burden of adjustment there. Its prescriptions tend to focus on belt tightening and institutional reform in deficit states rather than on other sources of imbalance such as surplus state policies, protectionism against deficit state exports, and moral hazard or reckless behavior in global capital markets.[61] Much of the criticism of Fund policies centers on this domestic focus. Critics of structural adjustment often argue that terms of trade are systematically skewed against poor developing states and that the causes of their imbalances often lie in protectionism or stockpiling practices of industrialized states. Similarly, criticism of Fund policies during the Asian financial crisis often revolved around the role played by global capital markets in the financial panics of states that had balanced budgets and high domestic savings rates. If global capitalists caused these crises, the criticism went, then why should they be bailed out by the Fund?[62] There are a variety of other external or systemic causes of payments deficits on which the IMF could focus analysis and policy intervention, but it has attended to only a few of these in favor of domestic remedies.[63]

The IMF's domestic-oriented approach persists for several reasons. It is pragmatic and tractable for policymaking. It also coincides with the preferences of many powerful member states who are surplus states, protect their agricultural markets, and are home to powerful global capitalists. But Great Power support alone cannot explain acceptance of Fund policies. If all the Fund was able to say to borrowers was, "You must implement this stabilization program because the G-7 states want you to," borrowers would rebel, publics in G-7 states would mobilize in protest, and Fund staff would quit. What makes the prescriptions of the Fund so authoritative is that they are undergirded by a body of economic analysis that is accepted by a large number of economists in many countries. The Fund's expertise creates some amount of agreement that certain basic features of the Fund's model and stabilization programs are right and true in some objective way. Widely shared agreement among economists across borders on certain modes of analysis and perceived truths is one component of the deference paid to the Fund's recommendations.

Objectivity and Quantification

While the content of its knowledge shaped the Fund's view of the world, the form of the knowledge, particularly its quantified and supposedly objective character, shaped the world's view of the Fund and its expertise. As discussed in chapter 2, one important reason we put bureaucrats like Fund staff "in authority" is that we understand them to be "an authority" on tasks at hand. We create bureaucracies so that well-trained experts can collect and analyze relevant data and devise objective, impersonal rules and courses of action based on those data. The Fund does this kind of work when it develops abstract economic models, collects data about countries, and then applies the models to derive policy recommendations.

This kind of objective rule- or method-driven expertise is particularly compatible with international bureaucracy because it helps to solves legitimacy problems for bureaucrats. When expertise is objective and embodied in abstract rules, mere personal judgment with all its idiosyncrasies disappears and is replaced by a set of universal rules that appear impersonal and impartial, ergo fair. We value policymaking of this kind not just because we think it will give us good policies that will accomplish our goals; we value it because we see it as disinterested and objective. Because analyses based on numbers, models, and rules seem impartial and fair, they are a defense against accusations of politicized and unprofessional behavior that can undermine bureaucrats' authority as experts. Indeed, it is the objective and depoliticized nature of these policy recommendations that allows them to garner political support and mobilizes people to implement the recommended policies.[64] As Max Weber and others have argued, this kind of expertise has widespread appeal in modern societies, democratic and authoritarian alike, but it is especially compelling to international bureaucrats who lack the mandate of popular election or divine right.[65]

The IMF uses rules to reason and also to justify and explain its decisions to its publics, and in this way it is no different from the UN Secretariat or UNHCR. But its form of reasoning is different because of its reliance on quantitative analysis. The Fund's analyses are rooted in statistics about national economies. Fields of investigation built on the scientific method, which is a set of rules for inquiry, exemplify this kind of expertise and have been the model for economics for decades. While quantitative analyses of statistics are not all the Fund does in its assessments, they are the core of these assessments; they are the basis upon which stabilization programs are formulated and justified—to member states, the executive board, and the broader public.[66]

Quantification plays a crucial role in this perception of disinterested analysis by experts.[67] To the extent that a messy, nuanced world can be rendered numerically in the form of statistics, reasoning about it can be made uniform by way of mathematics. Judgments and policy recommendations based on numbers can be checked (and challenged) by other experts in other places who may not share the political views or material interests of the policymakers. Quantification is thus a technology that helps deal with two important problems of the international political community—distance and distrust. To the extent that they can quantify the social world and develop mathematical models of important relations in it, experts can achieve strong intersubjective agreement on the nature of the world, the nature of its problems, and appropriate policy responses. These responses are made powerful by both the agreement among experts and the objective basis for their recommendations.[68]

One paradoxical implication of quantification is that bureaucrats become powerful only by making themselves appear powerless. It is only by giving up much of their subjective discretion to universal objective methods and by letting the numbers "speak for themselves" that their judgments become legitimate and accepted. This observation challenges the conventional view both among political scientists influenced by economic theories of organization and in the epistemic communities literature. Both hold that the power of expertise is rooted in information asymmetries that enable the possessor of information to manipulate outcomes.[69] Fund staff would disagree. Rather than seeing themselves as powerful, staff often complain that they are powerless, that borrowers and others do not listen to their advice. Greater expertise is often a problem to be overcome rather than an advantage in securing compliance. Fund staff believe that their proposals will be properly persuasive only to others who share their knowledge and can understand what their numbers say. Consequently, they work hard to eliminate information asymmetries and to promote macroeconomic expertise and knowledge among member states. The ability to exercise power is premised on forms of argumentation and reasoning that obscure the very existence of that power.

In order for the models and the statistics to have these sorts of effects, they must be accepted as valid. Bureaucracies do several kinds of important work in this regard. They establish universal rules about how categories are defined and how things are measured or counted. It was international organizations, mostly the UN and associated IOs (like the Fund), that set the guidelines for national accounts data after World War II.[70] They also help to determine what these categories mean and to resolve disputes regarding what sort of data should be collected and why. The Fund takes data collection issues very seriously and invests a great deal of resources in data collection. Not only does it have an active statistics department that publishes extensive data sets concerning members, but, especially in places where data are poor, Fund staff spend much of their mission time collecting, reviewing, and reconciling numbers pertaining to the national economy.[71] The numbers it publishes are not simply out there waiting to be discovered. They are the product of extended negotiation among staff and member government personnel. This is not to say that the data are bad or made up, nor that this is simply a measurement problem; it is also a conceptual problem. People must agree, first, on the categories of things to be measured. They then must agree on the definition of the categories and on rules about how measurements will be done. Further, they must agree on interpretation if they are going to use the statistics in policymaking. Someone catching fish for recreation in the United States may not be treated the same as a someone fishing for food in Thailand by a bureaucrat collecting data on fishing industry production or policy. When there are disputes about data, as there often are in Fund work, international bureaucrats are the arbiters. Richard Harper describes the Fund's role as one of sanctioning and even "sanctifying" data. Fund missions decide what are "good" numbers, legitimating some and rejecting others. In this sense, "missions are to some extent in the business of creating a moral order, an order upon which the Fund's analytical apparatus can operate."[72]

Once these categories and rules for data collection become widely accepted as valid (or at least reasonably so), they become the basis for policy interventions of all kinds at all levels. They create new categories, concerns, and public policy problems. For example, while states have always been concerned about state wealth, they tended to focus on the wealth of the king, the contents of the treasury, or, perhaps, the net worth of citizens. They were not concerned about the specific form of wealth as output we call gross domestic product until the creation of that statistical measure. The introduction of unemployment rates and poverty rates similarly restructured people's conceptions of desirable goals. Further, creation of a statistical measure shifts the focus of human action; it redirects policy toward manipulating that number. Economists, especially those in public bureaucracies like the Fund, have been an important source of these new measures as well as a source for intervention strategies to manipulate them. Thus, in a sense, statistics do not simply describe the world; they remake the world.[73]

Expertise, Failure, and Expansion

Application of the Fund's objective models has failed to stabilize borrower economies in a great many cases, and the Fund's response has consistently been to elaborate those models further, incorporating more and more aspects of domestic life into its stabilization programs. This dynamic runs counter to what most models of IO behavior would expect. Most would expect that an organization that consistently failed to achieve the goals members set for it would be punished. Expertise serves an important function here in that it makes failure intelligible, ergo excusable, to principals. It provides a basis on which the organization can not only deflect criticism and avoid punishment, but also justify expansion. The logic of Fund models suggests that program failures often result from omitting parts of the economy from the stabilization program, thereby justifying more expansive conditionality in the future. This is not Machiavellian manipulation by staff. Their conclusions are both earnest and logical, based on the frameworks governing their work. Since those frameworks are often shared by powerful states, they are generally accepted and expansion is sanctioned. Expertise thus helps us explain a pattern of expansion in the face of failure that makes little sense from other perspectives.

Our expertise explanation also provides an alternative to another piece of conventional wisdom about bureaucracy. The expansionary dynamic we find in the Fund is similar to William A. Niskanen's assumption that bureaucrats always act to expand their budget or turf, but expertise offers different reasons for this behavior. Niskanen attributes expansionary behavior to simple self-interest and power seeking. In this case, the argument would be that Fund staff actively want to expand their influence and look for excuses to do so. According to the dynamics of expertise traced here, however, conscientious experts trying to do their job can cause similar mission expansion, even when they prefer not to take on additional tasks or increase their turf because they do not have the resources or knowledge. They do so only because the logic of their task dictates that more must be done to accomplish it.[74]

Persistent mission expansion at the Fund thus raises some important theoretical questions for IO scholars, but it also raises normative questions. As their analytic frameworks draw them into spheres of economic and social life increasingly distant from their core macroeconomic competencies, the Fund staff's authority as experts diminishes and the possibility for poor policy rises. More fundamentally, as the Fund and other IOs expand their missions and intrude into more aspects of national or local societies, questions of accountability and representation loom large. These are crucial questions, not just for the Fund but for other IOs and for global governance more generally, and we address them in chapter 6.

4

DEFINING REFUGEES AND VOLUNTARY REPATRIATION AT THE UNITED NATIONS HIGH COMMISSIONER FOR REFUGEES

The United Nations High Commissioner for Refugees (UNHCR) was born with little autonomy and few prospects for expansion. States created UNHCR in 1951 to assist in the protection of refugees and to help states carry out their obligations under the recently signed Refugee Convention. Although the creation of the agency and the convention represented an unprecedented pledge to assist these neglected populations, states took care that their momentary humanitarian sympathies did not compromise their sovereignty. They designed an organization that was to do very little and do only what states told it to do.[1] They made UNHCR completely dependent on voluntary contributions from states and other sources for its funds.[2] They restricted its scope of operations to circumstances in Europe related to events prior to 1951. They gave the agency a three-year life span.

Yet UNHCR was able to capitalize on world events and use its authority to greatly expand both the groups of people it assisted and the kinds of assistance it could give. UNHCR's authority derived from an amalgamation of sources. From the beginning it had delegated authority. States entrusted it with the task of helping them carry out and coordinate their obligations under the Refugee Convention and with diffusing refugee law. UNHCR also had moral authority that derived from its mission to help protect refugees and from its standing as a humanitarian agency that acted in an impartial manner.[3] Its authority and influence were in no small measure due to its image as an advocate for the powerless. After years of experience in the field and work to develop refugee law, it also acquired expert authority. It became the lead agency in various relief exercises and humanitarian operations, coordinating and directing the actions of others. UNHCR was often placed "in authority" because of its formal roles and became "an authority" through its experiences in the field and standing in the international community.

Section I examines how UNHCR used its authority to both define the category of refugees and expand the organization's geographical scope and orbit of responsibilities. From the beginning, UNHCR was mandated to help protect refugees. UNHCR officials, however, felt that their initial mandate had unwarranted restrictions because it limited the definition of refugees to those who had been displaced as a result of events prior to 1951 in Europe, and it limited the meaning of protection to provision of legal services. Gradually UNHCR operationalized these concepts in ways that had important implications for the nature and extent of international obligations as well as the life chances of millions of people. The power of UNHCR was both constitutive and regulative: it involved defining the category of refugees so that it applied to more people in more places, and it allowed the organization to help regulate how states dealt with refugees and to provide protection in a fuller sense to displaced populations.

Section II examines the emergence of the repatriation culture at UNHCR and the organization's increased tendency to violate refugee rights in the early 1980s. A core element of UNHCR's protection mission is to find a permanent solution to refugee problems. Its founding statute explicitly mentions three solutions: asylum, third-country resettlement, and repatriation. Until the late 1970s the agency had an exilic bias, rarely considering repatriation as a permanent solution. Subsequently, the agency developed a policy that strongly favored repatriation, which, in turn, forced it to develop rules governing repatriation. At issue in this process is the relationship between rules regarding repatriation and the refugee regime's foundational principle of *nonrefoulement:* no state shall "expel or return *[refouler]* a refugee . . . to the frontiers of territories where his life or freedom shall be threatened." UNHCR, therefore, has to determine when and how repatriation can be carried out without violating this principle. This is far from simple. It is often difficult to poll tens of thousands of people to determine when they want to return and whether they know enough to make informed choices. It also can be difficult to assess whether the situation at home has appreciably improved. States rarely want to host refugee populations for long periods of time and therefore are quite keen to return them—by force if necessary. Alternatives in such situations are often bad and worse, and UNHCR is heavily involved in deciding the "least bad" of the alternatives.

Over the last several decades there have been growing reports that repatriation has been carried out in ways that violate the principle of nonrefoulement and a growing number of allegations that UNHCR is playing fast and loose with the principle of voluntary repatriation.[4] The standard explanation for this development points the finger at states. Shifts in the geography of refugee concentrations from Europe to the developing world, an expanding refugee population, and an increasing reluctance to resettle or grant asylum to large numbers of refugees have made states more insistent on swift repatriation as the best means of dealing with refugee situations. States increasingly view refugee rights and nonrefoulement as inconvenient obstacles when they have decided that it is time for refugees to go home. Under such circumstances, states will encourage or coerce their return. In the face of state demands, the reasoning goes, UNHCR has had little choice but to associate itself with forced repatriation, judging that it is better to compromise its principles and help however it can than to sit on the sidelines with its principles intact as refugees suffer more than they otherwise would.

While state pressures provide an important part of the explanation for the broad shift in UNHCR's preferences toward repatriation and for the many instances in which it is accused of violating refugee rights, UNHCR has its own independent reasons for viewing repatriation as the preferred solution to refugee problems and for developing rules that increase the probability that it will sanction involuntary repatriation even when state pressures can be resisted. Beginning in the 1980s UNHCR gradually developed a "repatriation culture"—a bureaucratic structure and discourse coupled with formal and informal rules that made repatriation UNHCR's preferred solution and, in fact, nearly synonymous with "protection." This culture shifted the operational meaning of "voluntary" so that the voice that counted was the agency's and not the refugees'. It also shifted the meaning of "protection" so that the ultimate form of protection was defined as getting refugees home as soon as possible. A consequence of this culture was that UNHCR favored repatriation under circumstances that potentially threatened refugee rights even in the absence of state pressures.

This case illustrates the normalization of deviance, which occurs when bureaucracies introduce incremental deviations from established rules because of new environmental or institutional developments, believing that these modest alterations do not heighten the risk of policy failure (see chapter 2). These exceptions can accumulate so that a policy that at an earlier time might have been considered a gross violation of acceptable practice later becomes normalized and acceptable. This normalization of deviance captures the evolution of UNHCR's repatriation policy beginning in the early 1980s. Faced with state pressures, the changing circumstances of refugees, and new rules and understandings that made getting refugees "home" appropriate and desirable, the agency attempted to revise the rules of repatriation so as to safeguard refugee rights. Over time, however, it revised these rules in ways that normalized behavior once considered to be deviant. Its repatriation exercises became increasingly risky and pathological. In section III we examine UNHCR's handling of the Rohingyan refugees in 1994. UNHCR authorized the repatriation of the Rohingyas from Bangladesh to Burma in ways that violated the principle of voluntary repatriation when state pressures did not force it to do so, and it returned refugees to a place where their lives were at grave risk.[5]

I. THE ORIGINS OF AN INTERNATIONAL REFUGEE REGIME AND UNHCR

There have always been refugees. Wars, political upheavals, and religious strife have caused people to flee their homes because they fear for their safety.[6] International migration flows of this kind are at least as old as the Bible. Prior to the twentieth century, decisions by governments to grant asylum were usually ad hoc and based on their attitude toward those seeking asylum.[7] There was no standardized procedure for determining who was and was not to be given asylum. Private voluntary agencies were sometimes organized to assist specific ethnic, national, or religious groups, and sometimes states cooperated with these groups, but there was no international mechanism for assistance. This lacuna is not so surprising when one considers that until the twentieth century states did not intensively regulate population flows. It was only with the rise of nationalism and the consolidation of national states in the late nineteenth and early twentieth centuries that governments began to introduce immigration laws, passports, and other legal and administrative barriers to entry.[8] These changes made possible and necessary the legal category of refugee, since it was only after these changes that individuals forced to flee their homes were unable to obtain citizenship or legal residence in another country. As John Stoessinger put it, "what distinguishes the refugee of the twentieth century is the immense difficulty, and often impossibility, of finding a new home."[9]

World War I, the Russian Revolution, and the HCR

Emerging state controls on entry set the stage for the massive refugee crisis that evolved because of World War I. The war itself displaced hundreds of thousands of people. The breakdown of the multinational empires in Austria-Hungary and Turkey and the creation of national states (often by ethnic cleansing) led to mass flight. The Russian Revolution and then the famine of 1921 produced over a million Russian refugees. With millions of people unable to go home but unable to find sanctuary elsewhere, Europe faced a grave humanitarian emergency.

Responding to these developments, in 1921 the League of Nations established the first international organization dedicated to refugee matters—the High Commissioner for Refugees (HCR). The commissioner's mandate was to help assist the Russian refugees. There were several reasons why states chose this moment to act. Many private charity groups were overwhelmed by the sheer number of displaced peoples and lobbied states to create a new international agency to aid the relief effort.[10] States were probably less influenced by these normative appeals or humanitarian motives than by narrow political interests and pragmatic considerations; these migration flows were having a destabilizing effect in Europe. However impure their motives, the willingness of states to establish an organization dedicated to refugees was a remarkable innovation given the previous pattern of sustained indifference punctuated by isolated acts of charity.

States established tight restrictions on the new agency. Although there were refugees strewn across Europe, Western states limited the HCR's work to people from Russia who claimed to be fleeing political persecution. This had two advantages. It ensured that the organization did not become involved in a potentially endless array of possible refugee obligations in other parts of the globe. It also directed the charge of political persecution at communist Russia (even though many of these individuals were not political refugees). States also restricted the HCR's mandate, making it a coordination—and not an operational—body. To ensure this limited field of activity, states gave the HCR a meager budget, which they claimed was plenty given its limited duties.

Notwithstanding this limited autonomy, the HCR widened its scope of activities over time, becoming involved in refugee crises elsewhere in the region and articulating a set of refugee rights. Much of the credit for its growing prominence goes to the organization's first high commissioner, the renowned Norwegian explorer Fridtjof Nansen. He exploited his credibility with Western governments, gained as a result of his extensive experience dealing with the repatriation of Russian war prisoners, to expand the agency's activities. Over the objections of these governments, Nansen insinuated himself into the political and refugee crises in Greece, Turkey, Bulgaria, and elsewhere. Such interventions proved to be a powerful precedent for more widespread international involvement in refugee issues.[11] In addition to this geographical expansion, the HCR successfully negotiated a set of refugee rights, including travel documents (the so-called Nansen passport), education, and employment (Nansen worked with the International Labor Organization to help refugees find jobs). For the first time there was an international agency that was assisting refugees—helping to define populations in need and what rights they might possess.

Although Nansen was able to extend his mandate, ultimately the HCR was wholly dependent on states to carry out its recommendations. When states did not want to cooperate, little was done for refugees, and, as would become painfully clear over the subsequent decade, states had gone about as far as they were prepared to go. In 1933 governments convened to consider a refugee convention. Largely written by Nansen's office, the draft treaty aspired to expand the definition of refugee beyond those fleeing communist Russia to include all people who were forced to flee and to assign them a bundle of rights.[12] States were not pleased. They had a difficult time imagining that refugees might have rights, held fast to the restrictive definition of refugee, and rebuffed the HCR's plea to recognize refugees outside the Russian context, in parts of Europe where internal and interstate conflicts were creating migration waves not covered in the HCR's original mandate. Their discussions led to a draft treaty that failed to define a refugee, refused to guarantee the right of asylum, skirted the issue of refugee rights, and neglected to deliver a strong endorsement of nonrefoulement. Even this weak document proved too radical for most states, for it received only eight signatures. The unwillingness of Western states to shelter undesirable groups became tragically clear over the next few years as they refused to permit the entry of Jews and other persecuted groups from Nazi Germany. Nansen's successor, James McDonald, tried to help the victims of Nazi persecution by publicizing their plight and imploring Western governments to follow through on their obligations, but they would have none of it. He resigned in protest. When states were unwilling to help those peoples whose own states had failed them, there was little HCR could do.

Although states had clearly demonstrated their limits in supporting refugees, the HCR had nevertheless helped to redefine where those limits were. States had fundamentally transformed their conception of refugee flows. Before World War I states rarely acknowledged any moral obligation toward refugees and certainly never dreamed of creating an international organization to handle their plight. Now they had done both. And despite scant resources and meager state support, the HCR proved remarkably effective, and at times ingenious, in its handling of refugee crises, expanding its geographical and functional scope. The fact that states now acknowledged special responsibilities to refugees provided a foundation on which future refugee advocates could build.

World War II, the Cold War, and UNHCR

Pressing refugee problems following World War II prompted states to undertake a series of efforts to create multilateral arrangements to deal with refugees, but they proceeded in a manner that reflected their limited sympathies. The European landscape was flooded with refugees and displaced persons. Initially states responded on an ad hoc and case-by-case basis, making individual arrangements for each asylum applicant. The first coordinated response came from the Supreme Headquarters Allied Expeditionary Force (SHAEF). However, its efforts were rocked by controversy when it forcibly repatriated great numbers of refugees and displaced persons, often to Soviet-controlled lands. Refugees cried out in mass protest and in several highly publicized cases committed suicide. The combination of the refugees' reaction and the reluctance by Western powers to suffer the political costs associated with turning over desperate populations to the Soviets led SHAEF to suspend nonvoluntary repatriation to these areas.[13] This unsettling episode contributed to growing support for the principle that repatriation must be voluntary.[14]

In November 1943 Western powers established the United Nations Relief and Rehabilitation Administration (UNRRA) to continue the work of settling the millions of refugees and displaced peoples. The agency quickly became ensnared in East-West conflict. At issue was whether UNRRA would be obligated to provide assistance to those individuals who refused to repatriate. The Soviets insisted that only those who returned home should be eligible for assistance, while the West asserted that individuals should be allowed to receive assistance even if they refused to repatriate. Lurking behind this debate over the principle of voluntary repatriation was old-fashioned politics—the West would not force individuals to return to Soviet-controlled lands, and the Soviets were unwilling to suffer this ideological slap. In the end the two blocs struck a compromise: individuals would not be forced to repatriate, but those who refused were eligible for only six months of assistance. As a consequence, the agency was unable to help the thousands of refugees who were reluctant to return home, had no home to return to, or refused to resettle in their current locale because they had been brought there against their will or as slave laborers.[15]

Despite the compromise formula, the United States was unwilling to be the chief financial patron of an organization that pressured individuals to return to the eastern bloc. Therefore, in late 1946 it took steps to kill the agency and replace it with the International Refugee Organization (IRO). This agency broke new ground in two respects. First, states formally recognized the right of refugees not to be repatriated against their will—the first time an international document stated this right in categorical terms. Second, they tied the concept of refugee to fear of persecution.[16] This turn of phrase was struck in part to assuage Soviet objections to harsher language that was more pointedly anti-Soviet (though its aim at the Soviet Union was inescapable). Defining refugees in relation to persecution had two important effects: it shifted determination of refugee status away from national origins and toward individual characteristics, and it promoted a definition that was more easily universalized because it was tied to generic properties and not to a specific nationality. The relatively well-funded IRO began its work on August 20, 1948, setting out to assist the nearly one million remaining displaced people, a task thought to require no more than five years. Over the next three years it spent nearly $400 million settling more than 700,000 refugees, but there remained roughly 174,000 old, weak, or orphaned individuals in various camps across Europe.

The very fact that refugee flows seemed to be a permanent feature of the international landscape swayed the UN's Economic and Social Council to discuss the termination of IRO and the creation of a more permanent refugee agency. These discussions led to the establishment of the institutional and legal pillars of a more permanent international regime built around UNHCR and the Refugee Convention. Because the debates over the Refugee Convention and UNHCR proceeded along parallel tracks, tackled comparable issues, and were waged by many of the same players, the outcomes were roughly similar. In both cases states laid the foundations for the international refugee regime, but these were narrow and shaky foundations, not intended to support any expansion. Although the European states were in favor of a robust regime, largely because they were shouldering the burden of the displaced populations, the United States successfully opposed the creation of a strong organization with a broad mandate.

The Establishment of UNHCR

Before formally establishing UNHCR in 1950, states held two years of discussions over core issues including the scope of the office, legal definitions, the operationalization of such basic concepts as protection and assistance, and the extent of the agency's autonomy. The Europeans and the Americans were at odds on these basic issues. Driven less by humanitarianism than by a desire to find a multilateral burden-sharing mechanism to reduce their individual costs, the European states envisioned a forward-looking and encompassing organization that could provide a robust international response to the post–World War II refugee crisis.[17] France, for instance, wanted a UNHCR that was strong, multilateral, permanent, independent, and empowered to raise its own finances. Other European governments sympathized with the French position.[18]

The United States, in contrast, wanted a limited agency that would cease to exist once the remaining European refugees were resettled. Indeed, it believed that the ultimate solution to the refugee crisis was economic development, which could be provided by the Marshall Plan.[19] In the meantime, and in the context of the deepening Cold War, the United States increasingly favored bilateral over multilateral policy instruments as a way to reduce the constraints on its policies and to avoid having to listen to the Soviets. Consequently, while the United States sanctioned the creation of UNHCR, it quickly moved to establish and support other refugee agencies, most famously the International Committee for European Migration and the United States Escapee Programme. Much to the disappointment of the Europeans and the satisfaction of the United States, UNHCR was created with few responsibilities, little autonomy, and few available mechanisms to establish any independent action that might extend its very limited functional and geographical jurisdiction.

Definition of a Refugee. The United States insisted on a highly circumscribed definition of a refugee because it wanted to settle IRO's account and then terminate any international structure to handle refugee matters. Accordingly, it favored a definition that was tied to recent European events. The European states, on the other hand, argued that refugees were a permanent problem in world politics that would require a permanent international solution, and thus sought to establish a definition to serve that end. Of a similar mind were former IRO staff, who lobbied vigorously for a more universal definition that would allow the organization to help those who feared violence but not necessarily persecution from governments. They and allied delegations pointed to the massive refugee flows occurring elsewhere, notably in South Asia and the Middle East, and to the establishment of the United Nations Relief and Work Agency for Palestine Refugees in the Near East, as compelling evidence that refugees fled not because of persecution but because of conflict and violent circumstances. IRO and other like-minded delegations used this fact to argue in favor of an expanded definition. The United States was unmoved, and the compromise favored its preference for a restricted definition.

In the end, a refugee was defined as any person who:

> as a result of events occurring before 1 January 1951 and owing to well-founded fear of persecution for reasons of race, religion, nationality, membership of a particular social group or political opinion, is outside the country of his nationality and is unable or, owing to such fear, is unwilling to avail himself of the protection of the government; or who, not having a nationality and being outside the country of his former habitual residence as a result of such events, is unable or, owing to such fear, is unwilling to return to it.

This definition's central feature is its narrowness, a reflection of states' desire to limit their responsibilities. UNHCR was born as a backward-looking rather than a forward-looking organization, and so it was expected to help those who already were refugees and not future refugees. A refugee had to have crossed an international border. States recognized that there were many displaced persons, but only one who had managed to fall on the other side of a territorial divide could be legally classified as a refugee. Refugees, moreover, were defined as those persecuted by their national governments.[20] Persecution further narrowed the definition of a refugee, for it omitted large numbers of peoples who might be forced to leave their country because of economic hardship, international and internal wars, famines, and authoritarian practices by their government.[21] Moreover, refugee status could no longer be extended to an entire population but instead could be conferred only on an individual. The effect was to potentially limit the numbers of individuals who might be classified as refugees by prohibiting blanket designations of entire groups.

Definition of Protection. There was such widespread acceptance that UNHCR would have a protection function that there was relatively little discussion regarding what protection meant.[22] Discussions that did occur revealed the expected differences between the United States and the Europeans, with the former favoring legal assistance only and the latter envisioning an extensive material assistance mission. Those in the U.S. camp wanted to omit financial and logistical assistance, which they believed were better handled by governments, private charity foundations, and international agencies like the International Committee for the Red Cross. Moreover, many key states were increasingly impatient with, and growing weary of, refugee flows that they believed "were by definition temporary" and would soon be a part of the remote past.[23] The Europeans, on the other hand, envisioned a more robust and wide-ranging arrangement. The U.S. vision largely carried the day.

UNHCR was to provide legal protection, offering refugees an "international legal bridge between periods of national sovereign assimilation."[24] Toward that end, UNHCR could assist refugees by "identifying them, issuing travel documents, assisting in obtaining recognition of their various legal statuses, and advocating ever more precise guidelines for handling recognized refugees."[25] As one UNHCR official summarized: "international protection implies a series of arrangements with institutional and legal aspects meant to provide for the specific position of a refugee as an alien resident who cannot claim the protection of his country of nationality and to ensure for the refugee, in the country of asylum, as close as possible to the status of national residents, particularly with respect to civil, economic, social, and cultural rights."[26]

Although states insisted that international protection was limited to a legal meaning, at the time UNHCR staff interpreted protection to include extralegal measures. As the first high commissioner stated in 1954: "It is clear that the international protection for which my office is responsible is wider than the legal and political protection with which previous international organizations concerned with refugees were charged."[27] In the staff's view, legal protection meant little without material assistance, including food, shelter, health services, education, social welfare, and possible employment.[28] Accordingly, UNHCR staff immediately adopted a more liberal interpretation of protection—one that included measures designed to maintain and improve the well-being of the refugee—even as states were insisting that such interpretations were out of step with UNHCR's statute.[29]

Future events, as we will see, enabled the agency to develop programs to match its broader vision.

Definition of Permanent Solutions. Although voluntary repatriation was one of the three permanent solutions envisaged by UNHCR—along with integration into the asylum country and resettlement to a third country—it was widely dismissed as a viable possibility in the 1950s. Indeed, during the debate over the establishment of UNHCR it was unclear whether repatriation would even be listed as part of the high commissioner's functions. France and the United States initially objected to its inclusion because they assumed that in this Cold War context repatriation meant sending refugees back to communist lands.[30] In the end, repatriation was eventually included as a possible permanent solution, but with little expectation of wide use.

In keeping with the times, UNHCR quickly established an exilic bias: the only conceivable solution for refugees was to reside permanently outside their homeland.[31] The bias against repatriation was stated clearly and consistently by the first high commissioners. In a 1955 address to the Nobel Institute, High Commissioner Gerrit Jan van Heuven Goedhart observed that voluntary repatriation was no longer a solution of much importance and that it would probably represent a solution for only 1 percent of all refugees. He later said that his office had no real mandate to pursue repatriation.[32] In 1957 High Commissioner Auguste R. Lindt made it clear that he did not consider repatriation a real solution.[33] In 1967, at the request of a member of the Executive Committee, the high commissioner said that it would be difficult but possible to prepare a document that would provide an overview of repatriation (which he never did).[34] This was not mere rhetoric divorced from practice. Over the 1955–62 period, the organization "directly assisted the repatriation of 251 refugees, the emigration of 16,613, and the local integration of 53,681."[35] The organizational culture from the top down was geared toward resettlement and third-country asylum, and the conception of international protection as a legal bridge toward resettlement was consistent with that exilic bias.

Organizational Autonomy. To match the restricted-action vocabulary, states gave the institution little autonomy. This result, once again, was much closer to the U.S. position, which favored establishing strong control mechanisms, than to the European position, which preferred an agency that had considerable discretion. The United States wanted the high commissioner to be subservient to the UN secretary-general, while the Europeans wanted an independent commissioner. The compromise was a high commissioner nominated by the secretary-general of the United Nations, who subsequently reported to the General Assembly. Moreover, UNHCR was obligated to report directly to an advisory committee of governments (which became the

Executive Committee in 1957) that was expected to closely monitor the agency's activities. UNHCR also received only a temporary operating mandate of three years (now it has a five-year term, renewable at the discretion of the General Assembly). At U.S. insistence, the organization had limited resources and little opportunity to develop any financial independence. Its $300,000 administrative budget came from the UN's general operating budget and was expected to cover its primary activities. In order to make sure that it did not gain financial independence, UNHCR was expressly prohibited from raising or spending money without prior approval of the UN General Assembly. The practical result was that UNHCR operated on voluntary contributions and not on assessments.

Although UNHCR was created with very little autonomy and could act only under the limited circumstances defined by its statute, within a few years it became apparent that the agency would be able to exploit its authority in order to challenge states and expand its scope of operations. Its authority had several sources. It had a moral authority owing to its standing as a humanitarian organization and as the protector and diffuser of refugee law.[36] Thus, lobbying and diffusing norms were part of its mandate. States directed UNHCR to promote the dissemination of the principles of refugee law and to make sure that states knew the law and were in compliance with existing statutes. It also began to promote the development of refugee law to "meet the demands of contemporary refugee situations."[37] UNHCR officials acted quickly and tirelessly to ensure not only that states honored their commitments under the convention but also that the general humanitarian principles covered in the statute were applied to "refugee-like" situations around the world that resulted from events occurring after 1951.[38] Portraying itself as an apolitical and impartial humanitarian organization also proved instrumental for establishing its authority, a self-presentation that was both sincere and strategic.[39] States and others quickly came to perceive UNHCR as a leading expert on refugee matters, with its expertise derived from its formal position in the international system as well as from its experience on the ground. Being "an authority" and "in authority" would prove critical to the agency's efforts to shape its own destiny and the future of the international refugee regime.[40]

The Refugee Convention

In fall 1950 the General Assembly passed the Convention relating to the Status of Refugees, which took effect on January 1, 1951. Like the debates over UNHCR, states' deliberations over the convention were shaped by recent experiences, the ideological divisions between the East and the West, and, critically, the differing views of the United States and Europe. The outcome was similar to that of their debates over UNHCR; states created a refugee convention that blended narrowly defined state interests and pragmatic humanitarianism, and that shielded them from open-ended commitments by narrowing the range of people who could claim refugee status and the rights they might possess.[41]

The definition of a refugee in the convention was slightly different and more restricted than that in the UNHCR statute. A refugee was defined as an individual "outside the country of his origin . . . owing to a well-founded fear of being persecuted for reasons of race, religion, nationality, or political opinion" as a consequence of events that occurred before January 1, 1951, in Europe. This involved four key restrictions. Most significant, the definition contained both geographical and temporal restrictions. Although UNHCR's statute also limited its activities to those situations caused by events prior to 1951, the convention further limited the legal definition of a refugee by adding a geographical element, "in Europe." The consequence was to place profound legal limits on UNHCR's activities. A third restriction reflected the individualistic thinking that prevailed at the time. "Strictly interpreted, this concept could be considered to exclude from the High Commissioner's mandate refugees or groups of refugees whose circumstances made it impossible to verify their eligibility individually."[42] For instance, UNHCR could not automatically confer refugee status on all exiles of Russian nationality but instead would have to determine refugee status on a case-by-case basis. All three restrictions would be assailed and substantially revised as a consequence of events over the next decade. Finally, the circumstances that caused flight were limited to persecution. Persecution was not crisply defined, though the experiences of World War II and the circumstances in the communist countries had a pervasive influence in creating the assumption that persecution involved political or religious affiliation.[43]

The Refugee Convention also delineated a bundle of rights for refugees. Because refugees are individuals who are not protected by their state and who have not been adopted by another, they no longer benefit from the legal protections afforded to citizens of a state. States rejected proposals that refugees have either a right to membership elsewhere or the right to asylum and instead opted to enumerate rights that refugees can expect in order to maintain some level of dignity and sustenance consistent with human rights conventions.[44] Toward this end, the convention stipulated that refugees should have access to national courts, the right to employment and education, and a host of other social, economic, and civil rights.

Perhaps the most fundamental right granted refugees was nonrefoulement: refugees cannot be returned to a country where they risk physical harm or persecution. This principle gives individuals the right to flee their homeland and to find sanctuary in another country, thus prohibiting both rejection at the frontier and expulsion after entry.[45] While states have rights to control their own borders, they must do so in accord with the principle of nonrefoulement. Nonrefoulement thus was responsible for the later concept of voluntary repatriation. Although never mentioned in the treaty, voluntary repatriation became a logical way of returning refugees while respecting nonrefoulement. Its presumption is that refugees cannot be returned to a situation they believe still presents the dangers that forced them to flee for their safety. Thus, what matters is not only that the situation at home has changed but that refugees have voluntarily consented to return. Note, however, that by conferring on refugees the right not to be repatriated forcibly but denying them the right to automatic asylum, the convention signaled that they might end up living in a transnational limbo. It was up to UNHCR to find creative ways to assist the millions of refugees who would be created around the world after 1951, devise solutions, and protect their rights.

UNHCR's Early Years

It was unclear whether UNHCR would survive much past birth because of its handicaps, powerful opponents, and dangerous rivals. Its shoestring budget provided for only the barest necessities, and its financial situation was so perilous that it required a three-million-dollar Ford Foundation grant in 1955 to stave off death. Because its mandate was limited to refugees produced by events in Europe prior to 1951, it was quickly going out of business as the number of Cold War refugees dwindled. The United States refused to have much to do with the agency, providing little diplomatic and no financial support. There were better-funded refugee organizations, often sponsored by the United States, that marginalized UNHCR and encroached on its modest jurisdiction.[46] Perhaps the only thing in its favor was a determined high commissioner, van Heuven Goedhart, who saw himself as the refugees' representative and the champion of their interests.[47] Dedicated personnel alone, however, were unlikely to save UNHCR or expand its budget and mandate.

UNHCR capitalized on world events and used its growing authority to rescue itself from oblivion and significantly extend its activities, mandate, and working definition of a refugee.[48] Beginning in the mid-1950s, a series of conflicts created refugee crises that were formally outside UNHCR's jurisdiction because the conflicts occurred after 1951 and/or because they were outside Europe. In each case a similar sequence of events occurred. The high commissioner strenuously argued that his office was morally obligated and well positioned to handle the new situation; member states, including, critically, the United States, agreed that the agency could play a valuable role; and the General Assembly authorized UNHCR's action, establishing a precedent for future exceptions and a more permanent expansion of UNHCR's mandate. Several cycles of this dynamic slowly but impressively expanded UNHCR's reach, eventually allowing it to provide legal and material assistance to those who were in refugee-like situations in all parts of the world. As High Commissioner Sadruddin Aga Khan reflected, "A concept of collective prima facie eligibility, prompted by events, thus gradually took shape. It departed from the individualist concept linked to the definition of the term 'refugee' in the Statute and Convention, and progressed towards a more pragmatic and human rather than legalistic approach to the refugee problem."[49]

Cycle I: Hungary

The October 1956 Soviet invasion of Hungary created a major Cold War crisis and triggered the flight of nearly two hundred thousand Hungarians. The question was how to handle the swell of refugees who were not only in need of international relief but also entangled in a superpower confrontation. UNHCR became the focal point for the international relief effort. Early in the crisis Austria formally requested UNHCR's assistance. The United States had already begun to soften its opposition to the agency and became more receptive to its assistance role. As a result, the General Assembly, over the objections of the Soviet Union, authorized UNHCR to take a commanding role in the assistance effort, a position backed by its assessment that UNHCR's previous experience made it well-qualified for this role.[50] This was the first time that UNHCR was given the "lead agency" designation.

Although political factors favored a growing role for the agency, it remained unclear whether it had legal jurisdiction. After all, this was 1956 and UNHCR was limited to events that occurred prior to 1951. In January 1957, however, an agency official struck upon an imaginative interpretation of UNHCR's statutory mandate that provided the legal cover for the agency: because the antecedents for this event could be traced to pre-1951 circumstances, the Hungarian crisis was within the agency's mandate.[51] The new high commissioner, Auguste Lindt, won over the General Assembly with this logic.[52] However, there was another legal issue to be smoothed over. UNHCR was supposed to determine on a case-by-case basis the status of each refugee. This was reasonable under more leisurely circumstances, but it posed a bureaucratic nightmare in this refugee crisis. Accordingly, UNHCR decided to give a blanket, temporary refugee designation to all those fleeing, deferring until later the bureaucratic procedure of determining whether an individual refugee had fled because of persecution. In the end, the Hungarian crisis demonstrated to states, first, the usefulness of having a nonpartisan agency deal with the humanitarian consequences of interstate conflict, and, second, the necessity of overcoming the restrictive features of the 1951 definition of a refugee if UNHCR was to play this role.[53]

Cycle II: Hong Kong

The 1949 Chinese Revolution further demonstrated the utility of UNHCR, drawing attention to the problems associated with an overly restrictive mandate and allowing the organization to introduce an innovative concept called "good offices" to overcome these restrictions. Thousands of mainland Chinese had been seeking refuge in Hong Kong, swelling the Hong Kong population by almost 25 percent and placing a heavy financial burden on Great Britain. High Commissioner Goedhart let it be known that his office was ready to assist if the complex political situation could be worked out. As one of the first Western powers to have established relations with mainland China, Britain wanted to avoid provoking a crisis by categorizing these populations as "refugees." Accordingly, it refused to recognize them as refugees, claiming that they were fleeing because of economic circumstances and not political persecution. It further concluded that UNHCR had no jurisdiction in a British colony. To complicate matters, Chiang Kai-shek's Taiwan represented China at the UN. While the Taiwanese government was happy to see UNHCR provide assistance to these refugees, it was willing to resettle only those who were politically or economically useful. Because refugees are those who experience persecution by their government, and because Taiwan was formally recognized as the government of China, many member states argued that those fleeing Mao were not bona fide refugees. There was no way that UNHCR, a member of the UN family that formally recognized Chiang as the head of the Chinese government, could become involved without some cover from the General Assembly.

The General Assembly finally sorted out the morass of political and legal impediments in November 1957 when it requested the high commissioner to use his "good offices" to encourage contributions to the Chinese refugees in Hong Kong who were of "concern to the international community."[54] The good offices formulation proved to be a sharp tool that gave the high commissioner the delegated and moral authority to expand his mandate in three ways. First, the concept allowed the high commissioner to assist refugees who were not formally part of his mandate. Statutory refugees were those created by events that occurred in Europe before 1951. Good offices refugees were those who did not meet these temporal and geographic restrictions. Second, UNHCR was allowed to assist good offices refugees without a determination that the government of origin was persecuting its population.[55] All the high commissioner needed to know was that they required international assistance. Third, good offices refugees usually needed not legal protection but rather material assistance, and the high commissioner was now authorized to help coordinate and provide that assistance. According to High Commissioner Félix Schnyder, the General Assembly's request that the high commissioner use his "good offices to encourage arrangements for contributions" was a pragmatic solution to an extreme problem, for the refugees outside UNHCR's mandate were in greater need of material assistance than legal protection. Over time the good offices concept became institutionalized and available as a tool to assist in new episodes.[56]

Cycle III: Algeria

The Algerian civil war provided the next occasion for the agency's expansion. When war broke out in 1954, Algerian refugees began fleeing into neighboring Morocco and Tunisia. By May 1957 the number of refugees in Tunisia had grown to nearly eighty-five thousand, and the Tunisian government went to UNHCR for assistance. The request proved to be an important challenge and opportunity for the agency. This was the first request from a Third World country, and it came at a time when the agency was expanding its operations in Hungary. High Commissioner Lindt was uncomfortable with the appearance of caring only for refugees in the West and wanted to expand his operations into the Third World, transforming the agency into a truly global refugee organization. He believed that the Hungarian crisis presented the required precedent because it permitted UNHCR to help refugees without determining their status on a case-by-case basis. Others in the agency, however, objected. Some worried that by accepting the challenge they would be accusing France—a Great Power, a member of the Security Council, and a country with a liberal asylum policy—of persecution. Others argued that the agency had no jurisdiction. Lindt decided to push the agency into North Africa, but only after he had smoothed the waters by working with Western powers and other relief agencies.

By late 1958, nearly two hundred thousand refugees were in camps in Morocco and Tunisia. This moved the General Assembly to authorize UNHCR to assist these refugees. General Assembly Resolution 1388 of November 20, 1959, drew the first-ever distinction between refugees within the mandate and those outside it and requested the high commissioner to use his "good offices" to transmit contributions and assistance to them. The significance of the resolution, according to High Commissioner Schnyder, was that the General Assembly chose not to specifically identify the groups to be helped but instead "refer[red] in general . . . to refugees who do not come within the competence of the United Nations."[57] Once again, UNHCR could confer blanket refugee status. But this time there was no debate as to whether such blanket designations represented a departure from acceptable practices, suggesting that acts once thought of as exceptions were becoming institutionalized. Reflecting on the relationship between the Hungarian, Hong Kong, and Algerian crises and UNHCR's new activities, Louise Holborn wrote that the emerging consensus position was that to respond effectively to these new and diplomatically difficult situations, the agency would require states to delegate the authority necessary to allow its actions to be viewed as "non-political."[58]

Cycle IV: Decolonization

During the 1960s a succession of refugee crises associated with decolonization in Africa produced new challenges and opportunities for UNHCR. The high commissioner determined to do everything he could to expand UNHCR's geographical reach and delivery of services, exploiting precedents and, most important, the concept of good offices for this purpose. At the dawn of the decolonization era and on his first day on the job in December 1960, the new high commissioner, Félix Schnyder, issued a press release indicating his intention of providing assistance to refugees in the developing world and claiming that the good offices concept was flexible enough to allow him to do this.[59] Agency staff had always chafed at a convention that implied that their moral obligations stopped in Europe and did not extend to all refugees, and they successfully used moral claims and now-available organizational vocabulary to increase its range.

Signaling its agreement, the General Assembly passed a series of resolutions that gave the high commissioner the legal language he needed to respond immediately to new situations in new places. For instance, in the context of the ongoing humanitarian and refugee crises in Africa, a 1961 General Assembly resolution authorized UNHCR to use its good offices to play a leading role in protecting and assisting refugees outside Europe. This resolution recognized once again that the agency might have to give blanket refugee designations if there were mass population movements and designated UNHCR as the principal agency in control of such situations.[60] The collective effect of these resolutions was considerable. They virtually obliterated any geographical restrictions. They permitted the agency to help those whose flight was due to armed conflict or other extrastatutory causes. They allowed the agency to provide both legal protection and material assistance, thus backing Deputy High Commissioner Aga Khan's observation that because the circumstances surrounding African and European refugees were vastly different, the agency had to provide vastly different and kinds of assistance.[61] They eventually erased the distinction between statutory and nonstatutory refugees. By the mid-1960s resolutions ceased to mention "refugees who do not come within the competence of the United Nations," in effect giving the agency the moral and legal authority to remove the distinction between different refugee groups in favor of a single, omnibus category.[62]

In the mid-1960s, UNHCR and states began to discuss whether and how to upgrade UNHCR's formal mandate so that it would be more consistent with practice. In 1965, General Assembly Resolution 2039 abandoned the distinction between new groups of refugees covered by good offices and the regular mandate refugees and simply requested the high commissioner to "pursue his efforts with a view to ensuring an adequate international protection of refugees and to providing satisfactory permanent solutions to the problems affecting the various groups of refugees within his competence."[63] The General Assembly also passed several resolutions that expanded the authority of the high commissioner. They freed him from having to seek approval from the General Assembly for appeals for each individual refugee crisis. They gave him authority to finance and coordinate permanent solutions to refugee crises without state approval. They established an emergency fund that he could deploy at his discretion.[64]

The UNHCR of the 1970s bore little resemblance to the UNHCR at its birth. Once it had needed a Ford Foundation grant to rescue it from starvation; now it had a firm financial floor, its budget had expanded manyfold over the years, and it was much better staffed. Once it had been "mainly a small European migration agency"; now it was a muscular assistance body and a major UN agency.[65] Once it had been constrained by a refugee definition that limited its assistance activities to people stranded in Europe as a consequence of pre-1951 events; now it had the jurisdictional and conceptual freedom to roam the world helping those fleeing not only persecution but also assorted political upheavals.[66] Once it had been limited to legal protection; now it was providing material assistance, sponsoring development projects, and serving as a full-service humanitarian operation.

Several factors account for this impressive organizational expansion. Refugee flows generated substantial global and regional problems, and states recognized that they needed an international agency that could handle these matters impartially. UNHCR had proven functional in earlier crises, and so states turned to it and gave it more discretion to act in subsequent refugee crises. State approval, then, was critical for allowing UNHCR to expand into new regions and to act in new ways without getting prior state authorization. But successive high commissioners were hardly passive agents waiting for state requests. Instead, they identified new problems and circumstances that the agency not only was obligated to help solve but also in which it could play an effective role; they then presented these principled and functional claims to states, attempting to convince them that it was in their interest to allow the agency to help refugees and address humanitarian problems. At each and every opportunity, the high commissioner was on the scene, arguing that his office had the expertise to assist, offering legal interpretations of the mandate that connoted that his office had the delegated authority, and using his moral authority to speak on behalf of the displaced. These authority-based claims helped the high commissioner convince states to lengthen UNHCR's leash and provided the conceptual range that gave legal protection and material assistance to nonconvention refugees.[67] Thus, when states explicitly or implicitly permitted UNHCR to venture into new geographic areas and accept new tasks, the general sequence was that UNHCR successfully represented itself as offering the best response to the situation and then states went along either by authorizing new action or by failing to object.

Perhaps the most important tool in the high commissioner's arsenal was the good offices concept. It gave him legal and political justification for action in "contingencies and situations on the fringe of the normal activities of the High Commissioner's office," allowing him to extend protection and assistance to new groups.[68] The concept was more than a legal wedge, however. It allowed the UNHCR to transform sticky political issues into apolitical, humanitarian concerns. Making a formal determination of a refugee crisis meant in essence accusing the refugee-producing country of persecuting its people. By invoking good offices, the high commissioner could assist in a humanitarian manner that skirted political accusations because it did not directly charge the refugee-producing country with persecution.[69] In this way, states, refugees, and UNHCR benefited from the good offices formulation.[70] It also allowed the agency to expand its services beyond legal protection to material assistance. Although some in the agency worried that relief was beginning to overshadow protection, the high commissioner insisted that the real issue for many refugees was not legal standing but rather basic needs.[71] Material assistance, unlike legal protection, also allowed the agency to maintain its humanitarian character. Increasingly "solution and protection were considered for most of this period as 'political' questions to be distinguished from the 'humanitarian' questions of relief: the former were to be outside UNHCR's concern, the latter was not so to be considered if the main states involved were to be of that opinion in each particular case."[72] Overall, the good offices concept, and the associated UN resolutions, hastened UNHCR's expansion and gave the organization more autonomy and discretion.[73]

The good offices concept was only one of several contributors to UNHCR's growing autonomy. The organization now could raise and dispense money without prior authorization from the Executive Committee. More important, its delegated, moral, and expert authority all contributed to autonomy. The cycles of crises in its early years dramatically increased its delegated mandate. Its rapidly accumulating experience from years in the field and its standing as the guardian of refugee law were making it expert at its tasks. UNHCR also had moral authority derived from its status as protector of refugees and its impartiality as a humanitarian agency. High commissioners were well aware that their influence depended upon this moral authority and the appearance of being above politics, so they worked hard to maintain that face.[74]

UNHCR used its growing autonomy and authority to help to constitute world politics and shape directly the behavior of states as well as the life chances of refugees and other displaced populations. As already discussed, UNHCR used its delegated authority and its moral authority to help give a new conceptual meaning to such basic terms as "refugee" and "protection," thus playing a role in determining how new situations were understood and categorized and in establishing new sets of standardized responses to these problems. This new conceptual, legal, and normative language shaped how states framed new events and debated the appropriate policy response. Consequently, it narrowed the range of policy choices available to them. At one time Western states could safely ignore refugee problems in parts of the non-Western world. This became increasingly difficult as UNHCR and other constituencies were able to capitalize on this discursive shift and argue that the comparability of circumstances justified the expansion of UNHCR into new areas and activities.[75] Behind the scenes UNHCR was shaping the agenda of the Executive Committee and thus helping to determine which issues were discussed and how they were debated. Much to their chagrin, states also discovered that UNHCR was now an agency with considerable stature, ready to remind them of their obligations under refugee law. Of course states continued to fall short of their obligations, but they increasingly attempted to bring their conduct in line with UNHCR's standards and, failing that, gave defensive justifications for why their policy was a legitimate exception. In these and other ways, UNHCR was able to use its authority to help constitute the very category of refugees and to then regulate how states treated them.

This growing authority had implications not only for states but also for refugees. UNHCR now had more authority over more displaced peoples who were categorized as refugees. As a consequence it was entitled to give them material and legal assistance, to think about permanent solutions, and to represent their interests. To the extent that staff used that authority and power to represent refugees' interests and protect their rights, refugees benefited by having an international body assigned to them. To the extent that the agency developed rules that might run roughshod over their rights, UNHCR's authority and control over their fates could leave them at risk.

II. THE REPATRIATION CULTURE

UNHCR now had global authority to help solve refugee problems. Beginning in the late 1970s, though, it shifted its proposed solution from asylum and third-country resettlement to repatriation. An increasing percentage of UNHCR's budget has been consumed by repatriation activities.[76] The percentage of refugee flows that eventually lead to a repatriation exercise has increased. The amount of time devoted by the Executive Committee to repatriation issues has also increased significantly over the last two decades. High commissioners have stated boldly that the organization will marshal its energies and resources in favor of repatriation, with Sadaka Ogata declaring the 1990s the decade of repatriation.

UNHCR's shift toward repatriation is partly the result of state pressures, but not entirely. UNHCR officials also were responding to new circumstances and to legal and normative developments that encouraged them to see repatriation as the presumptively more humane alternative. As they were drawn toward repatriation, however, they worried about how far they could go without jeopardizing their traditional protection mission, violating refugee rights and nonrefoulement. UNHCR officials debated and then gradually altered the rules governing repatriation in ways that were intended to hasten repatriation without putting refugees at undue risk. Over time, these changes led to the normalization of deviance and a repatriation culture—a bureaucratic structure and discourse coupled with formal and informal rules that made repatriation UNHCR's preferred solution and, in fact, nearly synonymous with protection. This repatriation culture made pathological behavior—the possibility that a humanitarian and refugee organization would violate refugee rights—more likely.

Systemic Pressures and Changes

Although states accepted that displaced groups could be reasonably categorized as refugees, they became increasingly impatient with the demands placed on them by the growing numbers of refugees. Until the late 1970s Western governments had not clamored for repatriation because most refugees who landed in their countries were from communist countries, and it was ideologically and politically unthinkable to send them back. However, the profile of the typical refugee changed in the 1970s. Whereas once she was from an eastern bloc country attempting to escape to the West, now she was from the Third World and frequently attempting to gain entry to Western states for what these states viewed as illegitimate, often economic, reasons. The changing profile led Western states to complain about the ever-expanding number of asylum requests.[77] In response, they began denying asylum and demanding reforms in asylum and refugee law to restrict access.[78] Perhaps more important, Third World states were becoming increasingly intolerant of refugee flows and demands. A watershed event was the 1979 decision by Southeast Asian governments to deny asylum to the Vietnamese boat people, forcing them either to return to Vietnam, which branded them as criminals, or to fall into the arms of pirates on the high seas. This was no isolated instance. Many Third World governments that had once tolerated and sheltered refugees were becoming inhospitable and openly hostile. In many respects, the reasons were understandable. After all, refugees impose tremendous financial, environmental, and political costs, often entangling the host country in an unwanted conflict with the refugees' national government. Many Third World governments now conditioned fulfillment of their international legal obligations on assistance from UNHCR, wealthy states, and NGOs, and there were an increasing number of refugees whose presence was barely, if at all, tolerated by states.[79]

The growing number of refugees and the growing reluctance of states to shelter and support them produced twin crises for UNHCR. UNHCR's financial and administrative health worsened when its budget skyrocketed because the dramatic increase in the number of refugees outstripped voluntary contributions by states. Although states were partially responsible for this crisis because of their failure to provide the requisite resources, that did not stop them from using the crisis to scrutinize UNHCR's budget and activities.[80] The climax of the budget crisis came in 1989 when the Executive Committee took the unprecedented step of not authorizing UNHCR's budget, opting instead to cut its programs by 25 percent and its staff by 15 percent. Unhappy with the expense of their humanitarian obligations, states reacted by reducing UNHCR's financial autonomy and discretionary capacity.[81]

The second crisis concerned UNHCR's protection and assistance mission. Western states and UNHCR officials agreed that the protection system was not working, but they disagreed over the nature of the problem. Western governments claimed that individuals were filing fraudulent asylum requests, often claiming persecution when they were simply seeking better economic opportunities. They demanded that UNHCR reduce the abuse and alter its protection practices in ways that favored repatriation, and they frequently used the Executive Committee to voice their views, to encourage UNHCR to seize the initiative, and to create conditions to permit repatriation under less exacting standards.[82]

UNHCR, however, believed that "the threat to protection came from governments" that were refusing to honor asylum law and were forcibly repatriating refugees.[83] Although certainly aware of abuses in the asylum regime, it also worried that states were using leaks in the system as a pretext to weaken the rights available to asylum seekers and refugees. It also favored repatriation, though unlike states it did not treat refugee rights as an inconvenient obstacle. While in the 1970s UNHCR seemed able to confront and work with governments simultaneously, during the 1980s its relationship became more adversarial and it worried that it was angering the very states on whom it was dependent to sustain its activities.[84] The financial and protection crisis meant that UNHCR was confronting extremely difficult times and considerable pressure to alter its policies.

Although states were exhorting UNHCR to favor repatriation, UNHCR on its own was already attempting to shift away from its exilic bias toward a more favorable view of repatriation. This shift occurred because of developments in refugee law, refugee activities, and ethical understandings of how to best serve the needs of refugees.[85] The Cold War context that had shaped refugee law in 1951 assumed the desirability of asylum and resettlement. Refugees leaving communist states and with little interest in returning were ideological symbols; sending them back was politically impossible, and there was certainly no end in sight for the conditions causing them to flee. But by the 1970s most refugees were from and in the Third World. They were escaping different kinds of conflicts or disasters and largely viewed their exile as temporary. This development stimulated a greater interest by legal experts in previously unexplored features of refugee law surrounding repatriation.[86] Moreover, the simple fact was that refugees *were* going home. In a movement that was generally undetected because officials were not looking, refugees were "spontaneously repatriating," returning voluntarily to their home countries without the assistance of UNHCR or other relief organizations. UNHCR began to argue that in these situations it should facilitate both their return journey and reintegration into their home societies.[87] The belief that asylum was the most humane solution was gradually replaced by the view that individuals had a legal and moral right to return home.[88] The legal, institutional, and ethical climate became oriented toward repatriation.

The changing international environment also made it easier for UNHCR staff to contemplate and implement repatriation exercises. Many staff insist that the Cold War precluded them from considering repatriation—an option that they had always desired when circumstances were right and that many refugee populations preferred. Accordingly, UNHCR staff responded to the changed environment after 1989 by adopting those policies desired by refugees. As one UNHCR official put it, "We were always interested in repatriation, but geopolitical factors prohibited it. So when the opportunity emerged to move toward repatriation, UNHCR jumped. And we always listened to what the refugees wanted during this period, and the difference is that now we were getting new refugees (not from the eastern bloc but from recently decolonized states) that wanted to repatriate."[89] UNHCR now had motive and opportunity to move toward repatriation.

Still, there remained important divisions within the organization over how to balance the pressure from states to repatriate with the principle of voluntary repatriation. The agency developed cleavages between "fundamentalist" and "pragmatist" camps on this issue. Starting from a more legalistic approach to repatriation that emphasized the roots of refugee law in human rights law, fundamentalists argued that the legal principles at the core of the organization's mission were sacrosanct and should not be compromised. Specifically, UNHCR could authorize a repatriation exercise only if refugees were surveyed to determine whether they were willing to return home and if they thought such a return no longer represented a threat of persecution or endangered their physical safety. If the agency allowed for deviations and compromises, fundamentalists argued, several consequences would follow. UNHCR would sacrifice its moral authority and its unique role as an advocate for the refugees. Even modest deviations from established norms might become institutionalized and endanger refugees. By following a line advocated by states, UNHCR would jeopardize its impartiality and independence. Fundamentalists tended to reside in the legal and protection divisions of the organization or were protection officers scattered in other parts of the organization, and they had powerful figures representing them, including the head of the Protection Division, Michel Moussalli.

Frequently occupying the office of the high commissioner and regional bureaus, pragmatists argued for flexibilty and against a rights-based policy. Repatriation could be principled, they contended. Refugees often wanted to go home, and often protection officers following legal principles were the last to realize it. Pragmatists believed that the organizational and doctrinal shift in favor of repatriation righted a defect in the system that tended to privilege rigid, legalistic application of rules by protection officers who knew little about the region in which they worked and could not appreciate the larger political picture of which refugees were a part.[90] Moreover, the situation on the ground was already putting many refugees at risk because states had little tolerance for them. Ignoring those risks would not make them go away. Instead, UNHCR had to try to minimize those risks. If states were going to forcibly repatriate, pragmatists argued, then the choice for UNHCR was whether to sit on the sidelines with its abstract principles or try to make the best of a bad situation and protect the refugees as well as it could. Refugee camps were hardly safe havens: they frequently placed refugees at risk and could even present a greater threat to refugees than the circumstances that triggered their original flight.[91] Fundamentalists, the pragmatists insinuated, might think that rights protected refugees, but in fact rights could stand in the way of true protection.

The high commissioners consistently advocated a more flexible interpretation of refugee law and a more pragmatic response. In 1985 High Commissioner Jean-Pierre Hocke observed that repatriation was now desirable because, first, the regional conflicts directly caused or exacerbated by the Cold War were winding down, and, second, there was no alternative.[92] That same year UNHCR held a Special Round Table on Voluntary Repatriation consisting of UNHCR staff and member states that gave UNHCR the go-ahead to promote repatriation where possible.[93] Hocke's successors, Thorvald Stoltenberg and Sadaka Ogata, continued to stress repatriation. In his statement to the Executive Committee on October 1, 1990, Stoltenberg announced: "My first ambition is that UNHCR should be prepared to seize all the possibilities for voluntary repatriation, which is the best solution for refugees, the most productive use of resources, and a concrete contribution to peace and stability."[94] In her 1991 address to the Executive Committee, Ogata stated that repatriation would be a prime objective of the organization under her watch and later dubbed the 1990s the "decade of repatriation."[95]

The Normalization of Repatriation

The pragmatists gained the upper hand during the 1980s and 1990s, and UNHCR increasingly and forcefully articulated the view that repatriation should happen as soon as possible and could occur even when circumstances were not ideal—an ideal situation being one where refugees volunteered to return home to a situation that no longer posed a threat.[96] States certainly kept pressuring UNHCR to relax its original position. But the agency refused to go as far as states, which bristled at the notion that refugees needed to be consulted regarding their assessment of the situation back home and their preferences. Instead, in a demonstration of considerable autonomy, UNHCR staff engaged in an active debate that considered how to balance longstanding principles regarding refugees rights, pressures from states, and new refugee circumstances. Slowly but steadily UNHCR allowed exceptions to the rules governing repatriation until these exceptions became the rule, which had the cumulative effect of producing repatriation culture. Next we trace the emergence of this repatriation culture in each of three forums—discourse, structure, informal rules—and show how these changes made repatriation more desirable, proper, and legitimate.

Discourse and Conceptual Change

Within UNHCR there was a marked change in how repatriation was understood in relationship to other solutions and operational concepts. Prior to the 1980s repatriation was one of the "permanent solutions" that UNHCR considered, but afterward it was *the preferred* solution.

> Until the 1970s, both the solution of voluntary repatriation and its counterpart of resettlement (not infrequently defined as resettlement and integration, which is a shorthand for settlement in a third country, respectively the country of refuge) were mentioned without specific preference attached to either one of them. From 1971 onwards, "voluntary repatriation" is isolated from the alternative solution in phrases like "recognizing the importance of voluntary repatriation as a permanent solution to the refugee problem." The preference for the solution of voluntary repatriation acquires an absolute character in 1983: "emphasizing that voluntary repatriation is the most desirable *and durable* solution to problems of refugees and displaced persons of concern to the High Commissioner," which it has since retained.[97]

The shift from "permanent solutions" to "durable solutions" is significant. "Permanent solutions" is the original term used in UNHCR's statute and had been understood since the earliest days of the organization to entail asylum and resettlement. The term "durable solutions" does not exist in the statute. It was coined by High Commissioner Poul Hartling at the end of the 1970s in the context of the failure of Southeast Asian countries to admit the Vietnamese boat people. According to Gervase Coles, Hartling

> endorsed a new concept of a "durable solution" which amounted effectively to a devaluation of the post-war notion of solution in relation to external settlement, i.e. naturalization, in favor of a new concept falling short of naturalization but including economic self-sufficiency, in the evident hope that this devaluation of the concept of solution—principally, it must be said, at the expense of the refugee—would induce the first receiving countries, with the additional encouragement of international aid, to keep the refugees within their territories. Whether a durable solution amounted to a solution of the problem of the refugee, or was a solution to another problem, was a question which was not examined at the time; indeed the concept of durable solution seems to have been scarcely evaluated at all from a legal protection perspective, as if it were a purely economic concept.[98]

As perceptively noted by Coles, Hartling intended the shift from permanent to durable to signal to potential host countries that repatriation—and not resettlement—was the solution. In other words, the high commissioner was suggesting that those states housing refugees need not worry that they would be expected to accept them on a permanent basis. Consequently, UNHCR would no longer push for resettlement as a solution and would allow states to repatriate refugees when possible. Stated more starkly, durable solutions became tantamount to repatriation, and references to durable solutions were intended to channel energies toward repatriation. This was a major change from the days when permanent solutions included resettlement and asylum.

Repatriation was supposed to be voluntary and to occur in a manner that honored the principles of nonrefoulement. Increasingly, though, many in the organization argued that these principles had been devised during a more idyllic period and that they failed to recognize complex reality in the refugees' countries of origin. If UNHCR had to wait until the letter of the principles was honored, they argued, then refugees might not ever go home. To make repatriation possible under less than ideal conditions, UNHCR introduced new categories of return, new concepts and terminologies that clearly differentiated repatriation under ideal conditions from repatriation under less than ideal conditions. For example, conditions in the home country did not have to improve "substantially" but only "appreciably" for safe return.[99]

Perhaps the most significant discursive and conceptual change was the reinterpretation of what was meant by the word *voluntary* in "voluntary repatriation." When UNHCR was considering the repatriation of individuals or small groups, it could reasonably determine the voluntary character of a decision to return. But in situations of mass flight, UNHCR faced the logistical nightmare of assessing voluntariness in large populations. Any operationalization of "voluntary" ran risks. If protection officers clung to the original standard, then they would be expected to conduct individual interviews. This highly complicated, involved process might well mean that refugees would be forced to live for long periods in exile and in camps. Alternatively, UNHCR officials could try to develop measures of voluntariness that were less dependent on the explicit consent of refugees. Consider the following observation by one UNHCR official:

> As a lawyer I can tell you that we can be creative with definitions, but while we believe in free will, we understand that this is not ever really the case. So how do we really determine voluntariness? There are so many ways to judge voluntariness. The key, however, is providing the refugees with information and the information that there has been an improvement of the objective conditions back home. We must have an objective threshold to measure safety.[100]

UNHCR's practical solution to this measurement problem was to substitute "objective" criteria for the slippery subjectivity of refugee consent. One consequence of this definition was to transfer authority over determinations of safety and voluntariness from the refugees to the bureaucracy—to UNHCR. Under the new understanding of voluntariness and the new method for determining it (via assessment of objective conditions), UNHCR became the decision-making agent to determine when repatriation was warranted.

These modifications to the meaning of voluntary repatriation opened the door to violations of refugee rights. UNHCR's willingness to consider repatriation under conditions it deemed objectively safe, but not ideal, meant that the difference between "safe" and "unsafe" had been narrowed, leaving refugees at greater risk. Its new discourse shifted decision-making authority away from those who were taking the risks—the refugees themselves. The organization had crafted a new concept of voluntariness that potentially violated the principle of voluntary repatriation because the decision to repatriate was no longer dependent on refugee consent or judgment about whether return was safe. These conceptual and discursive changes, in short, lowered the barriers to repatriation. As one high-ranking UNHCR official observed, "The definition of voluntariness has been stretched to the point that it violates refugee rights and informed consent. . . . That is a statement

The meaning of protection also came to include repatriation. UNHCR is mandated to protect refugees. Originally protection had a legal meaning. Then it acquired a material dimension; legal rights meant very little if refugees could not be sure of their physical survival and safety. During this period, though, protection increasingly became tied to repatriation. If resettlement and asylum were unavailable as permanent solutions, then refugees would have to linger in camps until the situation at home had improved. But these camps were hardly safe havens, and residents found themselves under threat from inhospitable host governments and bandits and thieves. Under such circumstances, the best way to protect refugees was to repatriate them.[102] High Commissioner Hartling pointed in this direction, and then High Commissioner Hocke deliberately altered the administrative meaning of protection so that it became more consistent with repatriation.[103] Protection now also meant repatriation.[104]

The desire to reduce the numbers of refugees and repatriate as soon as possible led to a greater interest in preventing refugee flows, getting at their root causes, and encouraging states to avoid situations that caused people to flee.[105] In the past the agency had steered clear of the domestic situation in the refugee-producing country for fear of venturing into political matters and sacrificing its humanitarian identity.[106] Now it gingerly moved in this very direction because of the desire to reduce the number of refugees.[107] Consequently, UNHCR began supplementing "activities related to traditional forms of protection . . . with increased activities within countries of origin. These activities have a dual purpose: to ensure the durability of the solution of voluntary repatriation through respect for fundamental human rights and the restoration of national protection for returnees; and to seek to prevent arising conditions which could leave people no choice but to flee."[108]

To encourage repatriation and reduce the causes of flight, UNHCR assumed new activities. It extended its already existing interest in economic development in an effort to improve the short- and long-term economic circumstances of refugees.[109] It became more deeply involved in the human rights situation in refugee-producing countries in order to improve refugee reintegration. When UNHCR first became involved in human rights in refugee-producing countries in the 1980s, it tried to avoid offending sovereignty-sensitive governments by asking for "safety and dignity" and not a marked improvement of human rights. Beginning in the 1990s, however, UNHCR became much more vocal about its human rights role, sometimes presenting itself as a human rights organization even as it continued to tout a standard based on safety and dignity that was much less offensive to home states.[110]

The desire to alter the circumstances in refugee-producing countries, though, contained its own dangers. One was that UNHCR's preventive measures might violate international law.[111] Specifically, an agency that was attempting to reduce the number of refugees by considering repatriation under safe conditions might discourage their flight, a danger acknowledged by the high commissioner: "In-country protection, e.g. through the establishment of internationally guaranteed safe zones, however, needs to be weighed against the rights of individuals to leave their own country, to seek and enjoy asylum or return on a voluntary basis, and not be compelled to remain in a territory where life, liberty, or physical integrity is threatened."[112] While this might have been a legitimate fear, the high commissioner gave assurances that "the object of prevention is not to obstruct escape from danger or from an intolerable situation, but to make flight unnecessary by removing or alleviating the conditions that force people to flee."[113] Still, the danger lingered.

UNHCR was now focusing on how to get refugees home and keep them there. Both a cause and a consequence of this emphasis on repatriation was the introduction of new concepts like safe return and voluntariness, and the reinterpretation of old concepts like protection. Such orienting concepts overturned the agency's exilic bias. This rush to repatriation contained possible threats to traditional refugee rights. The new concepts allowed UNHCR to claim the authority to determine whether returning refugees were no longer at risk. Now that the term "protection" was no longer reserved for legal protection but also included repatriation, it became more likely that those in the field and in Geneva would consider whether it was possible to repatriate in determining whether the situation at home was improving. The desire to reduce the causes of flight might also lead the agency to take action to reduce the chance that individuals would exercise their right to flee their homes.

Bureaucratic Changes

As plainly stated by UNHCR's "Note on International Protection," these conceptual shifts required a bureaucratic restructuring "in recognition of the inter-relationship between protection and solutions and refugee law and action."[114] If UNHCR was going to emphasize field operations and repatriation and downgrade legal protection, then it would be necessary to restructure the organizational chart. Prior to the 1980s the director of protection had control over and responsibility for protection in the field, and protection officers, many of whom had legal backgrounds, had a degree of bureaucratic power. In the 1980s, though, High Commissioner Hocke diminished protection's profile when he disbanded the Protection Division, created a new division called Refugee Law and Doctrine, and assigned to each regional bureau a protection officer who was to keep Refugee Law and Doctrine informed of any incidents in the region. As a result, protection officers lost considerable influence, and legal protection became only one element among many to be considered by a regional bureau in its assessment of refugee policy.[115]

Both opponents and supporters of these changes recognized that they were designed to alter UNHCR's definition of protection: UNHCR was no longer so willing to intervene to protect refugee rights and to challenge governments; it now meant to place a greater emphasis on repatriation and was willing to work with and recognize the interests of governments.[116] Although additional bureaucratic reshuffling over the following years restored some power to the protection officers, UNHCR's bureaucratic structure now significantly favored a more flexible and pragmatic interpretation of refugee law.[117]

Rules and Decision Criteria

These discursive and bureaucratic shifts shaped the formal and informal rules concerning repatriation. UNHCR's previous position was that four preconditions had to be satisfied before it became involved in a repatriation exercise: a fundamental change of circumstances in the home country; a voluntary decision by the refugees to return; a tripartite agreement between UNHCR, the host country, and the home country; and a return marked by dignity and safety. Well-intentioned people might disagree over whether these preconditions had been satisfied in any particular instance and thus whether a repatriation exercise could safely proceed.

Three important changes in the role these preconditions played in repatriation exercises supported speedy repatriations. First, UNHCR staff debated whether all four of these preconditions had to be satisfied unambiguously or whether they were benchmarks that served as useful checks and guidelines. In the face of growing pressure from states and the recognition that many home countries were rebuilding after violent conflicts, making safety problematic for citizens generally, UNHCR determined that it had to be prepared to act under less than ideal conditions. Second, UNHCR officials began to judge safe return in relationship to what existed in the camps, to treat the readiness of the government to accept the refugees as an indicator of an improved situation at home, and to consider whether an impatient host government might soon forcibly repatriate refugees. Third, UNHCR officials began to insist that additional factors had to be included in the repatriation calculus. Refugees had rights, but these rights should not automatically trump the rights of states or come at the expense of broader political objectives such as peacebuilding and regional conflict resolution. High Commissioner Hocke, for instance, hypothesized that voluntary repatriation of the "most vulnerable groups such as the elderly, the handicapped, the unaccompanied minors, etc. [might] demonstrate in political terms that despite the continuation of the conflict, the two states are willing as it were to insulate the problem."[118] The 1992 UNHCR "Note on International Protection" baldly stated:

> Criteria for promotion and organization of large scale repatriation must balance the protection needs of the refugees against the political imperative towards resolving refugee problems. . . . The realization of a solution in a growing number of refugee situations today is most likely where the solution is made an integral part of a "package" which strikes a humane balance between the interests of affected States and the legal rights, as well as humanitarian needs, of the individuals concerned.[119]

In a similar vein, UNHCR has suggested that repatriation is an important mechanism for rebuilding confidence in the country of origin and for successful peacebuilding.[120] While this position has merit, it upends refugee law. Instead of following upon political stability, repatriation is now understood as (or hoped to be) a potential cause of political stability.

Further evidence of a change in the rules regarding repatriation comes from "Notes on International Protection," the organization's updated statement on protection issues, and the *Handbook on Voluntary Repatriation.* Although both documents continue to stress the importance of refugee rights and safety, they also contain more flexible rules regarding voluntary repatriation, reflecting a conflict between the increasing desirability of repatriation and the safeguards against nonrefoulement. Indeed, the *Handbook on Voluntary Repatriation* contains several competing definitions of voluntariness, an ambiguity that facilitates a lower threshold.[121]

The *Handbook,* moreover, reveals a logical gap in the relationship between voluntary repatriation and protection that produces the view that repatriation can occur under less than ideal circumstances. On the one hand, it notes that in determining the advisability of a repatriation exercise, the voluntary character of repatriation, that is, the subjective willingness of refugees to return home, is more important than the objective situation that will confront the returning refugees. In this line of reasoning, the decision to return voluntarily vitiates the legal requirement that return occur only under safe conditions. Repatriation-happy officials might be tempted to manipulate, hide, or distort the information presented to the refugees in order to encourage a voluntary decision to repatriate. If so, the decision to repatriate would not be voluntary. On the other hand, the *Handbook*'s notion of voluntariness suggests that if the objective conditions have improved at home in relationship to life in exile, then voluntary repatriation can be proper, even if refugees do not give their consent. All roads lead to repatriation under the rules of the *Handbook.*

The UNHCR's organizational culture—its concepts, bureaucratic structure, and rules—was now structured in favor of repatriation. Repatriation had become the desired durable solution for refugees. The growth in repatriation exercises was truly impressive. Orienting concepts and categories such as "solution" and "protection" had altered appreciably in ways that made repatriation more desirable and likely. The movement away from protection and toward relief, the departure of many veteran staff, and the introduction of more pragmatic personnel profoundly altered the organizational culture in ways that watered down its human rights and protection orientation.[122] Refugees might not always be capable of assessing objectively where they would be best protected, and UNHCR might be forced into a guardian role. UNHCR also was encouraged not to wait for opportunities for repatriation, but rather to create them.[123]

The desire for repatriation had various spillover effects, including a growing interest in the conditions in the refugee-producing country and in the ways UNHCR could develop the conditions to make repatriation more likely, and a willingness to consider the rights and needs of refugees in relationship to other, more global and regional, issues such as state rights and peacebuilding.[124]

This repatriation culture did not appear instantaneously but instead was a consequence of incremental changes over the years in response to environmental demands, including resource constraints and state pressures, and interpretations by staff regarding how to respond to these pressures while safeguarding refugee rights. Formal rules were altered in ways that permitted a more relaxed interpretation. More important, UNHCR staff were operating according to new, informal rules and interpreting the formal rulebook in ways that gave them confidence that they could actively promote repatriation and operate under a more flexible policy without violating refugee rights. These revisions in the rules also introduced changes in orienting concepts such as "protection" and "voluntary," changes that substantially recalibrated the conditions under which a repatriation exercise could be sanctioned. The result of these incremental revisions was to shift profoundly the rules of repatriation so that a policy that might have been viewed as a risky exception in the early 1980s became normalized and accepted by the early 1990s. The normalization of deviance and the emergence of this repatriation culture increased the likelihood that refugee rights, including nonrefoulement, would be violated.

III. THE "VOLUNTARY" REPATRIATION OF THE ROHINGYAS

UNHCR's repatriation culture makes repatriation likely even in instances where there are other choices and state pressures are manageable. The 1994–95 repatriation of the Rohingyan refugees from Bangladesh to Burma was such an instance. This repatriation exercise was carried out at the discretion of UNHCR officials. There were no immediate financial pressures because the Rohingyan operation had a $600,000 surplus for 1995.[125] Certainly Bangladesh was pushing for repatriation as soon as possible, and UNHCR officials were worried that Bangladesh might send back the refugees against their will; violent acts had occurred in the recent past as Bangladesh attempted to force the refugees to return to Burma. But even UNHCR officials acknowledge that this pressure was not intolerable and that Bangladesh was not about to repatriate the refugees forcibly. "I don't agree," said one UNHCR official intimately involved with the decision, "that we bent because of excessive pressure from Bangladesh."[126]

UNHCR officials used a definition of voluntariness that violated the traditional principle of voluntary repatriation. Although the conditions had not changed in Burma, UNHCR officials "objectively" determined that the refugees would be better off returning as soon as possible because UNHCR could monitor their return and reintegration. Not only had the situation at home not changed, but there is compelling evidence that UNHCR manipulated information and bribed the refugees in order to get their consent. Moreover, UNHCR's determination to repatriate led it to bend standard procedures, avoid troubling questions, and disregard evidence that might have frustrated its repatriation plans. UNHCR officials might have had good reasons for doing what they did, believing that the situation was as good as it was going to get and that repatriation under less than ideal circumstances was better than coerced repatriation. But as one UNHCR official confessed, "The Rohingyan repatriation exercise pushed voluntariness to its absolute limits, possibly beyond recognition."[127]

Background

The origins of the Rohingyan people are not fully known.[128] It is widely thought that they are descendants of the first Muslims who occupied the northern Arakan province of Burma in the ninth century and that they came to be called Rohingyan after the name of the region in Arakan that they inhabited. Since this original settlement, other Muslims have migrated to this part of Burma, most recently in the period from 1891 to 1931, when British colonial practices encouraged labor migration, and after the 1971 East Pakistan civil war. When the Japanese occupied Burma during World War II, the Rohingyas remained loyal to the British and were promised an autonomous Muslim state in northern Arakan after the war as a reward (this promise was not kept). The political and security situation quickly deteriorated over the next few years. Deadly communal violence erupted in 1942, leading to the flight of thousands of refugees to India. In 1947 the Rohingyas formed an army, and soon thereafter the Rohingyan political elite asked the new president of Pakistan to integrate the northern Arakan into East Pakistan (now Bangladesh). The Rohingyan leadership probably did not win any allies in

Rangoon with its constant claim that it was a distinct ethnic group and its demands for autonomy or political independence.

Life got progressively harsher for the Rohingyas following the 1962 military coup (as it did for most Burmese). According to the Rohingyan political leadership, at this point the Burmese government attempted to encourage their migration by withdrawing its recognition of the group's status as citizens and by replacing their national registration certificates demonstrating Burmese citizenship with foreign registration cards. Denial of citizenship rights harmed the Rohingyan population's economic, political, and social circumstances. It was more difficult than ever to join the civil service, and those in the civil service were pressured to resign. It was more difficult to get an education because most schools were government run. Rohingyas were denied the right to serve in the army, which severely affected their status and political power. In 1977 the government increased its repression of the Rohingyas, which directly led to the flight of over two hundred thousand to Bangladesh by May 1978. Bangladesh was hardly a safe haven. Its cash-poor government had little interest in housing, feeding, and schooling these numbers and attempted to repatriate them by using physical coercion and ceasing their food supplies. These harsh tactics led to roughly ten thousand deaths, most of which were women and children.[129] When the current military government in Burma came to power in 1988, once again the whole society suffered, but it is arguable that the Rohingyas suffered more than most. The military junta prohibited the Rohingyas from voting in the May 1990 elections, and when widespread rioting followed those elections, the military government turned the Rohingyas into a scapegoat and common enemy, increasing the level of repression.

In response to this increasingly miserable existence in Burma, the Rohingyas continued to flee to Bangladesh. Before the rains of May 1991 nearly 10,000 fled Burma. By March 1992 there were nearly 270,000 Rohingyas in Bangladesh, making this one of the largest refugee flights in recent history. Arriving refugees told horrific stories of forced labor, rape, executions, and torture. At first the Burmese government denied the estimated number of refugees and argued that these were workers looking for seasonal employment and not individuals seeking a safe haven from Burmese persecution. Later, however, the government altered its line and argued that these were Islamic insurgents. Most reports noted that while there had been a radicalization of Rohingyan politics, which was seen as a direct consequence of Burma's repressive practices, most Rohingyas fleeing Burma were not radicals and genuinely feared persecution.[130]

The 1990s Refugee and Protection Crisis

By all accounts Bangladesh's initial response to this refugee wave was cooperative and welcoming. Helping to establish the refugee camps and providing badly needed supplies and assistance, the financially strapped Bangladeshi government showed tremendous compassion for the flood of refugees who were now camping along the Burmese border and near the town of Cox's Bazaar in southern Bangladesh. Although initially Dhaka was wary of outside intrusion, it eventually allowed various NGOs to provide badly needed material assistance, and then in March 1992 it permitted UNHCR to contribute to the assistance effort.[131]

The Bangladeshi government viewed the refugee crisis as a short-term problem and sought to resolve it through bilateral mechanisms, which was how it had addressed the 1978 crisis. On April 28, 1992, Bangladesh and Burma signed a memorandum of understanding (MoU) regarding the return of the refugees. As a solution, this MoU had three significant limitations. First, Burma was obligated to accept the return of "those refugees who could establish their bona fide residency prior in Myanmar prior to their departure for Bangladesh."[132] In other words, those who lacked residency papers or certificates of citizenship could be excluded. Given Burma's recent policy of stripping documents and papers from those crossing the border into Bangladesh, those excluded could number in the thousands. Second, the MoU required only that Burma involve UNHCR at an "appropriate time." While UNHCR did have a formal role in making sure that those leaving Bangladesh were doing so voluntarily, it was given no formal role in monitoring the return or reintegrating the refugees. This might have been less worrisome if the political and security situation in Burma had improved, but it had not. This points to a third limitation of the MoU: parties were planning a repatriation despite the ongoing human rights abuses in Burma. Indeed, one UNHCR cable reported that refugees were continuing to flee at the rate of fifteen hundred a day, providing compelling evidence that life was not improving for the Rohingyas.[133]

Increasingly worried that this short-term situation was becoming a long-term problem and a drain on its meager resources, Bangladesh began to forcibly repatriate many thousands of refugees in fall 1992 and to deny UNHCR access to the camps.[134] On September 22 the government's first repatriation exercise took place—without UNHCR involvement. UNHCR reported that this repatriation was "accompanied by considerable pressure (coercion) from the Bangladeshi authorities, who insisted that they could not give the refugees long-term asylum" and pointed to the protests and violence in the camps as evidence of this coercion.[135] In response to UNHCR's very public protests, Bangladesh and UNHCR signed an agreement on October 8, which allowed UNHCR to verify the voluntary nature of the repatriation exercise. UNHCR monitored the October 12 and 31 repatriation exercises, which it certified as voluntary. Bangladesh, however, denied the agency a monitoring role in several subsequent rounds, rekindling fears that the refugees were being coercively repatriated. UNHCR and other NGOs reported that refugees were being herded into cattle trucks and then dumped over the border. Because it was denied the right to supervise nearly 84 percent of those being repatriated, on December 22, 1992, UNHCR withdrew from the repatriation program and the refugee camps to protest the suspected refoulement.[136] Undeterred, the Bangladeshi government forcibly repatriated eleven thousand more individuals. After a sustained shower of criticism from UNHCR, NGOs, and the U.S. Department of State, in January 1993 Dhaka announced that it would cease its repatriation program and resume a joint program with UNHCR.[137] The protests had successfully caused the Bangladeshi government to alter its repatriation policy.

Over the next several months UNHCR attempted to negotiate new agreements with Bangladesh and Burma in order to restore the principle of voluntary repatriation and to establish a monitoring role for UNHCR on both sides of the border.[138] Negotiations proceeded slowly until a high-profile and much-publicized trip by High Commissioner Ogata to Dhaka on May 12, 1993, resulted in a new MoU between UNHCR and Bangladesh. Each believed that it had won some important concessions. UNHCR was pleased to gain unhindered access to the camps, to win the right to interview the refugees in order to determine the voluntary character of their decision to return, and to have Bangladesh (re)commit to the principle of voluntary repatriation. Bangladesh was delighted that UNHCR agreed to implement "promotional activities to motivate the refugees to return home once an international presence for observing reasonable conditions for the returnee is established in Myanmar and in line with the Agreement of 28th April 1992" between Bangladesh and Burma. By tying this new agreement to the previous MoU between Bangladesh and Burma, an MoU that required only that the local situation be safe before repatriation could proceed, Bangladesh believed that UNHCR was now on record as condoning a repatriation program under less demanding conditions than were entailed in their previous understanding.[139] With this agreement in hand, UNHCR turned its attention to Burma. On November 5, 1993, UNHCR and Burma concluded an MoU that permitted the refugees to return to their places of origin and allowed UNHCR access to all returnees in order to monitor their reintegration and verify that the Burmese government had issued them new identity papers.

Although these bilateral agreements and the new roles for UNHCR on both sides of the border signaled positive developments, these MoUs contained several disturbing features that hinted that the principle of voluntary repatriation might be bent. First, while they authorized UNHCR to determine whether the refugees had voluntarily agreed to return, recent history here and elsewhere gave reason to believe that such consent might be suspect. Second, they failed to state explicitly that the refugees should or could repatriate only after the security situation had substantially improved.[140] Several NGOs criticized this glaring omission, seeing it as a fatal flaw that suggested a new, more relaxed UNHCR policy toward repatriation. There was little evidence that the situation in Burma had improved or was about to improve, and UNHCR officials had no way of inquiring into the status of the roughly fifty thousand refugees who had been forcibly returned to Burma the previous year because they and the NGOs were denied access to them.[141] On this point local NGOs were quite distressed by UNHCR's behavior. Even though it had little detailed knowledge of the current conditions in Burma, UNHCR was nevertheless making strong statements about an improved situation, including the cessation of forced labor (making it virtually alone in the international community in that assessment).[142] Finally, while its MoU with Burma permitted UNHCR to monitor the return and reintegration of the Rohingyas, no detailed plan for this critical feature had yet emerged.

UNHCR officials were aware of the shortcomings of these agreements, but they used rules to defend them and their conduct. The first defense was that while these agreements might have more problems than most, all agreements have their deficiencies. Host countries always want the refugees to return quickly and home countries typically object to obtrusive monitoring measures that they view as violating their sovereignty. Therefore some compromise is necessary. UNHCR officials hoped that they could use the foothold provided by these agreements to correct their shortcomings. Moreover, the agreements successfully recommitted Bangladesh to the principle of voluntary repatriation and Burma to the principle of safe and dignified return, as well as handing UNHCR a significant monitoring role—all important victories. If UNHCR pushed too hard for the ideal agreement, it ran the risk that Bangladesh and Burma might carry out the repatriation without UNHCR's presence, a far worse outcome. Second, with a monitoring role and these agreements in hand, UNHCR had a mechanism to ensure that the governments did what they said they would do and a lever to hold them accountable if they did not. Third, repatriation rarely has the luxury of occurring under ideal circumstances, and refugees are frequently willing to return to situations that are less than ideal because their lives in the camps are insecure. Fourth, Burmese authorities did not recognize the Rohingyas as legitimate citizens (a chief reason they could claim persecution), and UNHCR officials worried that the longer the Rohingyas resided in Bangladesh, the less likely it was that Burma would take them back; in other words, UNHCR officials determined that the refugees had to return to establish residency. Fifth, the refugees' long-term protection was best guaranteed by getting them home rather than by having them linger in insecure camps. Although the evidence concerning refugee desire to return at that moment was shaky, in UNHCR's view this was a better time for repatriation than most because the organization could monitor the return to Burma. The force of all these rule-based reasons—and not manageable Bangladeshi pressure—caused

UNHCR officials to legitimate and authorize repatriation under conditions that suspended traditional refugee rights.

The ink was barely dry on both MoUs when Bangladesh began pressuring UNHCR to prepare a major repatriation exercise. Formally unveiled on December 19, 1993, the plan was designed to repatriate a total of 190,000 refugees at the rate of 18,000 a month (or 1,500 a day).[143] Even in the planning stage, however, there were distressing signs that the refugees might not voluntarily return to a situation they perceived as little different from the one they had fled. Refugees were still coming into Bangladesh, including some who had recently repatriated, so-called double-backers—hardly evidence that the refugees would willingly go back to or stay in Burma. Moreover, the refugees remained fearful that they would not have their citizenship rights restored and would be denied freedom of movement. They also were unsatisfied by the vague guarantees given by the military regime and continued to receive reports that life had not improved since their flight. In order to alleviate their fears, in January and February 1994 senior UNHCR staff visited Burma and returned to tell NGOs and the refugees that the situation had significantly improved and that it was now safe to go home.[144] The Bangladeshi government, sometimes in concert with UNHCR, conveyed a similar theme.[145] Despite these efforts the refugees were not budging from the camps, much to the annoyance of Bangladesh and the increasing embarrassment of UNHCR.[146]

Then, in late April 1994, several bombings in Burma led the government to insist that either UNHCR refrain from entering into key towns or that military personnel accompany UNHCR on its rounds. This development severely compromised UNHCR's ability to monitor areas of return, a key feature of the repatriation agreement. The refugees were more reluctant than ever to return, fearing both that the government might accuse them of being involved in the bombings and that UNHCR would not be able to monitor credibly their return and reintegration.[147] Despite these many setbacks and emerging concerns, the first repatriation exercise took place on April 30, 1994. Predictably, given the circumstances, the number of volunteers was far below what either Bangladesh or UNHCR had wanted. To complicate matters further, a massive cyclone swept through the area on May 2 and destroyed the camps, departure facilities, and reception points for the repatriation exercise. All repatriation efforts were virtually suspended until July.

There was scant evidence that most refugees wanted to return to a situation that they perceived as similar to the one that had triggered their flight. To better gauge their preferences and the reasons underlying them, UNHCR surveyed some of the refugee camps. Because Bangladesh controlled whom UNHCR could canvass, the first surveys were based on an unrepresentative sample of those refugees in the transit camps—that is, those who were about to return. Not surprisingly, these surveys revealed that most of those about to return to Burma wanted to do so. Beginning in July 1994, however, Bangladesh gave UNHCR permission to survey nontransit camps. These surveys revealed a completely different picture: the refugees were not interested in repatriating under the current conditions. In one camp only 27 percent of the refugees said that they wanted to return.[148]

Two UNHCR-guided events resuscitated this repatriation exercise. First, UNHCR conducted a second round of interviews in the same nontransit camp several days later and discovered that nearly 97 percent of all refugees wanted to return.[149] The exact cause of this rapid turnaround was unknown. UNHCR officials attributed the increase to a delayed bandwagon effect. NGOs, however, suspected coercion. Between the first and second surveys several refugees had been beaten by Bangladeshi officials for "antirepatriation" activities.[150] There was a meeting the day after the beatings between camp and UNHCR officials, and refugees widely believed that the camp official responsible for the beatings was not even reprimanded. From this episode refugees concluded that they would not be protected in the camps and that UNHCR, which was supposed to be their protector of last resort, was no guardian angel.[151]

In response, UNHCR shifted its policy from simply providing information for repatriation to actively promoting it.[152] When queried at the time, UNHCR officials explained that this new policy of promotion was warranted because the Rohingyas now wanted to go home and because the situation in Arakan had improved to the point that the refugees could return with safety and dignity. Furthermore, UNHCR had established a presence in Arakan and therefore could monitor the refugees' return and reintegration.[153] Because these factors made the situation "conducive" to return, UNHCR began promoting repatriation through questionable means.[154] Rather than trying to ascertain refugee preferences, UNHCR shifted the burden of action onto refugees, expecting them to seek out UNHCR if they did not want to return. It replaced the practice of interviewing refugees on an individual basis (a right for which it had fought hard in the past) with mass interviews that could scarcely ascertain refugee preferences. It also warned the refugees that if they returned to Bangladesh after being repatriated, they might be arrested for illegal departure by the Burmese officials.[155]

Many NGOs on the scene believed that UNHCR's justificatory claims had little foundation in fact and that the organization was sanctioning an involuntary repatriation program. How do we explain UNHCR's decision to accelerate its repatriation exercise at this moment and in these ways? Certainly, if Bangladesh was determined to repatriate the refugees, then UNHCR wanted to be on the ground to minimize the possible harm.[156] The alternative was to stand on the sidelines with its principles intact, but at the expense of refugee lives. However, as UNHCR officials readily concede, Bangladesh was not explicitly or implicitly threatening to forcibly repatriate the refugees.[157] Instead, UNHCR officials justified the repatriation on the grounds that the refugees wanted to return, that the situation had improved in Burma, and that UNHCR could monitor their return and reintegration. These rule-based claims are highly disputable. We evaluate each in turn.

The Desire to Return

UNHCR explained that repatriation was justified because the Rohingyas wanted to go home.[158] A central factor driving this conclusion was the previously discussed camp surveys. To explain repatriation's newly found popularity among the refugees, officials referred to a delayed bandwagon effect, claiming that the refugees had become more knowledgeable about the improved situation in Arakan and asserting that they had finally soured on life in the camps.

The refusal to entertain potentially disconfirming evidence is exemplified by the following story. UNHCR's report of a dramatic increase in the percentage of refugees who wanted to return to Burma sounded odd to several NGOs. Fearful that this repatriation was involuntary and that the refugees had not been properly informed of their rights and the conditions in Burma, these NGOs suggested to UNHCR that it replicate its survey. UNHCR refused. After intensive discussion over how to proceed, in February 1995 Médicins sans Frontières (MSF)–Holland conducted its own survey in the camps. The results raised serious questions regarding the claim that the refugees were voluntarily repatriating. The vast majority said that UNHCR had not informed them that they had the right to say no to repatriation, a key feature of any definition of voluntariness. And only 9 percent of the refugees who said that they wanted to return indicated their decision was based on their expectation that the situation in Burma was safe.[159] The summary conclusion of the MSF report was that the refugees wanted to return home but only after the situation had improved; they had agreed to return home at that time because they did not believe that they could stay in the camps, not because they though that the situation had improved in Burma. Médicins sans Frontières–Holland released its findings and joined with other NGOs in writing to UNHCR to protest its activities. UNHCR dismissed the validity of the survey and depicted the protests as unwarranted and unprofessional, though it did say that it would renew its efforts to ensure that refugees understood that they could refuse to be repatriated.[160]

As UNHCR officials concede, the organization's determination to promote repatriation was based not only on the refugees' preference but also and more fundamentally on *UNHCR*'s assessment of whether life was better in Burma than in the camps. As previously noted, UNHCR used a definition of voluntariness that privileged its "objective" assessment over the refugees' desire to return or the refugees' assessment of the situation at home. This represented an important shift from the factors that typically were used to determine whether repatriation was warranted. It changed whose voice counted. In UNHCR's objective judgment, the refugees could not remain permanently in exile and therefore would have to return at some time in the near future, and they were better off returning while UNHCR was present in Burma. This point is subtly but importantly made in UNHCR's 1995 *State of the World's Refugees:* "While the situation in Rakhine State of Burma may not be an easy one, the refugees *appear to have recognized* that it is better to go home now and to benefit from UNHCR's presence and program, rather than to remain in the refugee camps which offer them no future."[161] Whether the refugees recognized this is not at all clear. What is clear is that UNHCR recognized it.

The shift away from strict adherence to refugee preferences as the standard for repatriation and toward a comparative evaluation by agency officials privileged UNHCR's knowledge claims over those of refugees. Refugees, in this view, would have a difficult time objectively assessing the situation. They could not adequately take into account the short- and long-term prospects at home relative to the situation in the camps. Nor could they know how long UNHCR officials would be present and able to maintain some necessary safety features. The Rohingyan case was not unique in this regard. UNHCR's reliance on objective criteria rather than the subjective perceptions of the refugees has been observed as an emergent feature of other operations.[162] UNHCR might well be correct in its assessments. But the issue at hand is who gets to make that decision. To interpret voluntary repatriation in a way that assigns the decision to repatriate to others seems nonsensical if not perverse.

To support their claim that the refugees wanted to go home, UNHCR officials note that two hundred thousand refugees did return without physical duress. That is, no one put a gun to their heads and forced them over the border.[163] Their behavior, in this view, reveals their preferences. Even some UNHCR protection officers, however, doubt the claim that refugees voluntarily expressed a free choice to return. Instead, they suggest that the refugees' decision was probably influenced by UNHCR's manipulation of information and bribery.[164] UNHCR officials were claiming that life had improved in Burma and that the agency had a presence in Burma that enabled it to protect the refugees. But, as we will see below, these claims were exaggerated and misleading. Refugees were also offered incentives to return, including the standard assistance packages containing supplies and food, and a highly uncharacteristic offer of US$20, a vast sum in this context. When asked to speculate why so many refugees who once refused to go back to Burma had suddenly changed their minds, one protection officer said that it was because UNHCR "oversold" its presence and the human rights situation in Burma and offered each family $20 to return, which was more money than they had ever seen in their lives.[165]

Burma Is Better Than It Was

UNHCR claimed that repatriation could proceed because Burma was safe and conditions that had triggered refugee flight had improved. This observation ran counter to the claims of NGOs and even other UN agencies. NGOs continued to write scathing reports of the government's treatment of its population and the Rohingyan people, and the UN's rapporteur on human rights had been issuing damning statements concerning the military regime's repressive character and human rights violations. In fact, at the outset of the repatriation process UNHCR failed to certify that conditions had improved for the Rohingyas,[166] a startling omission that it later corrected by saying that the situation was likely to get better because of UNHCR's presence in Burma.

UNHCR's determination that the Rohingyas could and should return was based on the following factors. First, UNHCR claimed that life was improving for the Rohingyas in Burma. Most important, even though Burma did not recognize the Rohingyas as citizens, it was restoring some rights to them, and UNHCR hoped that the situation might be rectified in the near future.[167] Still, UNHCR did not consider this lack of full citizenship legitimate grounds for fear of persecution.[168] Second, UNHCR claimed that the Burmese government had fully complied with the MoU and responded positively to all of the agency's queries. For instance, UNHCR asked the government to respond to the allegations that it was engaging in forced sterilization, forced labor, and forced education for Muslim women in military-run schools, and it accepted the denial by the government without independent verification. Thereafter it dismissed information about such allegations as "mere rumors."[169] Third, UNHCR claimed that it could provide protection through its presence; that is, rather than bringing people to safety, UNHCR hoped to bring safety to people.[170] Finally, UNHCR officials insisted that while life was hard for the Rohingyas, it was no harder for them than for any other Burmese citizen or population group.[171] Simply put, because the Rohingyas were treated as horridly as other Burmese, they could not claim to be a persecuted people according to the 1951 convention definition.[172] UNHCR had a point. It is a matter of debate whether these people were, in fact, a persecuted minority under the 1951 definition (because everyone in Burma was suffering from the regime), but it was a very odd point for UNHCR to be making. After all, UNHCR had long argued against a narrow interpretation of persecution and in favor of a more flexible definition.[173]

The claim that life had improved in Burma was challenged not only by

NGOs but more importantly by Rohingyas who were continuing to flee from Burma, often including those who had recently repatriated. How could UNHCR explain this migration? UNHCR officials pointed to economic circumstances and traditional migratory patterns, noting that in the past this area had seen economically induced migratory patterns, particularly during the dry season. Many Rohingyas were also attracted to the economic safeguards provided by the refugee camps.[174] Although reluctant to classify these asylum seekers as economic migrants, UNHCR argued that because they left owing to economic circumstances, they should not be classified as refugees and should be denied access to the camps and other rights granted to refugees;[175] UNHCR staff were especially fearful that giving refugee status might encourage more flight. While NGOs and local populations conceded that economic factors played a role in their decision to flee, they explicitly linked their deteriorating economic conditions to their standing as a persecuted minority and to human rights violations.[176] UNHCR officials apparently were not persuaded.

Once UNHCR became committed to a repatriation program and the claim that life was preferable in Burma, disconfirming evidence was shunned. Again, UNHCR appears to have avoided asking the tough questions that might have undermined its desired policy outcome. Rather than conduct systematic or individual interviews with those who approached field officers, UNHCR made blanket designations. When UNHCR did interview new arrivals, it claimed that the purpose was to gather information on their general circumstances and needs and not to determine whether they should be granted refugee status.[177] "Moreover, the information UNHCR provides on 'protection issues' in Burma does not include any reference to the fact that hundreds, perhaps thousands, of Rohingyan would-be asylum-seekers have been stopped by Burmese border guards as they attempted to flee Burma—a fact that Bangladeshi border security officials on the other side of the border freely admit."[178] As Médicins sans Frontières–Holland succinctly put it: "To acknowledge their legitimate rights as asylum-seekers would call into question the whole logic of the repatriation program."[179]

By late 1995, confronted by consistent evidence that the human rights situation had worsened in Arakan and that refugees did not want to return to a situation that they believed might place them in danger, the Cox's Bazaar office unilaterally halted its repatriation activities. This decision brought it into conflict with the Geneva and the UNHCR-Rangoon offices.[180] Geneva claimed that the staff at Cox's Bazaar had rushed to judgment and should continue the exercise, and Rangoon contended that this was a temporary change because there was a new, less tolerant military commander and that UNHCR still had access to the region.[181] This incident exposed not only the differences of opinion within UNHCR pertaining to the conditions under which voluntary repatriation might occur but also the determination of Geneva to proceed with the repatriation program.

UNHCR's status as a judge of human rights conditions also raised some disturbing issues. It is not clear that the organization had enough information to substantiate its claims about conditions in Burma. When UNHCR asserted in June 1994 that the human rights situation had improved, it did not have unhindered or easy access to Arakan. It did not have enough staff in the field to monitor all the remote villages and towns, and it was almost always accompanied by the Burmese military when it made its rounds. In addition, UNHCR offered its appraisal of the situation in Arakan without a more comprehensive assessment of the situation in Burma.[182] The result was that while UNHCR held a potentially distorted picture of the human rights situation based only on limited observations of field officers, it declared that the Rohingyas could return to Burma in safety and with dignity.

Not only was UNHCR operating with limited information, but it probably had a strong interest in seeing an improving situation in Burma and little reason to seek out disconfirming evidence. UNHCR was highly committed to repatriating the refugees as soon as possible, but that possibility depended on an improvement in Burma's human rights situation. UNHCR, therefore, had a potential conflict of interest, leading some observers to suggest that UNHCR's repatriation imperative colored its assessment of the human rights situation in Burma.[183] Moreover, while UNHCR's role permitted it to challenge Burma's treatment of the Rohingyas, it had strong incentives not to do so since heavy-handed criticism might jeopardize its ability to stay in Burma and undermine its own claim that a safe and dignified return was possible. "In Burma, UNHCR has monitored through the lens of repatriation, which has a distinctly rosy hue, 'seeing' those factors that are positive to continuing the repatriation and playing down or ignoring (at least in public) those factors which call into doubt the repatriation exercise."[184]

Capacity to Monitor Return

UNHCR claimed not only that the situation had improved but, equally important, that it could monitor the safe return and reintegration of the refugees. Indeed, for UNHCR officials its mere presence in Burma compensated for some lack of improvement by providing leverage to make life better for the Rohingyas in the near future. A UNHCR cable concluded that it had a "meaningful presence enabling [it] to undertake a reasonable pro-active and re-active monitoring function of the well being of the returnees and the progress in the implementation of the movement and reintegration phases."[185] But UNHCR's capacity to monitor that return is dubious. It faced significant manpower, geographical, and logistical constraints that made it nearly impossible to play this role effectively.[186] At the outset of the repatriation exercise there was only one, very green, protection officer in the Arakan. Soon there were a few others but hardly enough to cover the entire area. Moreover, Arakan is a highly inaccessible region that has few paved roads, and whenever UNHCR officials did interview returnees they were almost always accompanied by military officials and forced to work closely with the Burmese Immigration and Manpower Department. Accordingly, UNHCR could not expect the returnees to give a candid assessment of their life after return.[187]

UNHCR was caught in a bind. It was committed to a repatriation exercise that depended on monitoring the return of the refugees—a difficult task under the circumstances. But if UNHCR was to openly question its ability to monitor the refugees' return, then the entire repatriation exercise might be jeopardized.[188] "UNHCR was in effect forced to choose between either sticking to principles and pulling out of any involvement in the repatriation . . . or accepting that a UNHCR presence must be conditioned on a pragmatic approach, the logic of which was that some presence was better than none at all."[189]

IV. CONCLUSION: THE POWER AND PATHOLOGIES OF UNHCR

From very humble beginnings UNHCR developed into one of the premier UN agencies. Few would have predicted this outcome at its birth. States created a UNHCR that had very little autonomy and a very limited mandate. The United States was only modestly supportive of the idea of the organization and then created alternative mechanisms to handle refugee issues. UNHCR's mandate was originally limited to refugees produced in Europe by events prior to 1951, which meant that it would soon go out of business. Yet the organization overcame these obstacles, expanding its reach to new regions and populations and providing various forms of assistance. Certainly this development could not have happened in the face of active state opposition, and there were important states that believed that a stronger organization was in their interest. But UNHCR did not wait for states to discover the relationship between those interests and an expanded organization. Instead, ambitious high commissioners seized on various crises and global developments to campaign for a broader mandate. Using their moral authority, high commissioners argued that nonconvention refugees should be eligible for the same protections as convention refugees. Using their expert authority, high commissioners argued that UNHCR had the experience on the ground to be not only a coordinating body but also a lead humanitarian agency, and to provide not only legal protection but also material assistance. Using their delegated authority, high commissioners claimed the right to provide an authoritative interpretation of refugee law and to diffuse it. High commissioners used these authority claims to convince states that they should permit the agency to become more deeply involved in refugee and humanitarian affairs and to legitimate those permissions through various authorizing resolutions by the UN.

By abetting the expansion of the concept of refugee, UNHCR helped not only to constitute world politics but also to expand its role in regulating activities on behalf of refugee populations. This expanding role meant that it had more control over refugee populations and solutions to refugee problems. Its preference about solutions shifted in the 1970s, away from exile and toward repatriation. State pressures certainly influenced Geneva's thinking on these matters; after all, states were beginning to bristle at the demands imposed by the international refugee regime, rolling up the welcome mat and demanding that refugees go home as soon as possible. But UNHCR staff also had independently determined that it was time to overcome its exilic bias and to help an increasing number of refugees who wanted to go home.

Although both states and UNHCR were increasingly oriented toward repatriation, UNHCR refused to go as far as states wanted and insisted on balancing repatriation and refugee rights. The active debate within the agency led it to develop new terminology, concepts, and rules that attempted to encourage repatriation without sacrificing refugee rights. Over time, however, initial deviations from organizational rules accumulated and led to a normalization of deviance, where rules governing repatriation that might have been unthinkable in the 1970s became mainstreamed by the 1990s. The emergence of this repatriation culture increased the possibility that UNHCR would sanction a repatriation exercise that violated the core principle of nonrefoulement, even when it was facing manageable pressures from states. Although most repatriation exercises do safeguard refugee rights, the cushion once provided by UNHCR has been reduced, leaving refugees more vulnerable than ever. The case of the Rohingyas is an example of this repatriation culture at work. To understand how UNHCR sanctioned a repatriation exercise that violated their rights and forcibly returned them to a situation that still threatened their physical survival requires an examination of the development of an organizational culture oriented around and for repatriation.

This discourse of repatriation not only created the possibility of pathological behavior but also underscored the sense in which UNHCR's power is one of domination, a notion we explore further in chapter 6. International organizations are able to deploy their authority not only to shape how actors classify and act on categories such as refugees, but also to shape the fates of those classified in these categories. UNHCR's discourse of voluntary repatriation combined with its growing authority to assess the human rights and political situation in the refugee-producing country puts it in a privileged position to judge whether the conditions warrant a repatriation exercise. In this way, the knowledge claims of UNHCR can easily overshadow the knowledge claims of the refugees. UNHCR has thus used its authority to shape how the world understands refugees and their circumstances, but also, potentially, to control their lives and determine their fates.

5

GENOCIDE AND THE PEACEKEEPING CULTURE AT THE UNITED NATIONS

In one hundred days, between April 6 and July 19, 1994, roughly eight hundred thousand Rwandans were killed in a genocide surpassing in speed and intensity all other genocides of the twentieth century. At the outset of the killing, the United Nations had twenty-five hundred troops on the ground. The Security Council's response was not to try to stop the killings but instead to withdraw the peacekeepers. During these first critical weeks the Secretariat did little to discourage the emerging consensus in the Security Council in favor of withdrawal. It failed to recommend an intervention to protect civilians or even to lay one on the table for serious consideration. Why would a UN staff that espouses and is empowered by humanitarian principles fail to recommend civilian protection in the face of such an onslaught?

One explanation is that the Secretariat responded to or anticipated the wishes of the states on the Security Council that did not find such intervention to be in their own national interests. However, this explanation does not square with the evidence. During the first weeks of the crisis some states on the Council did advocate an intervention, yet the Secretariat offered no support for their position. Further, there is no evidence that the Secretariat privately preferred an intervention but publicly recommended withdrawal because it anticipated the Council's rejection.[1] Instead, evidence makes clear that doing nothing to stop the genocide was the Secretariat's preferred policy. We investigate the role of the UN's peacekeeping culture in producing this result. We examine how the rules of peacekeeping that developed within the UN bureaucracy shaped the Secretariat's categorization of the violence in Rwanda as a civil war rather than a genocide, and how the Secretariat's understanding of Rwanda as a civil war led it to reject intervention as inappropriate and undesirable, even in the face of mass killings. A Secretariat that professed humanitarian goals used peacekeeping rules to conclude that a humanitarian intervention was not warranted to stop crimes against humanity.

To understand how the peacekeeping culture made this pathology possible requires a systematic consideration of the evolution of the rules and practice of peacekeeping. Specifically, it requires attention to the way peacekeeping rules defined when peacekeepers should be deployed and how they should act on the ground. As described in section I, peacekeeping was a creative response by the Secretariat and several member states to the 1956 Suez crisis. It originally entailed positioning lightly armed forces to monitor an existing cease-fire or political agreement between two contending states. Peacekeepers also were expected to follow rules about impartiality, consent, and neutrality. These rules certainly reflected geopolitical constraints of that time and the functions that UN forces were to serve, but they also reflected the sources of the Secretariat's authority. One important source of authority was its delegated mandate from states to promote peace, but one condition of this delegation was that the UN operate with the consent of parties to the conflict. The UN also had moral authority, but, again, this was conditioned on acting impartially in the conflicts. The Secretariat's power and influence rested on its authority, which in turn depended on being perceived as impartial and operating with consent.

Section II examines the post–Cold War reconsideration of the rules and practices of peacekeeping. New global pressures and opportunities prompted the Security Council and the Secretariat to expand the purposes of peacekeeping. Originally peacekeepers monitored a cease-fire between two states, but in these second-generation operations peacekeepers became involved in domestic conflicts and a host of new activities, among them saving failed states and providing humanitarian assistance.[2] This new social purpose of peacekeeping shaped the UN's bureaucratization in two principal ways. First, it led to the establishment of new units within the Secretariat such as the Electoral Assistance Unit that reflected its understanding of how to assist states in making the transition from civil war to civil peace. More important for our purposes, it led to a reconsideration of the rules of peacekeeping and, specifically, of whether the rules of consent, impartiality, and neutrality were appropriate and functional for these new conflicts, where the UN increasingly confronted violent opposition to its personnel and its mandate. In order to discharge its responsibilities in this new environment, the UN began to adapt these rules to include nonconsensual enforcement tactics.

At the very peak of its popularity the UN met several high-profile failures in places like Somalia and Bosnia. For the Secretariat, these failures represented a threat to the organization because they generated vocal opposition in important capitals and compromised its moral authority. To ensure that peacekeeping would be effective, and to shore up the organization's authority and political support, the Secretariat and the Security Council narrowed the conditions under which peacekeepers were deployed (emphasizing the need for stability on the ground before deployment) and restrained their actions in the field (reemphasizing consent and impartiality). Peacekeepers were no longer to be used in civil wars where there was no peace to keep.

The adaptation of the rules of peacekeeping had mixed results. Officials in New York believed that adapting the rules in these ways would improve the UN's chance for success in peacekeeping and restore the organization's authority and popularity. Yet this adaptation also planted the seeds for pathological behavior. One reason why the more expansive, second-generation rules had evolved after the Cold War was that the UN was responding to humanitarian emergencies, a form of action that Cold War politics had largely prevented it from attempting. Its humanitarian objectives, though, often conflicted with impartiality and consent. Humanitarian emergencies are frequently engineered by the combatants whose war aims are served by the catastrophe. The UN confronted a decision in these cases: either depart from the rules of impartiality and consent in order to confront the humanitarian emergency or allow these rules to determine the limits of its humanitarianism. In the late 1980s and early 1990s, it moved toward the former option; Somalia and Bosnia, though, caused it to retreat to the latter. By mid-1993 the organization was so badly scarred by these failures that respecting rules became an end in itself, eclipsing other organizational concerns. In an "irrationality of rationalization," the organization's rules of consent, neutrality, and impartiality helped to determine its goals—and made it undesirable to try to stop crimes against humanity.

Section III investigates how the peacekeeping culture—the rules governing when peacekeepers are deployed and how they operate in the field—shaped the way UN staff understood and reacted to the violence in Rwanda. The Security Council established UNAMIR (United Nations Assistance Mission for Rwanda) in October 1993 to oversee the Arusha Accords, which ended the civil war between the Rwandan Patriotic Front (RPF) and the Rwandan government. Instead of a peace process, however, UNAMIR confronted an increasingly dangerous security situation. Even before April 6, 1994, UNAMIR confronted civilian killings and threats to peacekeepers, politicians, and the Arusha process itself. After April 6, violence escalated dramatically with the eruption of civil war and mass killings. Despite changes in the scale and kind of violence, the Secretariat's response was the same: operate with the consent of the parties and do not use force. Why?

There is no evidence that the Secretariat wanted to intervene to protect civilians but was prevented by the states on the Security Council. Instead, evidence indicates that the Secretariat also preferred nonintervention and that this preference was a product of peacekeeping culture. During the pre-April period the Department of Peacekeeping Operations (DPKO) leaned on the peacekeeping rules and ordered General Roméo Dallaire, UNAMIR's force commander, to respond to the growing violence and threats to the Arusha process with consent-based means. When the violence escalated on April 6, the peacekeeping culture shaped the Secretariat's response in two important respects. It colored its categorization of the problem Rwanda presented. There were several possible ways to define the violence, including civil war, reciprocal clashes between the two ethnic groups, and ethnic cleansing and crimes against humanity. General Dallaire was providing evidence that Rwanda was both a civil war and a site of crimes against humanity organized by Hutu extremists against the Tutsi population. During April, however, the Secretariat categorized these killings only as reciprocal violence related to the civil war and as the most recent chapter in the long story of ethnic conflict between the two groups. The peacekeeping culture informed this conclusion. UNAMIR was designed to end a civil war. Its peacekeeping activities were created for this purpose, and pre-April predictions of what would happen if the peace process collapsed always involved the return of the civil war. Accordingly, when the post–April 6 violence erupted the Secretariat expected killing in Rwanda to be part of a civil war and saw what it expected to see. Indeed there is evidence that this is what the Secretariat *wanted* to see. At no time did DPKO or Secretary-General Boutros Boutros-Ghali seek information that might have caused them to alter their initial assessment. Why would UN officials find this assessment consistent with their organizational interests?

The peacekeeping culture also shaped the Secretariat's view of the appropriate response to the violence. If this was a civil war, the UN had no basis for involvement under peacekeeping rules since there was no peace to keep. Indeed, the rules of impartiality and consent were specifically designed to ensure that the UN avoided such unstable situations. Not only were civil wars an inappropriate use of peacekeepers, but any involvement would likely harm the organization because the UN would probably be blamed for failing to stop the violence. Applying the peacekeeping rules, the Secretariat recommended a course of nonintervention that was appropriate for a civil war and protected the organization's authority in world affairs. The Secretariat's construction of Rwanda then shaped the actions of member states. This view informed the Secretariat's presentations to the Security Council, steering the Council's debates away from any consideration of intervention. Thus, an "institutional ideology of impartiality" led the Secretariat to believe that it was appropriate and desirable not to try to stop crimes against humanity, or even recognize them as such, as the UN itself later acknowledged.[3]

I. THE EARLY YEARS

At the UN's founding, states gave the Security Council three mechanisms for maintaining peace and security. The first mandated states to make available to the Security Council their armed forces, facilities, and other assistance in the maintenance of international peace and security (article 43). It was left to future negotiations to specify the numbers and types of forces, along with the other facilities and assistance that states might provide. The United States was largely behind this measure. The second mechanism was designed to enable the UN to undertake "urgent military measures" and instructed states to designate, on a standby basis, air contingents for combined international enforcement action. This proposal was pushed largely by the Soviets and the Americans. The third mechanism was the establishment of the Military Staff Committee comprising the national chiefs of staff of the Security Council's permanent members (article 47). Pushed by Great Britain, the MSC was to advise and assist the Security Council on military matters, including the strategic direction of the armed forces that were put at the Security Council's disposal. Modest steps were taken in 1946 and 1947 toward implementing these proposals, but the onset of the Cold War completely extinguished any further interest. The sole military forces that operated under the UN banner during the early Cold War were the various military observer missions established between 1947 and 1956, a precursor to peacekeeping, and the UN-authorized but U.S.-run military operation in Korea.

Although the Office of the Secretary-General was disturbed by the paralysis and the shunting aside of the organization, there was little it could do because it had little autonomy or authority to initiate action.[4] At best, according to article 99 of the UN Charter, the secretary-general could bring to the Council's attention any matter he believed was a potential international security issue. In practice, though, the Secretariat understood that the Cold War left little role for this multilateral organization and little chance that the superpowers would allow the Council to oversee critical issues of international security. Moreover, the Security Council kept close watch on the Secretariat and generally opted for a "safe" secretary-general who knew his place. The fact that the Secretariat had no independent resources beyond what states were willing to provide through dues only underscored the lack of structural autonomy of the staff and secretary-general beyond the moral authority that came with the office.

The Suez crisis handed the UN the opportunity to invent peacekeeping.

The Israeli-French-British invasion of Egypt in October 1956 posed several dilemmas for member states, and there were few obvious solutions.[5] Both superpowers were strongly opposed to the invasion, though for very different reasons. The Soviet Union saw this as an archaic and desperate move by the colonial powers to retain their status and privileges in the Third World. It also perceived a potential challenge to its own self-arrogated role of defender of the rapidly decolonizing world and of Egypt in particular. In response, the Soviets took a publicly strident pose, threatening military action unless all three states withdrew immediately. The United States was outraged that three allies had undertaken what it viewed as dangerous and illegitimate action without its knowledge. (It was also upset that the action distracted attention from the Soviet invasion of Hungary and that it occurred just weeks before a presidential election). It was determined to extract all three from the area, preferably through diplomatic means but by force if necessary. Although the Security Council initially addressed the crisis, the presence of the veto-wielding British and French created an insurmountable barrier to effective action. Unable to determine a mechanism that would allow the French and the British to withdraw, the General Assembly became the formal site for most discussions, and the Security Council looked to the Secretariat for creative thinking.

The initial conversations that led to the invention of peacekeeping occurred between Secretary-General Dag Hammarskjöld and Canadian ambassador Lester Pearson. Hammarskjöld was initially cool to the idea of a major role for the UN. He became persuaded when he realized that this crisis provided an opportunity for the UN to demonstrate its relevance to member states on a matter of critical concern and that several member states strongly supported the idea. After close consultations with these states, Hammarskjöld announced the creation of a neutral force that would replace Britain and France and interpose itself between Egypt and Israel. Expressly prohibited from using force (except in self-defense) or from involving itself in the domestic politics of Egypt, the mandate of the United Nations Emergency Force clearly stated that it should "refrain from any activity of a political character in a Host State" and in no way "influence the military balance in the present conflict and, thereby, the political balance affecting efforts to settle the conflict."[6] The development of peacekeeping represented a major innovation. Although the UN was drawing from its previous experience with observer missions, it was now extending and revising this instrument in significant ways.[7] The new peacekeeping concept and terminology quickly became part of international peace and security, giving the UN a new policy instrument.

Between 1956 and the winding down of the Cold War in 1988, the UN conducted fifteen operations (the last one in Lebanon in March 1978) and developed some general rules of peacekeeping. The cardinal rules in this first generation of peacekeeping were consent, neutrality, and impartiality. Peacekeepers were to be deployed with the consent of the parties; they were to be impartial and function without prejudice to any side; they were to be lightly armed and use force only in self-defense.[8] These rules grew out of the strategic and political environments in which peacekeepers were deployed and the function that they were supposed to serve. Rarely placed where there was an ongoing conflict and never expected to enforce a peace, peacekeepers were authorized to monitor an already existing peace agreement and thus to help states stick to their political commitments, maintain a cease-fire, and avoid a return to war. The observations made in 1958 by Secretary-General Hammarskjöld regarding the importance of these rules remained valid for the next several decades. Peacekeeping operations, he stated, "must be separate and distinct from activities by national authorities" and must limit their role to addressing the "external [that is, international] aspects of the political situation," or else the "United Nations units might run the risk of getting involved in differences with local authorities or publics or in internal conflicts which would be highly detrimental to the effectiveness of the operation."[9] There were rare and highly controversial departures from these rules, most notably in the Congo, but such departures only reinforced the desirability of these rules.

These rules of peacekeeping also distinguished the UN as an international actor. In contrast to states, which are biased, use force, and do not necessarily operate with the consent of the parties, the UN used persuasion, was impartial and neutral, and operated with consent. These rules, in effect, not only told the UN who it was and how it differed from states but also connected peacekeeping to the UN's moral authority and thus the wellspring of its influence. Certainly, outgunned peacekeepers had little chance of imposing their will on more heavily armed states or of operating without states' consent, but UN officials also worried that if they compromised their impartiality then they would forgo a principal reason why states and others complied with their decisions.

II. AFTER THE COLD WAR

Just as the superpower confrontation of the Cold War paralyzed the UN and hamstrung peacekeeping operations, so the Cold War's decline led directly to the UN's resurgence and the more liberal use of peacekeeping. There were several reasons why the Great Powers turned to the UN. The superpowers had a mutual interest in winding down regional conflicts and found the UN a good forum for doing so. They also found the UN a useful place to dump intractable conflicts as well as conflicts peripheral to their core security interests. Furthermore, in an era of declining security resources and with emerging norms of security cooperation, the multilateralism of UN action legitimated security activities and offered the promise of burden sharing. Finally, Third World states championed a growing role for the UN, hoping that it might provide an institutional buffer between them and the increasingly powerful West.[10]

The immediate result was an increasingly busy Security Council overseeing more issues that fell under a widening definition of international peace and security. Previously, the Security Council had avoided such activities as electoral assistance and civilian policing because there was no strong demand from member states and because of the view that they violated the principle of noninterference. At the end of the Cold War, however, shared notions about what activities promoted peace and security expanded. There was growing demand for such assistance, and because the UN's authority and perceived impartiality gave it distinct advantages over states, there was a general interest in developing and employing its services in these areas.

According to the UN Charter, the Security Council has "primary responsibility for the maintenance of international peace and security" (article 24). This function also gives the Security Council the ability to "investigate any dispute, or any situation, which might lead to international friction or give rise to a dispute in order to determine whether the continuance of the dispute or situation is likely to endanger the maintenance of international peace and security" (article 34). The charter does not explicitly define what constitutes a threat to international peace and security; the Security Council has some discretion over this interpretation.[11] During the Cold War the norm of sovereignty and the desire of superpowers to restrict possibilities for confrontation led the Security Council to define threats to security primarily as disputes between states that were or might become militarized.[12] Widely supported by major and lesser powers alike, this working definition prevailed throughout most of the Cold War.

With the decline of the Cold War the Security Council began to widen the definition of threats to international peace and security. No longer content to restrict itself to interstate matters, it now became involved in a variety of domestic conflicts on the grounds that they had implications for international peace and security. Beginning with the UN operation to provide relief to the Kurds during the first Gulf War, the UN also expanded its definition of security to encompass humanitarian crises as, by their nature, related to security threats. As it moved from Iraq to Cambodia to Somalia to Bosnia to Mozambique to El Salvador, the Council altered the definition of threats to international peace and security in a way that permitted the UN's intervention in domestic space.[13]

UN staff welcomed and in many instances lobbied hard for this expanded definition.[14] The most famous and consequential manifestation of the UN's thinking was the secretary-general's report *An Agenda for Peace.*[15] At the request of the Security Council, Secretary-General Boutros-Ghali outlined his vision of the UN's future security role. He capitalized on the opportunity to deliver a more ambitious, far-reaching, and forward-looking proposal than was expected.[16] The heart of the document is a reconsideration of the meaning of security. International security, he argued, was best achieved not through military force and deterrence but through institutions and assurance; in such matters international institutions like the United Nations were central. State security, moreover, should not overshadow human security. Unlike states, which presumably were threatened by neighboring states, individuals were threatened by the lack of food, a crumbling economy, environmental degradation, political instability, and even their own governments. Empirically, it seemed, most security crises were no longer international but domestic, and the UN had to go where the action was. Boutros-Ghali used his institutional and moral authority to try to effect a sea change in how security was conceptualized and in what role the UN played in producing a more stable international order.

The UN was not only offering to help states regulate their relations in new ways to further mutual security but was also attempting to use its moral and delegated authority to shape the underlying constitution of world politics—its basic organizing principles and what actions were considered legitimate and desirable. It was also offering to spread these principles where they did not exist. As the international community's legitimation forum, the UN was best able to codify and institutionalize constitutive norms such as multilateral diplomacy, confidence building, human rights, and the rule of law.[17] The UN would both provide a seal of approval for such actions and promote them, directing its resources at those states that did not have the domestic ingredients of law, democracy, and human rights that would make them peaceful citizens of the international community.[18] Peacekeeping was to be a tool not only to regulate but also to constitute a new international order.[19]

Peacekeeping Expansion

Peacekeeping operations expanded in number and purpose. Between 1989 and 1994 the Security Council authorized twenty-six operations across the globe, doubling in five years the number authorized by the council in the previous forty, and expanding the number of soldiers sevenfold.[20] While some of these post-1989 operations resembled the classical prototype, most now were situated in much more unstable environments, where a cease-fire was barely in place if at all, where governmental institutions were frayed and in need of repair, where ragtag armies were not parties to the agreement, and where the UN was charged with complex tasks that were designed to repair deeply divided societies.

These new activities represented a fundamental change in the social purpose of peacekeeping operations. The UN now advanced the claim that conflict was best solved and peace best promoted through democratic institutions and the rule of law. As UN staff set out to create the stable and legitimate institutions that could foster national reconciliation, they had in mind particular models. There were not many models to choose from, and the post–Cold War move by many former communist states to remake themselves into "Western" states only narrowed the possible alternatives and increased the legitimacy of the Western model. The result was that peacekeeping and peacebuilding operations promoted a liberal and democratic model of domestic order as they attempted to constitute new states and societies.[21]

There were various organizational expressions of this orientation.[22] The UN expanded existing units and added new ones to accommodate these added tasks. A dramatically revamped and expanded DPKO now worked to integrate human rights into its operation and to coordinate with the Department of Humanitarian Affairs, the Electoral Assistance Unit, the Civilian Police Unit, and a newly created situation room. The expansion of DPKO, the increasing personnel, and the addition of new activities that blurred the distinction between political, peacekeeping, and humanitarian affairs necessitated the development of new hierarchies, new divisions of responsibilities, and new decision-making processes. As UN peacekeeping blurred into peacebuilding, and as security melded into development, departments that once had a relatively solitary existence now had to coordinate their relations and activities across the UN system.[23]

Rewriting Peacekeeping Rules

This expanded form of peacekeeping quickly ran into problems. Beginning in mid-1993 and as a consequence of organizational overstretch, failures in the field, and a perception that the original rules had been "strained to the breaking point,"[24] the UN reconsidered the rules of peacekeeping in two dimensions. It developed more explicit rules for determining when peacekeeping was a proper and effective instrument for international peace and security. The rapid increase in the number of peacekeeping operations after 1989 reflected not only growing demand for the UN's services but also the Security Council's willingness to consider peacekeeping as the answer to an array of security problems. By mid-1993 there was a growing fear that peacekeeping was fast approaching a crisis, leading the Security Council and the Secretariat to adopt more restrictive rules for deploying peacekeepers. The Security Council also reconsidered the rules for how peacekeepers should operate in the field. Many of these second-generation operations had drifted away from the holy trinity of consent, impartiality, and neutrality and utilized enforcement tactics. A series of setbacks, most notably in Somalia and Bosnia, were partially blamed on the failure to stick to the original rules of peacekeeping and led the UN to return to the rules of classical peacekeeping. The hope was that by returning to these original rules the UN would increase its chance of success in the field and its popularity and authority.[25] The so-called shadow of Somalia was deep and long: it caused the UN to become more restrictive regarding when peacekeepers were deployed and how they operated in the field, and it shaped the UN's actions in other operations, including Rwanda.[26]

Peacekeeping: When?

Although UN officials occasionally grumbled that the organization was being unfairly saddled with operations for which it had no real competence and was given inadequate support from member states (this was especially true of the Bosnian mandate), in the main they welcomed their newfound popularity. By summer 1993, however, many governments and UN staff were concerned that the UN was unable to implement its expanding list of delegated responsibilities. They worried that the UN was trying to do too much, too fast, often at the insistence of a Security Council that was all too ready to authorize first and ask critical questions second.[27] Organizationally, the UN was a large, cumbersome bureaucracy ill suited to the nimble action required for many of its new assignments.[28] After years of neglect, the UN was experiencing tremendous growing pains that were made doubly difficult by states that were ready to delegate new tasks but without the requisite resources. Highly publicized failures in places like Somalia and Bosnia—where the UN was outgunned, ineffective, and an unwitting partner to the conflict—dampened the support for the organization.

These widely recognized peacekeeping shortcomings stirred a broad debate about the conditions under which peacekeeping was effective and prompted the determination to find more restrictive criteria for deploying peacekeepers. Because of experiences in Somalia and elsewhere, the Clinton administration reassessed its initial enthusiasm for UN peacekeeping and concluded that it would use more restrictive criteria before authorizing an operation, including a more careful look at the purpose, modalities, and resources for the operation.[29] Various working groups of states at the UN, including the Contact Group on Peacekeeping Reform, devised a set of criteria that were intended to delineate the conditions under which peacekeeping was likely to be effective and when it should be selected. UN staff contributed to these discussions and urged the Security Council to develop some rules to limit the application of peacekeeping, and their cautionary words carried weight with member states. Kofi Annan, for instance, said that "nobody would disagree with . . . the U.S. . . . when they say there should be some guidelines for the council to determine when they take on a crisis and when they do not—provided it's applied in a flexible and practical manner."[30] On another occasion, he summarized the lessons he had learned from recent experiences: "Peacekeeping works when you have a clear mandate, a will on the part of the people to make peace. The inspiration for acceptable and viable peace can only spring from the leaders and the people in the country."[31] Jan Eliason, the former head of the Department of Humanitarian Affairs, vehemently argued for the establishment of firmer guidelines, particularly in situations of internal conflict and the use of force.[32]

By mid-1993 the Security Council began to articulate more restrictive criteria for authorizing a peacekeeping operation. For instance, in a September 1993 meeting with Boutros-Ghali, the five permanent members of the Security Council demanded a more careful review of peacekeeping operations to ensure that demands did not exceed capabilities and that new commitments were made only after fundamental questions had been resolved, including the precise nature of the operation's objectives and its material and political foundations.[33] The events in Somalia on October 3, 1993, increased the Security Council's determination to develop more rational and restrictive criteria.

The new guidelines (formalized several months later on May 3, 1994) stated that peacekeeping operations could be used when (1) there was a genuine threat to peace and security; (2) regional or subregional organizations could assist in resolving the situation; (3) a cease-fire existed and the parties had committed themselves to a peace process; (4) a clear political goal existed and was present in the mandate; (5) a precise mandate could be formulated; and (6) the safety of UN personnel could be reasonably assured.[34] Not only were these criteria generally consistent with the Secretariat's preferences, but the Secretariat had worked in close consultation with the Council in devising them.

Peacekeeping: How?

In addition to rethinking when peacekeeping should be authorized, the UN also reconsidered how it should be carried out. For some of the operations established between 1989 and 1993 the UN's rules of neutrality, consent, and impartiality still held sway, but many others were established in more unstable environments, thus raising questions regarding whether and when enforcement action might be appropriate. There were two developments here. Beginning with the Gulf War, the Security Council entered a new stage of peace enforcement and authorized several Chapter VII operations, where no consent was given by a recognized government (unlike Chapter VI operations, where peacekeepers are deployed with the consent of the parties).

Here, because no consent was given, these operations were not compatible with the classical rules of engagement.

The UN also became involved in civil wars and humanitarian assistance. In these "VI-1/2 operations"—which occurred in less stable environments than those associated with Chapter VI but did not rise to the level of all-out war associated with Chapter VII—peacekeepers had to deal with highly fluid situations in which they operated in a constant no-man's-land between consent and enforcement.[35] What did consent mean when there was no recognized government or when a beleaguered government invited the UN but other parties did not? What did neutrality mean when parties opposed the UN's presence and saw it as an unwanted intervention force? Were impartiality and neutrality functional and efficacious in the face of human rights abuses or crimes against humanity? What good was consent when parties obstructed the implementation of the mandate? These rules could transform the UN into an unwitting accomplice to ethnic cleansing and other highly undesirable outcomes by protecting perpetrators from UN action. The alternative was to enforce the mandate without parties' consent, thus potentially compromising the UN's impartiality. The UN was confronting on a daily basis these very tricky but very pressing predicaments in Haiti, El Salvador, Cambodia, Somalia, and Bosnia. With little experience in such matters and little time to carry out a lengthy debate, UN staff gingerly revised the rules in ways that left them more willing to use enforcement tactics.[36]

The dangers of this willingness to depart from consent and impartiality became clear by summer 1993. Chapter VII operations raised questions that the organization had not adequately considered, including how to establish unified command and control, what were the proper rules of engagement, and whether there was solid political will and a sound resource base to back up the operations. In response, the Security Council backed away from Chapter VII, and in those instances when it was required, favored delegating enforcement to states.[37] The Secretariat also retreated from a willingness to use enforcement mechanisms when confronted by recalcitrant parties. One UN aide asserted, "We at the United Nations believe that peace-keeping is not peace-enforcement, and that the two activities do not mix very well."[38] Even Boutros-Ghali, who once championed enforcement, tempered his initial zeal because of Somalia and Bosnia: "The United Nations is not able to do a huge peace-enforcement operation. This is the lesson of the last two years."[39] Returning from a trip to Africa in October 1993, he said that his new message to African leaders was: "The United Nations cannot impose peace; the role of the United Nations is to maintain peace."[40] This, he maintained, was the new "U.N. mentality."[41]

The UN was already returning to the classical rules of peacekeeping when the U.S. Rangers died in Mogadishu on October 3, 1993, an event that only reinforced the rules' perceived appropriateness. A blue-ribbon commission comprising longtime UN hands mandated to investigate the deaths of the UN peacekeepers in Somalia concluded that the mandate "was too pretentious in relation to the instruments and the will to implement it." It urged the UN to return to its traditional principles of consent, neutrality, and impartiality.[42] Sashi Tharoor, an assistant to Kofi Annan, suggested that these rules were important for guiding the conduct of operations in the field and that the willingness to stray from them had caused the UN many troubles. It was time to return to these rules in order to increase the UN's effectiveness in the field.[43]

A change in the rules would help the UN become more effective, and a more effective UN would be a more popular UN. In the wake of Bosnia, Somalia, and the first operation in Haiti, there was considerable fear that any more UN failures would spell the end of the UN. By embracing more restrictive criteria for when an operation was authorized, insisting that peace enforcement be undertaken only under special circumstances, and adopting a traditional notion of neutrality, UN staff could be more confident that the UN would be used only when appropriate.

A return to the original rules also was intended to help the UN protect its moral authority and influence, which were being compromised when it departed from impartiality and (unintentionally) picked sides. Reflecting on the Somalia experience, Kofi Annan said that "in these situations the impartiality of the force and the principle of consent of the parties are crucial. If you are perceived to be fair, you do not run the danger of being engaged. If you are seen as taking on initiatives that could change the military balance on the ground and favor one group or another, the troops that see themselves as disadvantaged might decide you've taken sides and declare war on you."[44] Jan Eliason warned in late 1993 that the UN must "adhere strictly to the guiding principles of humanity, neutrality, and impartiality. Once those principles are compromised, our legitimacy and utility are at risk."[45] Sashi Tharoor said that "this department is not in a hurry to recommend . . . any operation that would call for peace enforcement. . . . The moment we become party to a conflict, as happened in Somalia, we lose our capacity to fulfill other tasks."[46] UN officials believed that moral authority and impartiality were two sides of the same coin and that both were important for maintaining the UN's influence.

These rules shaped how UN officials determined whether a situation was appropriate for peacekeeping. Peacekeeping was appropriate when there was stability on the ground, the parties had consented, and there was progress toward a political resolution. Security Council members, particularly the most powerful ones, were clearly signaling a strong reluctance to consider peacekeeping under fire, which created external pressures to use these more restrictive criteria. However, UN staff also were having doubts of their own that the system could continue and had independently determined that peacekeeping should be used only in selected situations where there was peace to keep. A resource-strapped UN could not deploy peacekeepers to every conflict or humanitarian emergency. It had to develop criteria for selecting situations where it could succeed, and recent experiences and lessons learned suggested that these more restrictive criteria were most likely to ensure success.[47] Restricting peacekeeping in this way also had a political payoff: success in the field would increase the UN's stature in world politics.

This functional adaptation of peacekeeping rules, though, established the cultural ingredients for pathological behavior, in this case an "irrationality of rationalization" in which rules became ends in themselves. Peacekeeping now was understood to be inappropriate if there was no peace to keep, if the conflict was active, and if there was no consent. If consent and stability were once again prerequisites for the deployment of peacekeepers, then the UN, once again, would have to define the purpose of peacekeeping in a way that excluded situations where these did not exist. This made peacekeeping inappropriate during humanitarian emergencies since these rarely fit the revised criteria. The decision to restrict peacekeeping to moments of stability to the neglect of humanitarian catastrophes was not accidental—it was intended. Although UN staff remained concerned about how to protect civilians during humanitarian nightmares, one of the lessons learned from recent operations in places like Somalia and Bosnia was that UN peacekeeping could not accomplish this task. In order to discourage the organization from allowing its emotions to overrule reason, the Security Council and the Secretariat jointly constructed criteria that explicitly reserved peacekeeping for situations when there was a peace to keep.

Adhering to the rules of consent and impartiality also reduced the likelihood that the UN would became an agent of humanitarian intervention. During humanitarian emergencies there often is not a party that can provide consent, and to become involved in protecting populations at risk often means taking sides and violating the rule of impartiality. The functional adaptation of the rules of peacekeeping thus shaped how UN staff judged the sorts of goals it should pursue, leaving humanitarian protection an orphaned goal, inappropriate under most circumstances. This change made nonintervention, even in the face of crimes against humanity, seem sensible and responsible to UN staff, as the Rwandans soon discovered.

III. RWANDA

Before the genocide Rwanda was one of the most densely populated countries in the world, with seven million people divided between three ethnic groups: the Hutus, who made up 85 percent of the population, the Tutsis, 14 percent, and the Twas, 1 percent.[48] The origins of these different ethnic groups are not completely known, but during the precolonial period a stratified system developed in which the Tutsis came to occupy the upper rung of the political and economic ladder. In 1890 Rwanda was colonized by Germany, which ruled largely through the already established political system. As a consequence of Germany's defeat in World War I, Belgium inherited the Rwandan mandate. Motivated by a "scientific" ideology that determined that the Tutsis, who were presumed to have come from the north and were seen as having Caucasian characteristics, were racially superior to the native-born Hutus, the Belgians introduced political reforms, identity cards, and educational, administrative, and economic favoritism that institutionalized ethnic cleavages and Tutsi supremacy.

This system remained largely intact until the decolonization process in the late 1950s. Beginning in 1959 Rwanda was increasingly convulsed by violence and challenges to Tutsi rule as Rwandan independence approached. The issue was not Rwanda's territorial integrity but rather its future constitutional fabric and the relations between the majority Hutus and minority Tutsis. Views regarding the desirability of a democratic Rwanda predictably fell along ethnic lines; the Hutu population demanded majority rule and the Tutsi population worried that such governing principles would strip them of all political and economic power and leave them at the mercy of a very resentful Hutu population. Elections were held in 1961, and the Hutu-dominated parties predictably won the vast majority of seats and formally unseated the Tutsi government upon Rwandan independence on July 1, 1962. These events, known as the "Hutu revolution," triggered ethnic conflict and led to the flight of nearly two hundred thousand Tutsis to neighboring countries. From their exile many Tutsi refugees began organizing guerrilla attacks. The Hutu government lashed back, which led to more refugee flows and more counterviolence. Ethnic tensions remained high for Rwanda's first ten years.

In 1973 General Juvénal Habyarimana grabbed power and consolidated his rule through all possible political, economic, and ideological means, using the reins of government to establish control and a willing church to legitimate his rule. He also introduced a new modus vivendi for the Tutsis: stay out of politics and live in relatively safety. For the next sixteen years ethnic tensions subsided, and Tutsis experienced better living conditions. The economy, though not impressive even by African standards, grew as the development industry showered aid on a government that it deemed efficient, competent, and stable. Rwanda was hardly a paradise, but it had almost a showcase quality given its history and the neighborhood it inhabited.

By the end of the 1980s, however, a series of unconnected developments produced a crisis period for Rwandan government and society. There was a major economic downturn, owing largely to a drought and a drop in the price of coffee, Rwanda's major export and source of earnings. The international financial institutions began to offer structural adjustment prescriptions, which only exacerbated the burden faced by most sectors of society. The worldwide democratization movement of the early post–Cold War period caught up with Rwanda, leading to tremendous international and domestic pressure on Habyarimana to relax his grip and allow the semblance of democracy. He relented, and beginning in 1990 political space opened up and was quickly filled by over a dozen political parties representing divergent views, including both reformists and an extremist right determined to defend Hutu power and privileges.

Democratization brought not only Hutu extremists but also attacks from militant Tutsi exile groups rooted in the now large Tutsi refugee community. By the end of the 1980s nearly half a million Tutsis were living outside of Rwanda and were continually refused the right to repatriate (or feared for their physical safety if they did). In 1988 the children of the first refugee flights from the 1960s formed the Rwandan Patriotic Front (RPF) as a political and military organization with the goals of repatriating the Tutsi refugees and establishing a power-sharing arrangement with the Hutu-dominated Rwandan government. In October 1990 the RPF launched an offensive designed to topple the Rwandan government. Although the RPF's stated goal was to produce a society of ethnic tolerance, the civil war, in fact, had the unintended consequence of hardening ethnic cleavages and fostering more extremism in several ways. Even though many Rwandan Tutsis viewed the RPF as an alien force and rallied behind the government, Habyarimana played the ethnic card and branded the Tutsi minority a fifth column. At the same time, the RPF invasion led, ultimately, to the displacement of nearly one million people (mostly Hutus) to temporary shelters, where they became resentful of the Tutsis and prime recruits for extremist groups. The government invited French, Belgian, and Zairian forces to help the government fight the RPF; the French remained after a cease-fire was established and became the government's patron and protector, giving it practically unconditional support. The combination of the invasion, the beginning of political liberalization, and the negotiations with the RPF caused many in the inner circle (*akuzu*) and Hutu-centric political parties to fear that they were going to lose their privileges and to begin to contemplate the use of whatever means were necessary to defend their power.

The RPF and the Hutu government made some progress in their negotiations between 1990 and 1993, helped along by military stalemate and various international intermediaries. By late 1992 they had concluded several protocols, but in February 1993 the RPF launched a major attack against the Rwandan government because of the government's massacre of Tutsi citizens. The fighting continued throughout spring 1993 and was ended only by a French military intervention to prop up France's Hutu allies and a series of cease-fire agreements initialed at Arusha, Tanzania.

Establishing UNAMIR

The Arusha talks continued over the next several months, culminating in an agreement on August 3, 1993, that included provisions for a cease-fire, repatriation of Tutsi refugees, demilitarization and demobilization of the contending armies, and the establishment of a transitional government that would lead to a power-sharing arrangement between the Tutsis and the Hutus. As envisioned in the accords, an "international force" (that is, the UN) was to play various roles. It was to help provide security; monitor the cease-fire agreement and investigate all infractions; establish and maintain a demilitarized zone around Kigali; help maintain public security by monitoring the activities of the gendarmerie and police; and assist with the demilitarization, demobilization, and integration of the armed forces of the government and the RPF.[49] In short, the proposed international operation was to provide security during the peace process.

When the Secretariat presented the proposal for a peacekeeping operation to the Security Council on September 24, 1993, the Council had to address two basic questions. The first was whether to authorize the operation. To answer this question the Council asked if the proposed operation satisfied the emergent criteria governing the conditions under which a peacekeeping operation would be deployed. There had to be a working cease-fire, a comprehensive political process and timetable supported by the parties, and a clear vision of the roles to be played by the UN. From the Council's perspective, the proposed operation passed with high marks. As outlined in the Arusha Accords and now part of the mandate of the United Nations Assistance Mission for Rwanda (UNAMIR), the new force was to contribute to the establishment of a weapons-free zone in Kigali, monitor the cease-fire and the security situation, assist with demining and refugee repatriation, investigate accusations of noncompliance with the agreement by the parties, help coordinate humanitarian affairs, and investigate reports on the police and gendarmerie. From the Council's perspective, the agreement contained the requisites for settling an ethnic conflict and civil war, and the secretary-general's proposal for a UN force fit the criteria for establishing a peacekeeping operation.[50] Moreover, the parties appeared to be in full support of the accords, a point underlined by a visit from the RPF and Rwandan government to New York. Finally, the operation had the political support of a Security Council member, France. This meant that a powerful member of the Council was willing to help oversee the operation and would be upset if it was not authorized.

Once the Security Council had determined that it could authorize a force, the second question concerned how the peacekeepers would operate. The Council's discussions were taking place after a consensus had emerged on the need to return to the original rules of peacekeeping and after a hellish period in Mogadishu, which only reinforced the necessity of those rules. Consequently, the Council was unprepared to consider anything but a consent-based operation. A central issue, though, was how UNAMIR would provide security around Kigali. The Arusha Accords imagined a robust force patrolling much of Rwanda and providing security in a comprehensive manner. The UNAMIR mandate, though, took a more conservative approach. Specifically, it instructed UNAMIR to "contribute to the security of the city of Kigali, *inter alia,* within a weapons-secure area established by the parties in and around the city." UNAMIR was to establish an area around the capital that it would vigorously patrol, controlling the movements of militias and combatants and confiscating illegal weapons. It could conceivably seize weapons that crossed its path and were visible, but it was prohibited from forcibly disarming militias; such action would take it beyond the "Mogadishu line"—when peacekeeping slides into peace enforcement—and beyond the mandate. The Council authorized a limited force of only 2,548 personnel for all these tasks, half of the planning team's recommendation but the most that the Security Council (and mainly the United States) would approve. The Council justified this reduced number on the grounds that because the parties fully supported the plan, there was no need for a robust force. One implication of the force structure's limited size, though, was that in order to monitor all of Rwanda the force would have to be spread thin. This was not too troubling in peacetime but could certainly be problematic if the situation turned violent.[51]

The Security Council authorized UNAMIR on October 5, 1993.

The Culture of Consent

Headquarters could apply the classical rules of peacekeeping with few second thoughts as long as the security environment remained stable and the parties complied with the Arusha agreement. But the security situation soured quickly and the political process stumbled, leading to a debate between General Roméo Dallaire, UNAMIR's force commander, and DPKO over the appropriate course of action. Dallaire advocated a more forceful presence that included enforcement tactics, but the Secretariat's consistent position, one that was influenced by the peacekeeping culture, was that such tactics violated the rules of peacekeeping, might imperil the troops and the operation, and would sacrifice the UN's authority. DPKO cleaved to these rules even when faced with evidence of violations of the Arusha agreement that might portend not only bad faith on the part of the government but government-sponsored violence against peacekeepers and civilians.

Dallaire's telegram to DPKO on January 11, 1994, is the most famous instance of this disagreement about how to respond to violence. Dallaire communicated to headquarters that he had received fresh evidence of a plot by extremists to scuttle the Arusha Accords by massacring civilians and killing peacekeepers and that he intended to seize weapons in the basement of President Habyarimana's party headquarters in order to stop the plot. DPKO overruled Dallaire's plan and insisted that he use consent-based tactics. The contrast between these extraordinary predictions of violence and DPKO's standardized response has led many scholars and investigators to wonder how DPKO could ever have believed that such a response was appropriate.[52] The peacekeeping culture, we argue, helps to explain its behavior.

Since his arrival in Rwanda in late fall 1993, Dallaire had been increasingly aware of the dangers confronting the operation and the political process.[53] These fears intensified in early January 1994 when an informant, who claimed to be opposed to the Arusha Accords and to have close ties to the president and the Interahamwe (a Hutu extremist militia), warned that Hutu elites were planning to assassinate supporters of Arusha and to exterminate all Tutsis. Although the informant confessed that he was no friend of the political process, he was opposed to a plan whose objective was to "kill, kill, kill."[54] To transform the plan into reality, the Interahamwe was stockpiling and distributing weapons, creating lists for assassination, and organizing hit teams. The plan would begin the moment the political deadlock ended and the transitional government was established. Although the Interahamwe believed that it could successfully confront the RPF and its Tutsi allies, it did not want to fight a two-front war with the UN. To remove the UN, it plotted to assassinate Belgian peacekeepers, an act it believed would cause the UN to withdraw. The informant offered to take UNAMIR representatives to the stored weapons caches in the party headquarters of the president so that they could be seized before they were distributed in the very near future.

Dallaire telegrammed DPKO on January 11, communicating the informant's account, stating that he intended to carry out a raid on the weapons cache within the next thirty-six hours if the story checked out, and requesting advice on how to handle the informant's request for protection. Crucially, he believed that the mandate to help establish a weapons-secure area meant that UNAMIR was permitted to provide security in the expanded sense of the term, allowing him to use a range of tactics from consent-based activities to more aggressive measures, such as seizing weapons.[55] Indeed, by late December he had begun seizing weapons in public places, a move he believed was both permitted by the mandate and absolutely essential for the provision of security. Therefore, when Dallaire sent his communiqué he was not expecting headquarters to comment on his plan to seize the weapons but rather was looking for guidance about how to handle the informant's request for protection.[56]

DPKO's swift reaction was to order him to (1) terminate his plan to seize the weapons cache; (2) relay the information to the U.S., French, and Belgian embassies in Kigali (members of the contact group that were to help keep the peace process on track); (3) communicate to President Habyarimana that he must both halt these "subversive activities" and recover the weapons (Dallaire also was told to tell the president to take these actions within forty-eight hours and to threaten him with bringing the news to the Security Council); and (4) tell the informant that while they could not protect him and his family, they would not reveal his identity.

One possible explanation for DPKO's response is that it was acting as the Security Council's agent, reminding Dallaire of the Council's instructions as defined by the mandate.[57] Along these lines, Iqbal Riza, then assistant secretary-general for peacekeeping, explained: "We have to go by the mandate we are given by the Security Council. It's not up to the Secretary-General to decide whether they're going to run off in other directions." DPKO was telling Dallaire that UNAMIR could assist the parties in establishing a weapons-secure zone but it could not "go and recover weapons" on its own.[58] UNAMIR could inform the local authorities that it had knowledge of illegal stocks, a clear cease-fire violation, but it was up to the parties involved to request UNAMIR's assistance in confiscating these weapons. Because the mandate did not permit the seizure of weapons, the Secretariat would have to get Security Council authorization for this type of action.

One might conclude that the Secretariat rejected Dallaire's request simply because states favored this response. DPKO understood that the Council was in no mood to rewrite or reinterpret UNAMIR's mandate to allow Dallaire's proposed actions.[59] During the Council's initial deliberation regarding the authorization of UNAMIR there had been a brief discussion regarding how the operation might provide security, and it rejected the idea of a forceful stance in favor of more consent-based tactics. Therefore, while the Council might have acceded to the seizure of weapons in visible locations, it undoubtedly would have rejected the idea of storming sensitive political locations such as the party headquarters of the president. Furthermore, it had authorized a force structure that was barely sufficient for assistance and was hardly ready for the sort of enforcement action contemplated by Dallaire. Finally, there is little reason to believe that any new information such as that contained in the January 11 telegram would have changed the Council's mind.[60] At this moment the Council was busily overseeing the American withdrawal from Somalia and institutionalizing rules of consent and impartiality. For DPKO to suggest to the Council that UNAMIR needed to take such enforcement action would probably have raised strong images of Somalia and led the Council to wonder whether it had approved the initial operation because of false information.

An alternative possibility is that DPKO was not simply a conduit for the Council members' reluctance but was expressing its own judgment and preferences, in accord with its peacekeeping culture.[61] There is no evidence that DPKO considered or approved of Dallaire's proposal but then rejected it because of the Security Council's anticipated objection. Dallaire's account of his discussions with DPKO, for example, does not suggest that DPKO was interested in an intervention but felt constrained by the Council.[62] Instead, the evidence is that DPKO reasoned through the rules of peacekeeping and concluded that Dallaire's proposal was both inappropriate and a risk to the operation and the UN.

The rules of impartiality and consent shaped DPKO's interpretation of the mandate. Driven in part by recent experiences and the shadow of Somalia, the Secretariat returned to a more traditional concept of neutrality, impartiality, and the consent of the parties—even when the parties were violating key features of the mandate. Pointing directly to Somalia, Iqbal Riza claimed: "We're talking about this cable having come in January," just months after the Pakistani and American soldiers had been killed as a consequence of their enforcement tactics in Somalia. He continued:

> We were cautious in interpreting our mandate and in giving guidance because we did not want a repetition of Somalia. . . . We could not risk another Somalia as it led to the collapse of the Somalian operation. We did not want this mission to collapse.[63]

The rules of peacekeeping, reinforced by recent events in Somalia, thus led DPKO to predict that any enforcement operation might transform Kigali into another Mogadishu. Although the implication was that UNAMIR would have to rely on the consent and full participation of the very individuals who were storing and hiding weapons, this was consistent with traditional peacekeeping rules.[64] Moreover, if it did use enforcement action, especially in such a sensitive location, the UN might sacrifice not only its impartiality but also its ability to influence the parties in the future—because impartiality, in this view, represented the sole means of influence. DPKO thus responded to the telegram in a manner that was consistent with the revised rules of peacekeeping. It applied the rules of consent and impartiality: peacekeepers are not permitted to seize weapons stockpiles without the permission of the parties, but they are permitted to communicate violations of the cease-fire to heads of state.

The peacekeeping culture also shaped DPKO's understanding of appropriate responses to threats of violence and threats to the peace process. The Secretariat's consistent line (shared by UNAMIR officials and the Security

Council) was that the surest and least costly antidote to the existing and anticipated violence was the immediate establishment of the broad-based transitional government (BBTG). At Arusha the parties had agreed to establish the BBTG immediately, but opposition to the accords from the extreme right had blocked the implementation of this key provision.[65] The security situation, meanwhile, was becoming increasingly shaky, with periodic bouts of ethnic violence. Many observers believed that there was a strong connection between the paralysis in the peace process and the deteriorating security environment: the failure to establish the transitional government contributed to the deteriorating security environment, and the deteriorating security environment delayed the establishment of the transitional government. The only way to escape this infinite loop, according to UN staff, was to establish the BBTG.[66] In this view, the political process would accomplish what a military adventure could not, and without the risks. Although Dallaire kept insisting that a more forceful security presence was required to give the parties the confidence to establish the BBTG, the Secretariat's firm line was that he was to operate with the consent of the parties.[67]

The peacekeeping culture and DPKO's fixation on the rules of impartiality and consent also provide insight into why DPKO apparently minimized the threat of violence to civilians and peacekeepers. Recall that the informant said that extremists were planning to launch an attack on peacekeepers devastating enough to drive them out of the country, creating a clear killing field. Many commentators have expressed dismay that DPKO failed to take more seriously these threats to the operation and to civilians.[68]

The Secretariat defended its actions by insisting that DPKO's interpretation of the telegram's contents was reasonable given the types of messages that typically arrived from peacekeeping operations. Boutros-Ghali observed that while reports such as those contained in the January 11 telegram are treated with "utmost seriousness by UN officials, [they] are not uncommon within the context of peace-keeping operations."[69] Although Riza conceded that the telegram was unusual because DPKO did not typically receive messages foretelling violence "of this magnitude" or "with such predictions," it was still "a normal cable . . . [and] there are a number of cables that we get of this nature."[70] Because peacekeeping operations are by definition located in trouble spots where violence is either latent or manifest, there is a steady stream of reports of planned military activities by various local parties that portend an inflammation of violence and unrest. As bureaucrats who had accumulated considerable experience and expertise overseeing operations in many different locales, DPKO staff treated the violence in Rwanda as similar to the violence that had appeared in other postconflict settings.

The telegram was given high-level and unusual treatment, but in a manner consistent with what one would expect from a peacekeeping culture that fixes on the rules of neutrality and impartiality. As Riza stated, rarely do force commanders send messages predicting imminent attacks against peacekeepers and civilians, and high-ranking DPKO staff took the unusual step of conferring late at night to formulate an immediate response. But the evidence suggests that DPKO was animated not by predictions of violence but rather by Dallaire's proposed raid. Dallaire's response was a gross departure from DPKO's established routines for dealing with possible violence. Although UNAMIR peacekeepers had begun to confiscate weapons that had crossed their paths in public locations, it was quite another matter to aggressively seek out and seize weapons hidden in highly sensitive political locations. In its view, if the raid failed it would probably have fateful consequences for the operation and the UN. The botched raid in Somalia had led to dead peacekeepers, the virtual collapse of the United Nations Operation in Somalia, and a flurry of criticism leveled at the organization.

Consequently, DPKO viewed Dallaire's plan as inappropriate and dangerous. Evidence in support of this conclusion is contained in the closing words of DPKO's responding cable, which drew a connection between a departure from impartiality and dangers to the mission and the organization: "If you have major problems with the guidance provided above, you may consult us further. We wish to stress, however, that the overriding consideration is the need to avoid entering into a course of action that might lead to the use of force and unanticipated consequences. Regards." As Boutros-Ghali later reflected, "DPKO . . . emphasized that the responsibility for the maintenance of law and order must remain with the local authorities and that, while UNAMIR could assist in arms recovery operations, it should avoid entering into a course of action that might lead to the use of force and to unanticipated repercussions."[71] Following recent events in Somalia, undoubtedly the "unanticipated consequences" and "repercussions" included not only a failed mission but also a badly damaged organization.

In summary, the peacekeeping culture influenced the Secretariat's response to Dallaire's plan in various ways. Certainly the decision was consistent with the Council's preferences. But there is evidence that DPKO overruled the plan not because of the Council's anticipated opposition but because it independently concluded that the planned raid violated the rules of peacekeeping. Violations of the cease-fire and the mandate were to be taken seriously and reported, but peacekeeping forces should not use enforcement mechanisms to compel the parties to honor their commitments and fulfill the mandate. This was not only appropriate but prudent. If the operation failed, the effects might be devastating for the operation and the organization. Consequently, Dallaire should use consensual means, impressing upon the president that this clear violation of the cease-fire would not be tolerated and encouraging the parties to take the necessary political steps to get the peace process back on track and reduce the likelihood of a security meltdown.

The period between the secretary-general's December 30 interim report on Rwanda and the end of the six-month mandate in early April 1994 was defined by paralysis on the political front and deterioration on the security front. By early spring the violence had become so constant and alarming that the UN and members of the contact group (the United States, France, and Belgium) publicized the widespread killings and the dangers they posed to the Arusha Accords, the cease-fire between the RPF and the Rwandan government, and the overall success of the mission. Dallaire's cables repeatedly drew attention to the disintegrating security situation and requested permission to take deterrent action and seize the hidden weapons.[72] Dallaire was not alone in calling for a more forceful engagement. The Belgian foreign minister also appealed to the Secretariat for enforcement action, but he was equally unsuccessful.[73] Those requests were repeatedly denied by Boutros-Ghali and Kofi Annan, who insisted that the success of the operation was dependent on the will and consent of the parties and that the only way to confront the spiraling violence was by establishing the transitional government.[74]

UNAMIR's six-month mandate came up for renewal at the end of March, when the failure of the parties to establish the BBTG caused considerable debate in the Council over whether and for how long to renew the mandate. Eventually the Security Council overcame the initial objections of the United States and renewed the mandate, though for a more limited term, insisting that any renewal was dependent on the establishment of the BBTG. The Security Council approved a three-month extension on April 4 just as the mandate expired.

See No Genocide

On April 6 President Habyarimana was flying back from Dar-as-Salaam, where he was rumored to have overcome the remaining objections to the transitional government. The plane was shot down on the approach to the Kigali airport, killing both him and the president of Burundi. After the crash, the Rwandan military and the Interhamwe erected roadblocks around the city and began to round up and murder Tutsi politicians and moderate Hutus. A few days later the RPF and the Hutu government renewed the civil war. The Arusha Accords were for all intents and purposes dead. Within a few days civilian killings were spreading out of control. With only twenty-five hundred lightly armed peacekeepers scattered throughout an increasingly dangerous Rwanda, not only was UNAMIR unable to do much but its own existence was in peril. Ten Belgian peacekeepers were brutally murdered while protecting Madame Agathe Uwilingiyimana, the prime minister, on April 7. The UN feared that the remaining Belgian troops were marked for assassination and that the other troops were in danger because of the security situation and the lack of fuel, water, and food. Moreover, resupplying or rescuing the force was becoming difficult as the airport became a major battleground, increasing the risk for any approaching aircraft. The meager and badly supplied UN force was surrounded by a civil war and a civilian massacre.

After two weeks of debate, on April 21 the Security Council passed by consensus resolution 912, which reduced UNAMIR to two hundred fifty troops and restricted its mandate to the attempt to negotiate a cease-fire between the Rwandan military and the RPF. There were several reasons why it decided not to intervene. The Council wanted to protect the remaining peacekeepers, who were part of a fraying operation in a highly dangerous situation. No troops were available to reinforce the operation. The rules of peacekeeping told the Council to intervene only when there was a peace to keep, and recent events—including Somalia and a renewed crisis in the safe havens in Bosnia—reinforced the view that the UN was ineffective in active conflicts. The Security Council recognized the mass killings but focused on the civil war and treated the latter as the cause of the former.[75]

These same factors weighed heavily on the Secretariat and help to explain why it, too, was cool to intervention. But at the very moment the killings began, Roméo Dallaire communicated two critical pieces of information to DPKO and Boutros-Ghali that one might think would have caused the Secretariat to give greater consideration to an intervention.[76] Dallaire emphasized that the violence was not anarchic but organized. In an April 8 cable, he wrote:

> THE APPEARANCE OF A VERY WELL PLANNED, ORGANIZED, DELIBERATE AND CONDUCTED CAMPAIGN OF TERROR INITIATED PRINCIPALLY BY THE PRESIDENTIAL GUARD SINCE THE MORNING AFTER THE DEATH OF THE HEAD OF STATE HAS COMPLETELY REORIENTED THE SITUATION IN KIGALI. AGGRESSIVE ACTIONS HAVE BEEN TAKEN NOT ONLY AGAINST THE OPPOSITION LEADERSHIP BUT AGAINST THE RPF, AGAINST PARTICULAR ETHNIC GROUPS (MASSACRE OF CIVILIANS IN REMERA), AGAINST THE GENERAL CIVILIAN POPULATION (BANDITRY) AND AGAINST UNAMIR. DIRECT AND INDIRECT FIRE ON U.N. INSTALLATIONS, VEHICLES, PERSONNEL AND AFFILIATED AGENCIES (I.E. UNDP) WHICH HAS RESULTED IN FATAL AND NONFATAL CASUALTIES.[77]

In addition to sending cables, Dallaire claims that he highlighted ethnic cleansing in his daily telephone calls to headquarters.[78]

Dallaire also demanded reinforcements and an intervention in order to reestablish the cease-fire.[79] At the time he argued that if the international community showed its resolve and deployed reinforcements, then the Interahamwe and the presidential guard could be induced to halt their plans, the killings could be stopped, and the cease-fire could be restored. Hours after the plane crash Dallaire sent a message to New York saying, "Give me the means and I can do more." DPKO's immediate reply was that "nobody is interested in that."[80] There was a repeated cycle of requests for troops and their denial for the next several weeks.[81]

The failure of the Secretariat to relay information to the Security Council is puzzling. Simply put, there was a gap between what Dallaire was telling the Secretariat and what the Secretariat was telling the Security Council. Dallaire provided meticulous and graphic accounts of the violence, a diagnosis of the source of the violence, and constructive and conservative prescriptions for ending the violence. Specifically, Dallaire clearly articulated that alongside the civil war between the Rwandan government and the RPF there was a well-organized campaign to kill Tutsi civilians being carried out by the presidential guard, the Interhamwe, and other extremist militias. According to Dallaire, therefore, Rwanda was a civil war *and* a site of ethnic cleansing and crimes against humanity. The only chance to stop the ethnic cleansing, he argued, was a forceful response by the international community. Yet in its presentations to the Security Council, the Secretariat portrayed the violence as chaotic and related to the civil war and suggested that the killings were spontaneous, perpetrated by both ethnic groups, and not organized. It provided no concrete suggestions for reinforcing the mandate or stopping the violence.[82] Why did the secretary-general's office fail to bring Dallaire's analysis to the attention of the Security Council during its first two weeks of debates?

Again, it is possibile that the Secretariat was anticipating or responding to the wishes of the Security Council and decided to tell it what it wanted to hear. The problem with this explanation is that there is no evidence that the Secretariat was self-censoring. The various reports and inquiries into the Secretariat's behavior have not uncovered any systematic evidence that it privately desired an intervention but felt compelled to articulate an alternative course of action. By Dallaire's account, indeed, DPKO and the secretary-general failed to give him any encouragement for his proposed course of action; they concluded days after April 6 that the troops should be withdrawn, and insisted that UNAMIR must adhere to passive rules of engagement.[83] Even DPKO officials have not claimed that their failure to advocate intervention was caused by their deference to the preferences of powerful members of the Council.

Rather, the same peacekeeping culture that shaped the Secretariat's pre-April response also contributed to its categorization of and response to the deteriorating security situation in April and May when the genocide occurred. As various UN officials have defended their failure to transmit Dallaire's information to the Security Council, they have frequently insinuated that their "mistakes" came from a misinterpretation of the situation.[84] This "misinterpretation" had roots in the rules of peacekeeping. These rules led the Secretariat to receive and interpret new information in ways consistent with its pre-April understanding. It led the Secretariat to categorize Rwanda as a civil war and to conclude that peacekeeping was not an appropriate response.[85]

This explanation of the failure is consistent with arguments made by organizational theorists, who have noted that those in organizations tend to use the available scripts and rules to interpret information, and that past understandings generate a "systematic bias in favor of information consistent with information that we have already assimilated."[86] The tendency to cling to preexisting beliefs and to reach premature closure is heightened during a crisis, when decision makers are operating under tremendous stress. Under such circumstances they do not have time to collect all available information and determine the probabilities of all the possible consequences of different policies. Abridging the decision-making process, however, can introduce biases. One bias comes from the fact that decision makers, like all individuals, usually rely on their personal experiences to judge the likelihood of an outcome. In addition, people tend to pay more attention to negative than to positive events. These biases can lead them to overestimate the possibility of major perils.[87]

The evidence suggests that these factors weighed heavily in shaping the Secretariat's understanding of Rwanda as a civil war to the neglect of the crimes against humanity. The crisis situation, moreover, might have made it much less receptive to alternative information, information that might have caused it to focus on the crimes against humanity. The willingness to stick to these existing assessments arguably was reinforced by the fear of the political consequences for the organization if it intervened and failed.

Once a Civil War, Always a Civil War

A core problem for UN staff was figuring out what kind of situation Rwanda was. Before individuals can know how to act, they must first define the situation and create a representation of the problem.[88] In this context, the pressing issue was how to categorize the violence. There was no doubting the return of civil war between the RPF and the Hutu government. There also was no doubting the rapid pace and scale of the civilian killings. But there was uncertainty regarding the exact nature of the killings and their relationship to the civil war. These killings might have been an offshoot of the civil war. Or individuals from the different ethnic groups might have been using the opportunity created by renewed war to replay what some viewed as ancient ethnic hatreds. Finally, it was possibile that the ethnic killings were organized and directed by extremists from one population group against the other. How the Secretariat categorized the violence in Rwanda had important consequences for its recommended action. If it saw the violence as civil war or longstanding mutual ethnic conflict, then, according to the rules, peacekeeping was not appropriate. If it saw the violence as organized ethnic extermination, then there was a justification for intervention.

The Secretariat continually emphasized the civil war and treated the civilian killings as a manifestation of that war.[89] This conclusion followed from the Secretariat's prior way of categorizing Rwanda and its previous understanding and predictions of what sort of violence would follow if the Arusha Accords collapsed. It was a civil war that had led to the Arusha Accords, and UNAMIR was established to monitor the cease-fire between the warring parties and to help oversee the Arusha Accords. For the most part headquarters explained the pre-April violence as an endemic part of all political transitions, compounded in Rwanda by the failure of the parties to establish the transitional institutions. The pre-April violence, in other words, was connected to the stalled political process and not to preparations for a genocide. Accordingly, those in New York linked the eruption of violence after 6 April to the return of civil war. Riza explained that he and other UN officials mistakenly viewed the ethnic killings as related to the political process:

> Everybody was concentrating on the political aspects [meaning the Arusha Accords and the transition government]. Everyone was preoccupied with a political solution. A transitional government should have been established by the thirty-first of December. Here we were going through January, February, and March without this government. This was the first priority, and [we] had the conviction . . . that if they had a political solution, then the violence would subside. In other words, the violence was not connected to a planning of a genocide, nobody saw it like that. *It was seen as a result of a political deadlock.*[90]

Because UN officials tended to see the pre-April violence as connected to a political process that was designed to end a civil war, it continued to see the post-April violence as part of a political process that had collapsed into civil war.[91] Because, as Riza observed, "our mandate was not to anticipate and prevent genocide," the Secretariat could not see it coming.[92] The Secretariat's mandate was to anticipate and help stop a civil war from returning, so that was all it could see.

The presumption that an ethnic civil war would lead to mutual killings also followed from the UN's prior understandings of the nature of the violence. Ethnic killings in Rwanda, observed Iqbal Riza, had deep roots, dating back to 1960.[93] The ethnic violence that the UN was now witnessing was nothing new, in his view. Because this was an ethnic conflict, then almost by definition the killings were reciprocal. Along these lines, Boutros-Ghali consistently portrayed the violence as part of ethnic conflict and time and again called on both parties to stop targeting civilians.[94] Thus the Secretariat was inclined to presume that this recent round of fighting was the latest installment of a long pattern.

The fact that the Secretariat was operating under tremendous stress also means that it would have been highly resistant to alternative information that might have contradicted its initial assessment. Research on decision making within organizations in similar situations suggests that UN officials would reach "premature cognitive closure," interpreting new information so that it remained consistent with past interpretations and disregarding new information that was inconsistent with them. This helps to explain the UN failure to incorporate fully the significance of Dallaire's observations. To complicate matters, UNAMIR was providing different assessments of the situation to DPKO in New York. While Dallaire was painting a very bleak picture of a situation that might be arrested with a determined action by the international community, the secretary-general's special representative there, Jacques Booh-Booh, was offering a different assessment that suggested that the UN should withdraw (and Booh-Booh led by example when he departed Kigali for Nairobi on April 21).[95] Such conflicting interpretations undoubtedly reinforced the tendency of the Secretariat to rely on its initial assessments.

The definition of Rwanda as a civil war also would have been reinforced by how DPKO evaluated the gains from a successful intervention relative to the losses from a failed intervention. The gains to be made from halting a civil war and stopping civilian bloodshed were difficult to calculate. In this post-Somalia environment, where the Secretariat believed that the chances of success were low and that its next failure might be its last, it understood that a failed intervention would have disastrous consequences for the organization. Consequently, UN officials had little incentive to incorporate information that might point them toward an intervention.

The desire to play it safe may have led not only to a passive stance with respect to how incoming information was interpreted, but also to an unwillingness to ask tough questions that might have forced officials to reassess the need for an intervention that they did not want. For instance, the secretary-general had only one brief phone call with Dallaire before April 21; in this momentary exchange, Boutros-Ghali told Dallaire to prepare to evacuate Kigali and did not bother to ask Dallaire for his observations or recommendations.[96] Indeed, in Dallaire's account New York was most concerned about how to evacuate the foreign nationals and UNAMIR forces and asked remarkably few questions about the nature of the civilian killings. New York apparently did not want to ask any questions that might generate uncomfortable answers.[97]

If a Civil War, Then . . .

The Secretariat opposed intervention during these first weeks. Its opposition is evident in the way it presented this option to the Security Council and member states, in both formal and informal discussions. Although the secretary-general occasionally listed intervention and reinforcement of the troops as a possibility, he almost always did so in a manner that directed conversation away from a serious consideration. In the Security Council the secretary-general continually emphasized the need to protect the UN forces and insisted that if they could not be protected through the immediate dispatch of reinforcements then they would have to be withdrawn from Rwanda.[98] The Secretariat's communications with possible troop contributors also discouraged them from signing up. As Dallaire writes, "We had been forwarding our radio logs to the UN at the end of the day, as requested by the DPKO, a practice we carried on until the end. I thought that if the UN knew what we were dealing with day to day, someone might still come to our aid. Instead, the log was used to inform troop-contributing nations of the state of risk to their national contingents, effectively scaring them off."[99] When the secretary-general finally did present an intervention option to the Council on April 20, he insinuated that UNAMIR was asking for ten thousand troops, while Dallaire was requesting reinforcements of only five thousand.[100] According to Dallaire, "Maurice [Baril, DPKO's military advisor] had made it very clear to me on several occasions that no one was interested in Rwanda, and now, because of the escalating risks, they were even less interested."[101]

There are several reasons why the secretary-general would have opposed intervention. The troops on the ground were hardly in shape to undertake complex military operations. Basic provisions were running dangerously low, and the Belgian troops, the backbone of the operation, were planning to depart, leaving behind a military force of decidedly uneven quality—a point continually emphasized by Dallaire in his communications with headquarters.[102] These factors certainly influenced the secretary-general's desire to withdraw the peacekeepers to a safe location, a view that he first expressed in his April 9 letter to the Security Council, outlining the possibly unavoidable need to evacuate UN personnel and foreign nationals, and that he emphasized over the next thirteen days.[103]

Also, because Rwanda was a civil war there was no basis for intervention. The rules of peacekeeping now prohibited peacekeeping in a civil war and in the absence of a stable cease-fire. The Arusha Accords and the cease-fire had been replaced by the return of civil war between the RPF and the Rwandan army. To compound matters, the RPF, worried that a UN intervention might be a cover for another effort by the French to rescue their Hutu allies, warned that it might treat a UN force as hostile. The rules of peacekeeping, therefore, advised against intervention. Proceeding in this direction was both appropriate and would avoid the risk of another failure in the field that might cause collateral damage to the organization.

The rules of peacekeeping not only discouraged the Secretariat from recommending an intervention but also shaped its position on how peacekeepers might be used in this volatile situation. The Secretariat warned UNAMIR against undertaking a protection operation.[104] The rules of impartiality and consent combined with recent experiences in Somalia and Bosnia suggested that peacekeeping was unable to play that protection role, and Dallaire's own uncomplimentary assessment of the condition of his troops certainly reinforced those conclusions. Consequently, beginning April 7 and then continuing throughout this critical period, the Secretariat commanded UNAMIR not to undertake protection operations or to defend civilians—even though paragraph 17 of the rules of engagement allowed UNAMIR to use its weapons to protect civilians against crimes against humanity.[105] On the morning of April 7, Iqbal Riza instructed Dallaire "not to fire unless fired upon."[106] On April 15, DPKO suggested that the Security Council should consider whether peacekeeping operations should be assigned such tasks as protecting civilians.[107] A few days later, when the Secretariat was actively considering the withdrawal option, DPKO instructed UNAMIR to consider how to transfer the civilian populations to one of the belligerents, stating that these populations had "taken refuge" and failing to acknowledge that they were under "UN protection."[108]

The rules of peacekeeping also made it difficult for the Secretariat to imagine a military option that simply protected civilians from harm rather than actively fighting the Hutu government. The difficulty in imagining such an option was undoubtedly reinforced by the simultaneous crisis in Gorazde, a safe haven in Bosnia that was under attack by Bosnian Serb forces. "Options to reinforce UNAMIR were always put by the Secretariat in terms of an enforcement operation, suggesting intervention between the two armies, rather than maintaining or increasing troop strength to protect civilians."[109] This was the case even though UNAMIR was actively engaged in such protection exercises, sometimes with as few as a handful of soldiers guarding thousands of individuals.

If an intervention was inappropriate and unwarranted, and if protection was dangerous, then the Secretariat's time and resources were best spent trying to arrange a cease-fire. From the opening shot of the war on April 6 through its end several months later, the Security Council and the Secretariat concentrated their energies on securing a cease-fire between the warring parties. Indeed, this is a nearly standardized response by the Secretariat to any sort of violence, present in other circumstances and equally present in the face of war crimes.[110] Although this might have been the only reasonable option, the UN continued to seek a cease-fire even when it became abundantly clear that an RPF victory represented the only possible end to the genocide, that no cease-fire was obtainable, and that a cease-fire might accelerate the ethnic cleansing because it would allow the *génocidaires* to concentrate their energies on the killings.[111] The cease-fire was both an end and a means to an end, which goes some distance toward explaining why the Secretariat (and others in New York) was so fixated on the need for a cease-fire to the neglect of all other possibilities such as protecting civilians. The insistence on the cease-fire above and beyond all other policy responses derived from a culture of consent and neutrality.

The Road Not Taken

There is no way of knowing whether an alternative representation of Rwanda by the secretary-general might have altered the Council's decision, but there is counterfactual evidence to suggest it might have. The delegated, expert, and moral authority of the secretary-general and Secretariat provided levers that might have been used to follow a different course. In constructing the UN, states delegated some agenda-setting power to the staff. The Secretariat is expected to write a report and deliver informal observations and recommendations prior to the Council's debate. Its observations frequently provide the parameters of the Council's discussions, shaping which options are given serious or slight consideration. The Secretariat has some expertise gained from its experience in various peacekeeping operations. It also has moral authority that flows from the presumption that it is more impartial and unbiased than states.[112]

During the first week of the crisis beginning on April 6, the Secretariat had the opportunity to use its authority to seize the initiative and help define the Security Council's policy toward Rwanda. As made clear by various reports, the future of UNAMIR was still an open question because Belgium was still on the ground. There was a debate in the Council over the efficacy and purpose of an intervention, and the Council was actively seeking information and recommendations from the Secretariat.[113] The secretary-general, therefore, could have used his delegated, expert, and moral authority to shape the debate. The UN was assumed to have more accurate and detailed information regarding what was happening because its forces were still present while the diplomatic corps was evacuating Rwanda; therefore, its possession of information and experience gave it expert authority to shape what constituted reasonable and unreasonable options given the circumstances. The secretary-general also had the moral authority to make a principled case for an array of options. Ibrahim Gambari, who at the time was Nigeria's ambassador to the UN and the nominal head of the nonaligned bloc in the Security Council, has speculated that had Boutros-Ghali made the case for a modest intervention to stop crimes against humanity, it might have changed the Council's decision. "If the secretary-general had made a pitch [for intervention] then it would have given us moral backing, it might have really changed things. Yes, it would have highlighted the double standard [lots of assistance for Europe and nothing for Africa]."[114] As it was, Boutros-Ghali's authority and presentation reinforced the positions of those who argued that the rules of peacekeeping meant that there was no basis for an intervention.

IV. PEACEKEEPING AND THE IDEOLOGY OF IMPARTIALITY

There are good reasons why most standard explanations for the UN's role in international peace and security focus on the states of the Security Council and not the staff of the Secretariat. The Security Council was designed to give privileges and provide protections to the Great Powers. Powerful states on the Security Council usually control what does and does not happen. The UN Charter provides for few formal avenues of autonomy for the secretary-general or his staff. The Security Council members, and especially the veto-wielding states, keep a close watch on the Secretariat and have demonstrated a reluctance to allow the office to gain much autonomy in critical matters of international peace and security. What autonomy the secretary-general has derives largely from his authority. He is "in authority" owing to the formal roles delegated to his office and "an authority" owing to his moral position and his standing as a representative of the international community.

This limited authority of the secretary-general means he can rarely engage in policy that runs against the well-defined interests of powerful states. He can try to reframe policy to fit within those interests or help states recognize additional interests, but direct opposition is unlikely to be successful. An example is the creation and expansion of peacekeeping. Although Dag Hammarskjöld and Boutros Boutros-Ghali, respectively, were able to use their authority and autonomy to help create peacekeeping and then develop second-generation peacekeeping operations, these actions were supported by key member states. Others agreed because they were persuaded by staff (and other states) that these changes served their interests. When this ceased to be true (for example, after Somalia and Bosnia), the secretary-general had little choice but to back off. States were not providing the resources and support required for a growing agenda of intervention and conflict management, and the organization's inability to deliver good results was endangering its very survival. In these circumstances, retrenchment was attractive. Returning to the organization's original rules of peacekeeping in limited, consensual circumstances protected the UN's credibility and ensured its survival.

Yet return to these rules regardless of the circumstances meant that the organization had no tools to deal with violent humanitarian crises. In fact, the rules generated indifference to such crises. They created an organizational culture where it was tolerable, even desirable, to disregard mass violations of human rights not only in Rwanda but elsewhere, most famously in Srebrenica in July 1995. Rwanda, in this respect, was not an unfortunate mistake. It was the predictable result of an organizational culture that shaped how the UN evaluated and responded to violent crises.

One important piece of evidence that Rwanda was symptomatic of a pathology has been the legitimacy crisis caused by the staff's failure to at least try to stop the genocide. The apparent willingness of the UN to subvert its own self-professed goals of humanitarianism and protection of human rights led many observers to question the legitimacy of the UN, and UN staff also felt themselves to be facing a crisis of authority in part because they had failed to do what was expected of them during the onset of the genocide. The paradox here is that at the time of the Rwandan crisis the Secretariat's self-understanding of how to best preserve its moral authority was tied to the rules of consent and impartiality. But soon thereafter it was the willingness to adhere to these rules in the face of genocide that threatened its moral authority as perceived by many publics. Although UN officials tried to put the best face on their actions, relentless questions and pressure forced them to begin to acknowledge that their behavior was unbecoming and that perhaps part of the reason was the emergence of an "institutional ideology of impartiality."[115]

Kofi Annan attempted to address this ideology, in part by encouraging member states to reconsider the rules governing humanitarian intervention. In his address to the General Assembly in 1999, an address that followed the UN's failings in Bosnia and Rwanda and the controversial interventions in Kosovo and East Timor, he made an argument in favor of a duty to intervene in the face of crimes against humanity, citing Rwanda as an exemplary case.[116] Presumably making the case for humanitarian intervention will send a signal to UN staff that humanitarian concerns must always be considered when weighing the possibility and desirability of intervention. Annan's insistence that the UN and the international community develop a consensus regarding how humanitarian interventions are to be conducted also represented his attempt to use the UN's moral authority to create an international environment that might allow the Secretariat to better carry out the organization's humanitarian assistance goals.

6

THE LEGITIMACY OF AN EXPANDING GLOBAL BUREAUCRACY

International organizations are central actors on the stage of world politics. They are not simply passive collections of rules or structures through which others act. Rather, they are active agents of global change. They develop new policy ideas and programs, manage crises, and set priorities for shared activities that would not exist otherwise. They do not work in a vacuum. States, NGOs, business firms, and other IOs all may have a hand, sometimes a heavy hand, in an IO's work. The fact that IOs have autonomy does not, after all, make them omnipotent. Their attempts to coerce, persuade, bargain, and otherwise shape the actions of others may encounter varying degrees of resistance or cooptation, just as we see in all relationships among international actors. But without understanding the contribution of IOs to political processes and outcomes, we cannot understand the very character, evolution, and regulation of the modern international polity. A world without IOs would be a very different world from the one in which we live.

If IOs are autonomous actors in world politics, then it becomes important to ask: What kinds of actors are they? How do they behave? What purposes do they pursue? and What sorts of effects do they have? A central goal of this book has been to develop theoretical tools for answering these questions. Starting from the fact that IOs are bureaucracies, we have developed expectations about the sources of their autonomy, how they exercise power, the kinds of dysfunction they might exhibit, and how they might evolve. Each of our cases explored these issues, refining and investigating hypotheses in different ways.

In this concluding chapter we explore two issues that cut across our cases and raise profound questions about the relationship between international organizations and the changing nature of both world politics and global governance. First, we examine the matter of organizational change and expansion. The IOs we examined have steadily expanded in both size and mandate since their founding, a characteristic common to many IOs. To the extent that IR theory has considered this phenomenon, it would expect this expansion to be the result of delegation from states. Theories of the bureaucracy and our cases, however, suggest that dynamics originating within IOs themselves play an important role. Further, most IR theorists would expect expanded IO activity to be focused on promoting interstate cooperation, which they see as the primary function of IOs. However, many of these bigger IOs are tackling issues that extend far beyond the regulation of interstate relations. They are creating new actors, tasks, and goals that transform the character of global politics itself.

Second, we ask: Is this expansion that is producing an increasingly bureaucratized world a good thing? One's theoretical starting points tend to drive one's normative conclusions. Those who adopt liberal or neoliberal theoretical precepts tend to see expanding IOs as positive because international organizations help to resolve collective dilemmas and problems of interdependent choice, foster international cooperation, and bring about a more rationalized world that is organized around fundamental liberal values such as liberty, autonomy, markets, democracy, and nonviolent conflict resolution.

Adopting a bureaucratic starting point, though, leads to a more mixed normative position. International organizations do perform important and valuable functions, but they also carry costs. These costs, moreover, arguably expand as IOs expand, and they pose serious challenges to the legitimacy of IOs that we explore in the concluding section. On the one hand, action by IOs is accepted as legitimate because IOs are perceived as rational, technical, and relatively objective servants of widely shared values most of which are broadly liberal in character. The IMF, UNHCR, and the UN respectively pursue financial stability through markets, refugee protection through rule of law with human rights, and peacekeeping with relative impartiality. However, IOs have never received high marks as exemplars of democratic decision making, and as they take on more and more functions their lack of accountability and transparency has raised serious questions about their procedural legitimacy. One consequence of global bureaucratization, then, is undemocratic liberalism. Although IOs might be celebrated because of the liberal values that they claim to champion, their increasingly detached and undemocratic character should be of concern to scholars and practitioners alike.

I. ORGANIZATIONAL EVOLUTION AND EXPANSION

International relations scholars have given little thought to the evolution of international organizations in large part because they have been fixated on the conditions under which states establish IOs and why they design IOs the way they do.[1] To the extent they do think about IO change, most IR theorists assume that factors outside IOs—state demands or environmental changes—are its cause; they cannot accommodate the notion that IOs might be agents in their own evolution. Realist theories presume that because Great Powers control IOs, any change must come from Great Powers' demands. Neoliberal institutionalism, similarly, suggests that IO change will be a reflection of changing state preferences and a functional need to be more efficient and effective.[2] Although world polity perspectives decenter the state and foreground a global culture, they, too, are ill equipped to imagine how IOs might be agents shaping their own futures because they hold that the global cultural environment constitutes IOs and drives their behavior. Principal-agent approaches acknowledge that IOs are purposeful actors that presumably might pursue internal reorganization and initiate their expansion into new areas, but because they lack any explanation of IO interests, they cannot say what changes IOs will pursue or why.[3]

IOs change for reasons that cannot be attributed to state demands or external pressures alone. Instead, IOs are active agents in their own change. States did not command the IMF to adopt a more ambitious policy regarding balance-of-payments difficulties; IMF staff were involved in making sense of past failures and argued for new policy directions as a way of trying to fulfill their basic mandates. UNHCR expanded its orbit by persuading states that it could play a useful function in new areas of the world and in new policy domains. After the Cold War the Secretariat was actively involved in helping to imagine what sort of programs and functions it might perform as it took on new peacekeeping and peace-building operations. States certainly played a role in these changes. They may initiate change with calls for reform, and they may block (or slow) it, but IOs themselves play a large role in determining the character and content of that change.

To Expand or Not to Expand?

If IOs have some control over their evolution, when, why, and how will they choose to change? To take up the "when" question first, IOs do not always choose to take on new tasks. While the overall trend line suggests that IOs are expanding in size and scope, there are moments when IOs resist opportunities and even explicit invitations to expand. These moments are theoretically important for two reasons. First, they provide further evidence of IO autonomy. Many of our examples of autonomy in this book concern new tasks IOs take on, but, logically, resistence to new tasks that states or others push on IOs is also evidence of autonomous action. IOs are not always imperialistic and sometimes even resist requests to increase the scope of their responsibilities. For a long time the IMF and World Bank rejected demands by powerful states to extend their economic analyses to include social and environmental policies. When they finally relented, they did so in a way that largely changed the formal requirements for these analyses but kept in place the informal norms that minimized their impact.[4] In early 2000 UNHCR resisted an invitation by the Security Council to add responsibility for protecting all internally displaced persons (IDPs) to its existing mandate to protect refugees (who have crossed an international border).

The second reason why these moments of self-control are theoretically interesting is that they draw attention to the fundamental question of IO interests. What do IOs want that would lead them to resist (or pursue) expansion? Realism and neoliberal institutionalism have not given this question much thought, largely because these theories presume that states hand IOs their interests. Scholars who do treat IOs as actors, like principal-agent analysts, either impute interests that are unsustainable empirically (for example, they assume that IOs want to maximize their budget, which makes little sense for IOs such as the IMF that are not funded through budgetary appropriation), or induce interests from their empirical data, which is hard to justify theoretically in these frameworks.[5]

The sociological perspectives, on which we draw, make IO interests a subject of inquiry rather than assuming them and make bureaucratic culture central to the investigation. Our conceptual apparatus and empirical studies suggest that delegated mandates, as well as professional norms and moral principles, are all important sources of IO interests. Our empirical studies reveal the active processes of debate and contestation within these organizations as staff draw on these sources to make sense of new situations, articulate new goals, and develop new rules that will make their organizations relevant to member states and other constituencies. Our studies also suggest that IO staff can, at times, decide that the organization is best served by staying close to home and doing what it does best.[6] IO staff can be reluctant to take on new missions if they believe they lack the expertise and organizational mandates to carry them out, or if they believe the missions will take them into politicized areas that might compromise their authority (and thus a source of their autonomy).

Our cases suggest, however, that over time the debates and contestations within large public bureaucracies tend to yield self-understandings and interests that favor expansion, and our theoretical understanding of the nature of bureaucracies provides several reasons why. Specifically, our cases suggest that the sources of IOs' authority provide part of the answer. Most large IOs are created with broad aspirational goals that legitimate them as actors and represent an important source of their authority. The IMF's broad mandate is to promote stability and growth in the world economy, UNHCR's is to protect refugees, the UN's is to promote peace and security. These are widely shared social values, and serving these broad goals is crucial to legitimating these IOs as actors. However, IOs are also created as pragmatic political compromises, usually with deep limitations imposed by suspicious states on their organizational capacities and mandates. Thus, IOs are authorized and empowered by moral or aspirational claims that are much broader than their specific mandates or capacities. Over time, the former tend to exert pressure on the latter: limited organizational structures make it impossible to fulfill broad mandates, creating reasons for diverse actors to press for organizational change, usually expansion.

The cases suggest several specific mechanisms by which this expansion might come about. One is learning from failure. If the organization has broad goals but limited range of action, it is unlikely to succeed in many of its endeavors. Learning from past failures, staff are likely to draw the conclusion that to carry out their mandate they need to expand their sphere of action, and they use failure to push states to allow this. For example, IMF staff did not expand conditionality eagerly, in pursuit of more turf, but reluctantly as a result of failure.[7] The organization's consistent inability to stabilize many borrower economies led staff to conclude that more and more aspects of the economy needed to be incorporated into stabilization efforts. Many staff (and state members) would have preferred a narrower mission, but prevailing economic expertise at the Fund told staff that they could accomplish their mission only by tackling new and different features of economic life in their borrower members. Dictating public spending and other aspects of the economy would have been considered unacceptable interference in domestic affairs at the time of the Fund's founding. It has become routine as staff (and others) have "learned" that involvement in such matters is essential to overall stabilization.

A related and more general form of this phenomenon is the way broad legitimating principles motivate people both inside and outside the organization to push for expansions beyond limited mandates and structures. Broad legitimating principles often sit uneasily inside bureaucratic boundaries and structural constraints. People animated by and committed to the moral claims or expertise underpinning the organization are likely to chafe at these bureaucratic strictures. At UNHCR, pressure to expand came from a mismatch between the organization's originally limited capacities and the general principles of refugee protection that legitimated it. States created UNHCR to handle refugee problems in Europe that were caused by events that occurred prior to 1951. Yet UNHCR's authority comes from universal humanitarian principles that logically and ethically should apply everywhere. From early on, staff, states, and other concerned actors animated by these moral principles pushed for expanded protection. World political events conveniently supplied a steady stream of refugee crises around which to make these appeals. In repeated cases, states agreed, some readily, others grudgingly, to accept the claim advanced by UNHCR that it could play an important and impartial role in solving these refugee problems and that there was no ethical defense for protecting refugees in Europe but ignoring them elsewhere.

The Secretariat's role in the creation of peacekeeping also can be understood as a result of its willingness to capitalize on world events to allow the organization to make positive contributions to the broad mission legitimating the organization—promoting peace and security. States delegated an extremely broad mission to the UN without simultaneously creating the organizational infrastructure to carry out those tasks. This gap between the organization's raison d'être and organizational constraints that made it impossible to carry out that mandate meant that the organization was both irrelevant and ineffective. Peacekeeping can be understood as the result of efforts by UN staff to address these broad goals under severe geopolitical and resource constraints in a pragmatic but influential way. The post–Cold War expansion and development of peacekeeping represented another impressive instance in which the organization capitalized on new environmental circumstances to extend its already existing tools for conflict resolution into new areas.

Change driven by this mismatch between broad goals and limited organizational capacity is one manifestation of a general bureaucratic characteristic, noted in chapter 2. Bureaucracies, by their nature, try to rationalize the world by defining it into neat categories and mapping each task or category of problem onto a specified solution or set of standard rules for action. However, this rationalizing effort is always fraught with tension because the world's complexity and connections defy the bureaucratic boxes. When the UN Secretariat was asked at the end of the Cold War to become more involved in international peace and security, it quickly found that its interstate peacekeeping mechanisms did not address the sources of many of the most potent conflicts that it was expected to consider. To deal with these sources of conflict, the organization needed to go deep into the heart of domestic politics, and it created a new category of practices called peacebuilding to accomplish its mission. When UNHCR began combating the causes of refugee flight and helping refugees repatriate and reintegrate with dignity, it, similarly, had to become involved in domestic politics. It began to propose such concepts as state responsibility, arguing that conditions *within* refugee-producing states needed to be addressed in order to prevent refugee flows. This, though, required the organization to become more invested in development work and to figure out how to build responsible states.[8]

Our cases also suggest that IOs change and expand not only through adaptation but also because of creative agency. Organization theorists have written extensively on adaptation, highlighting how much of organizational change comes reactively from the incremental alteration of the organizational rules in response to shortcomings and new environmental circumstances.[9] International organizations certainly exhibit this kind of reactive incremental change. Yet at times IOs can also be proactive—engineering change, transforming the organization and the environment, and thus exhibiting creativity.[10]

Application of rules, norms, and scripts to new situations always requires some creativity and invention. Not surprisingly, then, creative agency is most likely to occur at moments of rapid global change as IO staff draw from the existing bureaucratic culture to extend and project their authority. During periods of historical continuity actors are likely to rely on the tried and true and have little incentive to deviate from established routines. However, periods of rapid global change or "unsettled states" are defined by tremendous uncertainty.[11] New conditions pose new challenges to fulfilling mandates and may threaten the relevance or entire mission of the organization, thus giving IOs an incentive and reason to imagine alternative possibilities.

As IOs propose solutions that extend and expand their reach, they draw from their existing stocks of knowledge to reimagine the organization's goals and transform existing structures.[12] They exhibit sense-making characteristics that are common to organizations.[13] More specifically, our cases suggest two mechanisms by which IOs are able to use their authority to change their roles and overcome previously existing constraints. First, IO staff can be the source of new ideas and new solutions in policy debates. Their status as being both "an authority" and "in authority" on areas related to their mission positions them well both to generate new ideas and to have those ideas heard and respected. For example, when UNHCR volunteered to become a lead agency for the broad humanitarian efforts undertaken beginning in the 1970s, it argued that its prior experience providing material protection in the field made it a logical and legitimate choice for this new role.

Second, IOs may act as coalition builders in policy arenas where states and other actors disagree or are uncertain. Their role as impartial technocrats and champions of the international community's interest over particularistic national interests is often helpful here. Thus, when the Secretariat suggested an expanded role for the UN after the Cold War, it drew from widespread understandings that because the UN was an impartial agent of the international community, it was best positioned to help resolve domestic conflicts that threatened people's lives and regional stability. Similarly, IOs can build alliances with like-minded actors, both states and NGOs, to create momentum for preferred policies, raising the cost of opposition for those with different preferences.[14] UNHCR was able to use previous precedents, its "good offices," and alliances with newly decolonized countries to expand its orbit and overcome opposition from a wary United States, which only a few years before had opposed the idea of a UNHCR with a global mandate.

The Pathologies and Power of Expansion

If IOs are able to use their authority to recast their roles and expand their activities, what are the effects of this expansion? In this book we have been particularly concerned with the pathologies and power of international organizations. IOs almost always justify their reforms on the grounds that these changes will make them more efficient and effective at their tasks and better able to serve their constituencies. The IMF expanded conditionality to stabilize borrower economies. The Security Council revised the rules of peacekeeping to make peacekeeping "effective when selected." UNHCR staff broadened the menu of refugee solutions to deal with more refugees and fewer countries willing to host them.[15]

Yet the bureaucratic tendencies toward pathology discussed in chapter 2 and the evidence in our empirical chapters both suggest that organizational expansion might increase the likelihood of pathological behavior. Like most organizations, the UN Security Council, the IMF, and UNHCR accumulated new tasks, mandates, and functions. Sometimes these new tasks were complementary, but at other times they could demand contradictory behaviors. Some IMF staff claim that they cannot accumulate new goals and mandates, such as poverty alleviation and environmental protection, without compromising macroeconomic goals more central to their mission. As UNHCR becomes committed to helping reintegrate refugees into their home countries, it also becomes committed to the claim that the home situation is improving, thus potentially undermining the claim of persecution from potential asylum seekers.[16]

This kind of goal conflict can create cultural contestation within the organization, as different subunits are assigned and become attached to different goals. Irreconcilable goals can also promote adherence to rules at the expense of ends, or the irrationality of rationalization that Weber worried about. The UN Secretariat argued during the peacekeeping expansion of the early 1990s that it could not be placed in conflict situations like Somalia where it was expected to be both a party to the conflict and a neutral, impartial intermediary. Its failure to resolve these dilemmas led it to retreat to strict rules of impartiality in Rwanda and to avoid any active attempt to stop violence. The result was to induce an "institutional ideology of impartiality" even in the face of genocide.[17]

The expansion of IOs also has clear implications for their power. IOs use their authority to expand in ways that both help constitute how the world is organized and give IOs more control over a transformed world. These two types of power can be thought of as "power as constitution" and "power as domination."[18] With their constitutive power, IOs can reconfigure social space. When IOs create and extend new categories, they can draw connections and establish networks between previously disconnected actors, establish new forms of horizontal and vertical linkages, and create new categories of action that shape new kinds of actors and establish new sorts of activities.[19] When the Secretariat extended the notion of peacekeeping to include peacebuilding, it not only presented a categorical umbrella that bundled together a host of diverse actors but also drew connections between these actors in ways that allowed them to discover convergent interests. Over time human rights workers from local districts and nongovernmental organizations and civilian police trainers from member states and international organizations intermingled in the same space and realized that they each had a vested interest in seeing the emergence of professionalized police forces that were committed to the rule of law.[20] Constitutive power also enables IOs to define new interests and new tasks (such as protecting human rights, promoting development, peacekeeping), as well as to constitute and legitimate new actors to carry out those tasks (human rights monitors, technical assistance missions, peacekeepers). In this way, they create new interlocutors and new constituencies, both for themselves and for other actors, notably states. Finally, constitutive power allows IOs to persuade other states and other actors to accept new preferences and value new policy goals.[21] IMF officials have used their extensive technical assistance operation to teach states both the mechanics and the virtues of liberalized economic policies. UNHCR officials, similarly, have spent considerable energy lobbying states to change their policies, their laws, and their regional arrangements, sometimes in ways that represent an advance on existing legal instruments, thus helping to constitute state interests and policies.[22]

These effects reconfigure not just international social space but domestic social spaces as well. As IO governance activities expand, they are not only helping to create a new structure to world politics but are also working to create and constitute new domestic societies. IOs appear to be steadily expanding their mandates in a convergent direction: all are increasingly involved in the domestic affairs of states, and, specifically, all are trying to create durable, modern nation-states that are organized around democracy and markets.[23] The IMF routinely tries to teach states what it means to have a market economy. The UN Secretariat, the Organization for Security and Co-operation in Europe, and a panoply of other international organizations are trying to reconstruct democratic and rule-of-law states with certain identities and interests.[24] UNHCR is now involved in helping to build "responsible states" that will no longer produce the conditions that trigger refugee flight. European Union expansion includes not only increasing the number of members but also constituting these members as particular kinds of actors that can be part of the community.[25] IO expansion, in short, entails creating particular kinds of states with particular kinds of interests.

The ability of international organizations to frame problems as global and to use the discourse of the international community to justify and legitimate their intervention in domestic, interstate, and transnational spaces represents not only an exercise of power as constitution but also, at times, an exercise of power as domination. The hallmark of bureaucratic power, as Weber defined it, is "authority legitimated." Modern bureaucracies exercise power with some element of consent. But scholars of bureaucracies have routinely noted that bureaucracies also are agents of domination. Those who control the machinery of bureaucracy and staff its offices can force the people on whom the bureaucracy acts to behave in ways they would not choose. Such power to compel, leaving no ability to resist or oppose, is domination. Hannah Arendt, who despairingly referred to bureaucracy as "rule by nobody," worried that those who staff bureaucracies would become dehumanized and unthinking servants of rules that controlled the lives of millions, who frequently had little choice but to accept the dictates of the office holder.[26]

The bureaucratization of world politics means that international organizations have more authority than ever before and therefore have more power over other actors than ever before.[27] Expertise is central to their ability to dominate and control. As Zygmunt Bauman warned, "The essence of expertise is that doing things properly requires certain knowledge, that such knowledge is distributed unevenly, that some persons possess more of it than others, that those who possess it ought to be in charge of doing things, and that being in charge places upon them the responsibility for how things are being done."[28] IMF and World Bank officials might believe that because of their training and knowledge they understand the sort of economic medicine that sick countries need to swallow in order to get on the road to recovery, but from the perspective of the Third World patient these IOs are exhibiting power, even domination.

IOs promote a particular, mostly liberal, moral vision in world politics, and determining this moral vision is itself an act of power in the most fundamental sense. As Amartya Sen has argued, the institutionalization of a particular meaning of development at many international development organizations silences and disadvantages much of the world's population.[29] Although bureaucrats present the rules in a value-neutral way and portray themselves as having no power, bureaucratic power includes the ability to use rules, regulations, information, and decrees in ways that compel others to act. For the Rohingyas who did not know the ins and outs of international refugee law and did not know they had the right to decline repatriation to

Burma, UNHCR was exhibiting power in its most consequential form.[30] The bureaucratization of world politics means that global bureaucrats have authority to act in powerful ways. Sometimes this can mean emancipation, at other times domination.

II. LEGITIMATE GLOBAL GOVERNANCE AND UNDEMOCRATIC LIBERALISM

Global bureaucratization can be understood as the expression of two central components of global culture—rationalization and liberalism. Max Weber introduced the concept of rationalization to capture the process whereby modes of action structured in terms of means and ends, often using impersonal rules and procedures, increasingly dominate the world. Weber clearly saw rationalization as a historical process that was coming to define all spheres of life, including the economy, culture, and the state. Liberal ideas have seen a similar, perhaps related expansion across the globe. Liberal political ideas about the sanctity and autonomy of the individual and about democracy as the most desirable and just form of government have spread widely, as have liberal economic notions about the virtues of markets and capitalism as the best (and perhaps the only) means to "progress."[31] These two cultural strands have constituted IOs in particular ways, and IOs in turn have been important transmitters of global rationalization and global liberalism.[32] Rationalization has given IOs their basic form (as bureaucracies), and liberalism has provided the social content that all IOs now pursue.

IO Legitimacy

Although rationalism and liberalism are generally conferred tremendous legitimacy in modern world society, the two do not always sit well together. IOs, which combine the two at their heart, experience legitimacy problems as a result. Most ethical and philosophical understandings of legitimate rule center on the state, and the state is presumed to be representative of a community. We have an extensive theoretical apparatus for understanding how and why states are legitimate actors and why they may legitimately direct their citizens. We have far fewer notions about how or why global governance and rule by international organizations might be legitimate.[33]

The legitimacy of most modern public organizations depends on whether their procedures are viewed as proper and correct (procedural legitimacy) and whether they are reasonably successful at pursuing goals that are consistent with the values of the broader community (substantive legitimacy). An ideal-typical liberal democracy enjoys both types of legitimacy. Democratic procedures legitimate the state and the successive governments chosen by the governed. The liberal ends pursued by these governments (individual freedoms, economic growth gained through private property rights) are widely valued, ergo legitimate, and, in an ideal world, the government is reasonably successful at delivering those valued goods. Scaling up, this suggests that global governors and IOs may be legitimate because they were installed (or created) and continue to act through legitimate procedures, and because they help the broader community maintain and spread its values. IOs do, indeed, make these claims, but critics have likewise challenged their legitimacy on both of these grounds.

Many international organizations legitimate their actions by pointing to proper procedures used to make decisions, usually procedures involving participation by member states. Their actions are proper, they claim, because they reflect the will of members as expressed through these procedures. Indeed, one liberal notion legitimating these IOs is their voluntaristic and contractual origins. Many IOs, and most of the flagship IOs, were created by voluntary choices of member states, which designed the governing structure themselves. This social contract character, whereby members living in a "state of nature" voluntarily enter into agreements for self-betterment, is a powerful legitimating device for these organizations, drawing on deeply embedded liberal contractarian ideas. These contractual and voluntaristic notions, moreover, inform much of neoliberal institutionalist and principal-agent scholarship investigating these IOs, although the normative implications are often not explored in that work.

Yet, other features of IOs undercut their procedural legitimacy. As a practical and historical matter the degree of voluntarism involved in a state's decision to join an international organization is debatable. It might be little more than a legitimating myth that IOs have every reason to propagate.[34] Opting out of the IMF is not a viable option for most countries, particularly weak ones. More generally, the structure and decision-making rules of these organizations often raise questions about representation and accountability—two cornerstones of the broadly liberal notions that undergird IOs. Few international organizations operate according to standard democratic voting procedures, and many have weighted schemes that reflect power considerations. Votes in the IMF are explicitly tied to economic wealth; by design, poor borrower states have minimal say in the organization. Other IOs operate according to one state, one vote, but this is hardly democratic representation for individuals, since the entire population of China gets the same vote as the population of the Seychelles Islands. Many of those same IOs also have an inner sanctum that gives the most powerful states control over the most central issues, like the Security Council at the UN. Finally, many of the formal decision-making bodies are reserved for state representatives and exclude the peoples, children, indigenous groups, refugees, and others upon whom the organization acts. Much of the current dissatisfaction with global governance generally and international organizations specifically stems from champions of "the people" who believe their interests have been forgotten (if they were ever understood). This issue is certainly the focus of protests against international financial institutions, but it is also central to discussions within the European Union, where opinion polls consistently show that publics believe the Union is an elite project and are deeply skeptical about its virtues.

IOs also claim legitimacy on substantive grounds, because they promote values and pursue goals shared by the international community. When observers discuss the legitimacy of international organizations they are concerned with whether their activity "effectively promotes societal welfare, as defined by the audience's socially constructed value system."[35] In practice, many of these goals and values have a decidedly liberal quality, particularly since the end of the Cold War. The IMF's economic policies are unabashedly liberal, promoting private property and free markets around the globe. Other IOs, including the UN and UNHCR, have slowly come to accept the protection of individual rights, a liberal value, as part of their missions. The extremely powerful and expanding human rights regime that is pushed by a wide variety of IOs and is used to legitimate their activities has a strongly liberal cast since it makes individual rights a nonnegotiable trump card in many political situations. Even technical and service-oriented IOs frequently draw from broad liberal claims when they argue that standardization will facilitate cross-border exchanges that promote global welfare.[36]

The substantive legitimacy of IOs has been frequently challenged, however, when IOs are not effective in achieving their goals and when these goals are seen to serve particular interests rather than widely held values. The general presumption is that organizations should be judged by what they accomplish, and if they do not deliver what they promise then their lack of effectiveness injures their legitimacy.[37] Determining whether an organization has been effective is not easy, however, and effectiveness (like dysfunction) is often in the eye of the beholder. Some organizations may produce outputs that are difficult to measure, making it extremely difficult to determine whether they are effective.[38] How, exactly, are organizations like UNHCR or the IMF supposed to measure success? Moreover, different standards of effectiveness might be applied to the same event. For instance, while the Secretariat believed that the UN operation in Somalia was a mild success because it saved hundreds of thousands of lives, it was widely viewed in the United States as a failure because of the deaths of eighteen American Rangers.

While internal dynamics and organizational pathologies may prevent IOs from delivering on their promises, ineffectiveness also results from the lack of financial or political support from member states—especially powerful ones. As former secretary-general Boutros Boutros-Ghali liked to say, the

UN is only as powerful and effective as its member states. To secure needed resources, IOs often must tailor policies to specific interests of the powerful, but in doing this, their impartiality and nondiscriminatory principles may be compromised. IOs thus face a dilemma: effective performance requires reliance on powerful member states, but that same reliance can undercut an IO's substantive and procedural legitimacy when it undermines the appearance of impartiality and objectivity. Financial bailouts from the IMF and peacekeeping missions by the UN are more likely in countries of concern to powerful members, particularly the United States. UNHCR often finds that because of member states' pattern of contributions, refugees from regions that are of strategic relevance to powerful member states are better cared for than are refugees from nonstrategic regions. Critics of these organizations have been quick to point out such facts as evidence that these organizations may serve the realpolitik goals of the strong rather than the general welfare.

Lack of consensus on what goals or values are universally desired or welfare-promoting has plagued IO claims to substantive legitimacy on a variety of fronts. The World Bank and the IMF champion particular notions of economic organization that might seem legitimate to the staff and many of their most powerful clients but are not necessarily legitimate to borrower governments, their populations, or activist groups. These challenges to the policies of IOs have become sharper and more frequent as IOs have become more deeply involved in the domestic affairs of states. Historically, many IOs have maintained their apolitical appearance and claim to impartiality by respecting state sovereignty; but as they have beome more involved in domestic issues, this has become increasingly difficult. UNHCR's early definition of humanitarianism respected state sovereignty, and the agency did not become involved in the domestic circumstances of refugee-producing countries. When UNHCR started to address the causes of refugee flows, it began working to increase the political, economic, and social rights of minorities at risk in ways that made maintaining an apolitical persona all but impossible.

Procedural and substantive legitimacy can be tightly linked, and IOs are very much aware of these connections as they undertake reforms to counter criticism. In response to concerns that opaque procedures give voice to the powerful (who have resources to learn the ropes) but silence the weak (who do not), many IOs have attempted to increase transparency, democratic deliberation, and local participation and representation. Opening decision-making processes can do more than increase procedural legitimacy, though. It is also intended to produce policies that will better serve those previously excluded and so be more substantively legitimate. For example, procedural lack of representation, lack of transparency, and lack of accountability have been centerpieces of attacks on the IMF, World Bank, and World Trade Organization from both antiglobalization campaigns on the left and various reform efforts on the right. These criticisms have teeth because of perceptions that illegitimate procedures produce substantively unjust consequences, and opponents have been energetic in publicizing such outcomes. Conversely, unwelcome results can often be sold politically if they are produced by procedurally legitimate processes. For instance, the World Bank and the IMF now recognize that something like consent of the governed is essential to their legitimacy and have used participation as a surrogate for consent. In order to increase their procedural and substantive legitimacy, both now promote "ownership" of sometimes painful economic reform programs, encouraging borrower states to participate (or at least appear to participate) in the construction of these policies. Whether ownership and participatory development actually achieve these goals is a different question, but the reasons they are attempted flow directly from legitimacy problems faced by IOs.

Increasingly, legitimate procedures involve transparency, democratic deliberation, and local participation and representation, and as many international organizations reform they are attempting to introduce mechanisms that reduce their opaqueness and give voice to those who have had none. Again, the IMF has undergone a revolution in transparency, posting on its website vast arrays of borrowing agreements and other information that was closely held by member states ten years ago. It is less transparent, however, about its own internal deliberations. Although UNHCR and the UN Secretariat have attempted to provide more timely information regarding their activities through the use of new technologies, it still is difficult to get information about their decision-making processes. Overall, because few international organizations meet basic standards of procedural legitimacy and most are unlikely to implement such procedures in the near future (in part because states would not allow it), they are likely to continue to have their legitimacy questioned.[39]

IO Accountability

Lack of transparency and the growing prominence and power of international organizations also raise concerns regarding their accountability. There is little doubt that mechanisms of accountability have not kept pace with the power and reach of international organizations. Such developments become all the more troubling when it is recognized that IOs have autonomy and can develop in ways that are not sanctioned by their creators. An accountability relationship exists when "an individual, group, or other entity makes demands on an agent to report on his or her activities, and has the ability to impose costs on that agent."[40] This definition, though, invites further distinctions. Accountability, as Robert Keohane argues, has internal and external dimensions.[41] Many activists, scholars, and policymakers tend to focus on the issue of internal accountability, in which there is a formalized and institutionalized relationship between a principal and an agent. The principals (states) provide the delegated authority and resources for the agent (the IO), and the agent then is accountable to the principal.[42]

However, accountability also has an external dimension. As international organizations grow in power and scope, more populations are vulnerable to their policies than ever before. As Robert Goodin nicely summarizes: "Vulnerability amounts to one person's having the capacity to produce consequences that matter to another. Responsibility amounts to his being accountable for those consequences of his actions and choices."[43] Members of the Security Council did not clamor for an investigation into the Secretariat's behavior in Rwanda and Srebrenica in large part because they were equally blameworthy and therefore had little interest in breaking the collective silence. Instead, it was those who were affected by the Secretariat's inactions, Tutsis and Bosnian Muslims, who demanded that the Secretariat be made accountable. Significantly, when Secretary-General Kofi Annan finally delivered his belated apology for the UN's failures, he delivered it not to the formal principals but rather to the victims and their relatives.

As international organizations grow in power and scope, more groups will be interested in holding IOs accountable for their actions. While states are sometimes the source of these demands, increasingly NGOs and other nonstate actors are conducting patrols and pulling fire alarms.[44] Various NGOs were responsible for bringing attention to World Bank policies regarding the building of large dams and successfully got the World Bank to alter its policies.[45] In the case of the Rohingyas, although some indigenous movements protested UNHCR's policies, those with the most power and voice and who were best able to hold UNHCR accountable were Western NGOs. The growth of external accountability raises the possibility that IOs might not be able to satisfy all their constituencies concurrently. As UNHCR action has created (and constituted) new constituencies, particularly advocates for refugees, contradictions between the demands of these groups and those of member states have made crafting policies increasingly difficult. This is not to say that UNHCR cannot be accountable to several constituencies at once. Indeed, the staff spend a great deal of time explaining to states why UNHCR policies must also satisfy refugee advocates and explaining to refugee advocates why policies must satisfy states. But just as it is difficult to serve two masters, it is difficult to be accountable to different constituencies that have different expectations regarding what constitutes proper behavior.

Accountability matters because of the presumption that its absence means that those in power have the capacity to act without regard for those who authorize their actions and for those whose lives are affected by those actions. Accountability can take different forms—legal accountability, political accountability, or just simply being forced to give a public account of one's actions—and different forms may be acceptable in different contexts.[46] However, accountability of some kind is essential since it is accountability that, at least in part, makes IO rule legitimate and separates it from domination.

Undemocratic Liberalism

Scholars studying democratization, especially in the developing world, have worried that the use of democratic procedures will outstrip the spread of liberal values, creating "illiberal democracies" at the national level.[47] At the global level, we see the opposite problem: international organizations often use undemocratic procedures in the pursuit of liberal values, thus creating "undemocratic liberalism" in global governance. Global governance is legitimated by its pursuit of liberal goals—human rights, growth through markets. Yet international organizations are unabashedly undemocratic, and procedures for consent of the governed are very weak. Harmonizing the substantively liberal goals of these organizations with procedures that, if not democratic, at least provide some accountability and representation will be an ongoing task that is essential to the long-term legitimacy of global governance.

If scholars of international organizations have not been particularly concerned with undemocratic, unrepresentative, and unaccountable features of IOs it is because their theoretical lenses have until recently viewed IOs as a progressive and liberal force in a dangerous, largely illiberal, world. Given such dispositions the concern for many scholars and policymakers has been not the oversupply but rather the undersupply of international organizations. Most approaches to the study of international cooperation and global governance look to create international institutions as solutions to the world's problems. Institutions are the singular answer to promoting interdependence and solving the myriad of collective action problems in environmental, economic, and security affairs because they offer rational, impersonal, and nonviolent means of dealing with conflict and enable states to overcome narrow self-interest and achieve long-term cooperation. They also are valued because of the view that they help to bring about progress, nurturing development, security, justice, and individual autonomy.

Yet the liberalizing and rationalizing processes associated with global bureaucratization might come at a steep price. One hundred years ago Max Weber observed that Prussia was becoming bureaucratic. He welcomed this development, recognizing that it would enable an increasingly complex society to coordinate its activities in a more rational, objective, and peaceful manner. He was further heartened by the realization that the bureaucracy was helping to inculcate in his fellow citizens the liberal, rational values that he prized. But he also recognized that a bureaucratic world had its own perils, producing increasingly powerful and autonomous bureaucrats who could be "spiritless" and driven by rules, who could apply those rules in ways that harmed the people whom they were expected to serve, thus creating an "iron cage." Weber understood that the very bureaucracy that was needed to keep a society democratic, prosperous, and healthy might also undermine society's well-being.

What Weber observed at the beginning of the past century at the domestic level we observe at the beginning of this new century at the global level. States have built a panoply of international and regional organizations that are intended to help them facilitate interdependence and manage its excesses. Without international organizations, states and peoples would be less able to reap the fruits of commercial exchange, find nonviolent dispute mechanisms, and solve their environmental problems. International organizations are not only helping states and nonstate actors coordinate their activities and promote their interests, however. They are also shaping which activities the international community values and holds in high esteem. Beginning in the nineteenth century and continuing into the twenty-first, international organizations have been disseminating the liberal values that are the foundations for a global liberal culture. But the very source of their power to do good might also be the source of their power to do harm, to run roughshod over the interests of states and citizens that they are supposed to further. Managing our global bureaucracy and learning to exploit its strengths while moderating its failings will be an essential task.

ABBREVIATIONS

BBTG	broad-based transitional government
DPKO	Department of Peacekeeping Operations
ED	executive director
HCR	High Commissioner for Refugees (League of Nations)
HRW	Human Rights Watch
IDPs	internally displaced persons
IMF	International Monetary Fund
IO	international organization
IR	international relations
IRO	International Refugee Organization
KWSA	Kigali weapons-secure area
LCHR	Lawyers Committee for Human Rights
MoU	memorandum of understanding
MSF	Médicins sans Frontières
NGO	nongovernmental organization
RPF	Rwandan Patriotic Front
UNAMIR	United Nations Assistance Mission for Rwanda
UNHCR	United Nations High Commissioner for Refugees
USCR	U.S. Committee for Refugees

NOTES

PREFACE

1. Susan Strange, "Why Do International Organizations Never Die?" in B. Reinalda and B. Verbeek, eds., *Autonomous Policy Making by International Organizations* (London: Routledge/ ECPR Studies in European Political Science, 1998), 213–20.

2. Michael N. Barnett and Martha Finnemore, "The Politics, Power, and Pathologies of International Organizations," *International Organization* 53, no. 4 (1999): 699–732.

CHAPTER 1. BUREAUCRATIZING WORLD POLITICS

1. Union of International Associations, ed., *Yearbook of International Organizations, 2003–2004*, 40th ed., vol. 1B (Munich: K. G. Saur, 2003), 2,738, app. 3, table 1. This figure includes only intergovernmental organizations (IGOs) of the type classified as "conventional" in the *Yearbook*. The *Yearbook* lists an additional 1,700 IGOs under "other international bodies" as well as 6,584 conventional nongovernmental organizations (NGOs) and an additional 11,749 NGOs under "other international bodies." For quantitative analyses of the expansion of IOs, see Cheryl Shanks, Harold K. Jacobson, and Jeffrey H. Kaplan, "Inertia and Change in the Constellation of International Governmental Organizations, 1981–1992," *International Organization* 50, no. 4 (1996): 593–627; Michael Wallace and J. David Singer, "Intergovernmental Organizations in the Global System, 1815–1964: A Quantitative Description," *International Organization* 24, no. 2 (1970): 239–87; Richard Cupitt, Rodney Whitlock, and Lynne Whitlock, "The (Im)morality of International Governmental Organizations," in Paul Diehl, ed., *The Politics of Global Governance: International Organizations in an Interdependent World* (Boulder: Lynne Rienner, 1997), 7–23.

2. In this book we use the term *international organization* to mean intergovernmental organizations. We define an international organization as an organization that has representatives from three or more states supporting a permanent secretariat to perform ongoing tasks related to a common purpose. This minimalist definition is consistent with that adopted by Harold Jacobson, *Networks of Interdependence: International Organizations and the Global Political System* (New York: Knopf, 1979); Clive Archer, *International Organizations*, 3rd ed. (New York: Routledge, 2001); and Inis Claude, *Swords into Ploughshares*, 4th ed. (New York: Random House, 1971).

3. Stephen D. Krasner, ed., *International Regimes* (Ithaca: Cornell University Press, 1983).

4. For a range of statements that correspond to this argument, see Kenneth Abbott and Duncan Snidal, "Why States Act through Formal International Organizations," *Journal of Conflict Resolution* 42 (1988): 3–32; Mark Thatcher and Alec Stone Sweet, "Theory and Practice of Delegation to Non-majoritarian Institutions," *West European Politics* 25, no. 1 (2002): 1–22.

5. For an extended discussion, see Barnett and Finnemore, "Politics, Power, and Pathologies."

6. On this point see Michael Barnett, "Authority, Intervention, and the Outer Limits of International Relations Theory," in Tom Callaghy, Robert Latham, and Robert Kassimer, eds., *Authorities and Interventions in World Politics* (New York: Cambridge University Press, 2002); and John Agnew, "The Territorial Trap: The Geographical Assumptions of International Relations Theory," *Review of International Political Economy* 1, no. 1 (1994): 53–80. For other IR scholars who see authority as polymorphous, see John Ruggie, "The New Institutionalism in International Relations," in his *Constructing the World Polity* (New York: Routledge, 1998), 59–61; Rodney Bruce Hall and Thomas Biersteker, eds., *The Emergence of Private Authority in Global Governance* (New York: Cambridge University Press, 2002); A. Claire Cutler, "Locating 'Authority' in the Global Political Economy," *International Studies Quarterly* 43, no. 1 (1999): 59–83; Martin Hewson and Tim Sinclair, eds., *Approaches to Global Governance Theory* (Albany: State University of New York Press, 1999); A. Claire Cutler, Virginia Haufler, and Tony Porter, eds., *Private Authority and International Affairs* (Albany: State University of New York Press, 1999); Richard A. Higgott, Geoffrey R. D. Underhill, and Andreas Bieler, eds., *Non-state Actors and Authority in the Global System* (New York: Routledge, 2000); Yale H. Ferguson and Richard W. Mansbach, *Polities: Authority, Identities, and Change* (Columbia: University of South Carolina Press, 1996); and Ian Hurd, "Legitimacy and Authority in International Politics," *International Organization* 53, no. 2 (1999): 379–408.

7. As Richard Ashley observed, "The power of an actor, even its status as an agent competent to act, is not attributable to the inherent qualities or possession of a given entity. Rather, the power and status of an actor depends on and is limited by the condition of its *recognition* within a community as a whole." Ashley, "The Poverty of Neorealism," in Robert Keohane, ed., *Neorealism and Its Critics* (New York: Columbia University Press, 1984), 291–92, italics in original. Cited in Stefano Guzzini, "A Reconstruction of Constructivism in International Relations," *European Journal of International Relations* 6, no. 2 (2000): 173.

8. Descendants of centuries-old theories, the "neo" versions of realism and liberalism dominated IR theory throughout the 1980s and 1990s. Both depart from their classical forerunners in focusing primarily on states in an attempt to promote more scientific theorizing. They disagree over whether states pursue relative or absolute gains. Neoliberals, theorizing that states aim for absolute gains, see a larger role for international organizations. See John Mearsheimer, "The False Promise of International Institutions," *International Security* 19, no. 3 (1994–95): 5–49; David A. Baldwin, *Neorealism and Neoliberalism* (New York: Columbia University Press, 1993).

9. Andrew Moravcsik, "A New Statecraft? Supranational Entrepreneurs and International Cooperation," *International Organization* 53, no. 2 (1999): 267–306.

10. Burkhart Holzner and John Marx, *Knowledge Application: The Knowledge System in Society* (Boston: Allyn and Bacon, 1979).

11. Pierre Bourdieu, *Outline of a Theory of Practice* (New York: Cambridge University Press, 1977), chap. 4.

12. Three exceptions are Ernst Haas, *When Knowledge Is Power: Three Models of Change in International Organizations* (Berkeley: University of California Press, 1990); Giulio Gallarotti, "The Limits of International Organization," *International Organization* 45, no. 2 (1991): 183–220; and Duncan Snidal, "Political Economy and International Institutions," *International Review of Law and Economics* 16 (1996): 121–37. For a perspective that also links bureaucratization to undesirable outcomes, see Tony Waters, *Bureaucratizing the Good Samaritan: The Limitations of Humanitarian Relief Operations* (Boulder: Westview Press, 2001).

13. Snidal, "Political Economy and International Institutions."

14. Terry Moe, "The Politics of Structural Choice: Toward a Theory of Public Bureaucracy," in Oliver Williamson, ed., *Organization Theory from Chester Barnard to the Present and Beyond* (New York: Oxford University Press, 1990), 116–53; Amy Zegart, *Flawed by Design: The Evolution of the CIA, JCS, and NSC* (Stanford: Stanford University Press, 1999).

15. Alexander Wendt, "On Constitution and Causation in International Relations," *Review of International Studies* 24, no. 5 (1998): 101–18. Also see John Ruggie, "What Makes the World Hang Together," *International Organization* 52, no. 3 (1998): 855–86.

16. Clayton Roberts, *The Logic of Historical Explanation* (University Park: Pennsylvania State University Press, 1996); Alexander George, "Case Studies and Theory Development: The Method of Structured, Focused Comparison," in Paul G. Lauren, ed., *Diplomacy: New Approaches in History, Theory, and Policy* (New York: Free Press, 1979), 43–68.

17. There is an older literature that was quite attentive to IOs as organizations and was interested in the relationship between how they were put together and how they acted. See Robert Cox, Harold Jacobsen, et al., *The Anatomy of Influence: Decision Making in International Organizations* (New Haven: Yale University Press, 1974); Robert Cox and Harold Jacobson, "Decision Making," *International Social Science Journal* 29 (1977): 115–35; Gayl Ness and Steven Brechin, "Bridging the Gap: International Organizations as Organizations," *International Organization* 42, no. 2 (1988): 245–73; and Robert S. Jordan, "'Truly' International Bureaucracies: Real or Imagined?" in Lawrence Finkelstein, ed., *Politics in the United Nations System* (Durham: Duke University Press, 1988), 424–45.

18. Karl E. Weick, *Sensemaking in Organizations* (Thousand Oaks, Calif.: Sage, 1995), 104.

19. See Alfred Schutz, *On Phenomenology and Social Relations* (Chicago: University of Chicago Press, 1970); and Fritz Ringer, *Max Weber's Methodology: The Unification of the Cultural and Social Sciences* (Cambridge: Harvard University Press, 1997). For scholars who write against the traditional bureaucratic politics approach and include more cultural and interpretive analysis, see for instance Emery Roe, *Narrative Policy Analysis: Theory and Practice* (Durham: Duke University Press, 1994); Jerome Bruner, *Acts of Meaning* (Cambridge: Harvard University Press, 1990); James G. March, *Decisions and Organizations* (New York: Basil Blackwell, 1988); James G. March and Johan P. Olsen, *Rediscovering Institutions: The Organizational Basis of Politics* (New York: Free Press, 1989); and James G. March, "Understanding How Decisions Happen in Organizations," in Zur Shapira, ed., *Organizational Decision Making* (New York: Cambridge University Press, 1997), 9–33.

CHAPTER 2. INTERNATIONAL ORGANIZATIONS AS BUREAUCRACIES

1. Martin Albrow, *Bureaucracy* (London: Pall Mall Press, 1970). There is a huge literature on bureaucracies. In addition to Weber, other classics include Philip Selznick, "An Approach to a Theory of Bureaucracy," *American Sociological Review* 8, no. 1 (1943): 47–54; Chester Barnard, *The Functions of the Executive* (Cambridge: Harvard University Press, 1940); Philip Selznick, *TVA and the Grass Roots: A Study in the Sociology of Formal Organization* (Berkeley: University of California Press, 1953).

2. David Beetham, *Bureaucracy*, 2nd ed. (Minneapolis: University of Minnesota Press, 1996), 9–12.

3. For statements by Weber and his interpreters, see Max Weber, "Bureaucracy," in H. H. Gerth and C. Wright Mills, eds., *From Max Weber: Essays in Sociology* (New York: Oxford University Press, 1978); Max Weber, *Theory of Social and Economic Organization* (New York: Oxford University Press, 1947); Beetham, *Bureaucracy;* Nicos Mouzelis, *Organization and Bureaucracy* (Chicago: Aldine, 1967); Peter Blau, "Critical Remarks on Weber's Theory of Authority," *American Political Science Review* 57, no. 2 (1963): 305–16.

4. James G. March, Martin Schulz, and Xueguang Zhou, *The Dynamics of Rules: Change in Written Organizational Codes* (Stanford: Stanford University Press, 2000), 9.

5. Krasner, *International Regimes;* Robert Keohane, *After Hegemony* (Princeton: Princeton University Press, 1984); and Lisa Martin and Beth Simmons, "Theories and Empirical Studies of International Institutions," *International Organization* 52, no. 4 (1998): 729–53. International law also has treated this function of rules. See Anthony Clark Arend, *Legal Rules and International Society* (New York: Oxford University Press, 1999), and Thomas M. Franck, *Fairness in International Law and Institutions* (New York: Oxford University Press, 1995).

6. See, for instance, Weick, *Sensemaking in Organizations;* Peter Manning, "Organizations as Sense-Making Contexts," *Theory, Culture, and Society* 14, no. 2 (1997): 139–50.

7. See Adam Kuper, *Culture: The Anthropologists' Account* (Cambridge: Harvard University Press, 1999), for a good account of anthropology's treatment of culture. See James C. Scott, *Seeing like a State* (New Haven: Yale University Press, 1998), and Michael Herzfeld, *The Social Production of Indifference: Exploring the Symbolic Roots of Western Bureaucracy* (Chicago: University of Chicago Press, 1993), for cultural accounts of the bureaucratic state and its tendencies and consequences.

8. Diane Vaughan, *The Challenger Launch Decision: Risky Technology, Culture, and Deviance at*

NASA (Chicago: University of Chicago Press, 1996), 64. For discussions of organizational and bureaucratic culture, see Lynn Eden, *Whole World on Fire* (Ithaca: Cornell University Press, 2004), chap. 2; Joanne Martin, *Cultures in Organizations: Three Perspectives* (New York: Oxford University Press, 1992); Mats Alvesson, *Cultural Perspectives on Organizations* (New York: Cambridge University Press, 1993); Mary Jo Hatch, "The Dynamics of Organizational Culture," *Academy of Management Review* 18, no. 4 (1993): 657–93; and Gertrude Jaeger and Philip Selznick, "A Normative Theory of Culture," *American Sociological Review* 29, no. 5 (1964): 653–69.

9. See Edgar Schein, *Organizational Culture and Leadership*, 2nd ed. (San Francisco: Jossey Bass, 1992), 52, 70–71.

10. Alvesson, *Cultural Perspectives on Organizations*. Students of militaries have long been aware of this phenomenon and have studied its consequences. See Morris Janowitz, *The Military in the Political Development of New Nations* (Chicago: University of Chicago Press, 1964); John J. Johnson, ed., *The Role of the Military in Underdeveloped Societies* (Princeton: Princeton University Press, 1962); Elizabeth Kier, "Culture and French Military Doctrine before World War II," in Peter Katzenstein, ed., *The Culture of National Security: Identity and Norms in World Politics* (New York: Columbia University Press, 1996), 186–215; and Jeffrey W. Legro, *Cooperation under Fire: Anglo-German Restraint during World War II* (Ithaca: Cornell University Press, 1995). This view also is prominent among students of business history. See Kenneth Lipartito, "Culture and the Practice of Business History," *Business and Economic History* 24, no. 2 (1995): 1–41.

11. Ann Swidler, "Culture in Action: Symbols in Strategies," *American Sociological Review* 51, no. 2 (1986): 273–86.

12. John L. Campbell, "Institutional Analysis and the Role of Ideas in Political Economy," *Theory and Society* 27 (1998): 378; Ellen Immergut, "The Theoretical Core of the New Institutionalism," *Politics and Society* 26, no. 1 (1998): 14–19.

13. Richard Handler, *Nationalism and the Politics of Culture in Quebec* (Madison: University of Wisconsin Press, 1988); Vaughan, *Challenger Launch Decision*.

14. For a sampling of different perspectives from the large literature on authority, see Hannah Arendt, "What Is Authority?" in *Between Past and Future* (New York: Viking Press, 1968), 91–142; Bruce Lincoln, *Authority* (Chicago: University of Chicago Press, 1994); Joseph Raz, ed., *Authority* (New York: Cambridge University Press, 1990); Max Weber, *Economy and Society* (Berkeley, University of California Press, 1978); Barry Barnes, "On Authority and Its Relationship to Power," in John Law, ed., *Power, Action, and Belief: A New Sociology of Knowledge* (New York: Routledge, 1986), 180–95; Richard B. Friedman, "On the Concept of Authority in Political Philosophy," in Joseph Raz, ed., *Authority* (New York: New York University Press, 1990), 56–91; Peter Winch, "Authority," in Anthony Quinton, ed., *Political Philosophy* (New York: Oxford University Press, 1967); and Richard Flathman, *The Practice of Political Authority* (Chicago: University of Chicago Press, 1980).

15. Lincoln, *Authority*.

16. Weber, *Economy and Society*.

17. We thank John Boli for this insight. Also see William Fisher, "Doing Good? The Politics and Antipolitics of NGO Practices," *Annual Review of Anthropology* 26 (1997): 439–64; James Ferguson, *The Anti-politics Machine: "Development," Depoliticization, and Bureaucratic Domination in Lesotho* (New York: Cambridge University Press, 1990); Cris Shore and Susan Wright, "Policy: A New Field of Anthropology," in Shore and Wright, eds., *Anthropology of Policy: Critical Perspectives on Governance and Power* (New York: Routledge, 1997), 3–41; Anne-Marie Burley and Walter Mattli, "Europe before the Court: A Political Theory of Integration," *International Organization* 47, no. 1 (1993): 41–76.

18. Danesh Sarooshi, *The United Nations and the Development of Collective Security: The Delegation by the UN Security Council of Its Chapter VII Powers* (New York: Oxford University Press 1999); Robert Keohane and Joseph Nye, introduction to Joseph S. Nye Jr., and John D. Donahue, eds., *Governance in a Globalizing World* (Washington, D.C.: Brookings Institution Press, 2001), 1–43; Abbott and Snidal, "Why States Act through Formal International Organizations"; Mark Pollack, *The Engines of Integration? Delegation, Agency, and Agenda Setting in the European Union* (New York: Oxford University Press, 2003).

19. For a good discussion of delegation, see Jonathan Bendor, Amihai Glazer, and Thomas Hammond, "Theories of Delegation," *Annual Review of Political Science* 4 (2001): 235–69.

20. Abbott and Snidal, "Why States Act through Formal International Organizations."

21. For a similar treatment of moral authority, see Rodney Bruce Hall, "Moral Authority as a Power Resource," *International Organization* 51, no. 4 (1997): 591–622.

22. For the discourse of intervention and the projection of "doing good," see Fisher, "Doing Good?"

23. This issue of expertise has obvious connections to the logic of delegation, as well. For a general discussion, see Roger Smith and Brian Wynne, eds., *Expert Evidence: Interpreting Science in the Law* (New York: Routledge, 1989); John Scott, *Power* (Cambridge: Polity Press, 2001), chap. 5. For the specific discussion of international organizations, see Ernst B. Haas, *Beyond the Nation-State: Functionalism and International Organization* (Stanford: Stanford University Press, 1964); and Thatcher and Sweet, "Theory and Practice of Delegation to Non-majoritarian Institutions."

24. Steven Brint, *In an Age of Experts: The Changing Role of Professionals in Politics and Public Life* (Princeton: Princeton University Press, 1994).

25. Brint, *In an Age of Experts;* Elliot Friedson, *Professionalism Reborn: Theory, Prophecy, and Policy* (Chicago: University of Chicago Press, 1994); Edgar Schein, "Culture: The Missing Concept in Organization Studies," *Administrative Science Quarterly* 41, no. 2 (1996): 229–40.

26. This distinction is developed by Friedman, "On the Concept of Authority"; and Lincoln, *Authority,* 3–4.

27. Thatcher and Sweet, "Theory and Practice of Delegation to Non-majoritarian Institutions."

28. Abbott and Snidal, "Why States Act through Formal International Organizations"; Thatcher and Sweet, "Theory and Practice of Delegation to Non-Majoritarian Institutions."

29. For the general argument as applied to bureaucracies, see Daniel Carpenter, *The Forging of Bureaucratic Autonomy: Reputations, Networks, and Policy Innovation in Executive Agencies, 1862–1928* (Princeton: Princeton University Press, 2001), 355; Roger Noll and Barry Weingast, "Rational Actor Theory, Social Norms, and Policy Implementation: Applications to Administrative Processes and Bureaucratic Culture," in Kristen Monroe, ed., *Economic Approaches to Politics* (New York: HarperCollins, 1991), 237–58.

30. This is reminiscent of the literature on the relative autonomy of the state, where evidence of state autonomy was limited to those moments when the state went against the core interests of the capitalist class.

31. For the general argument, see Martha Finnemore, *National Interests in International Society* (Ithaca: Cornell University Press, 1996), esp. chap. 1; and Jeffrey Pfeffer and Gerald Salancik, *The External Control of Organizations* (New York: Harper and Row, 1978).

32. For instance, as Weber argued, power "is the possibility of imposing one's will upon the behavior of others," established authorities exhibit power because they have the right to command and others the obligation to obey, and domination is virtually identical with the "authoritarian power of command." These quotes are cited in Reinhard Bendix, *Max Weber: An Intellectual Portrait* (Berkeley: University of California Press, 1972), 290–91. Social theorists have continued to debate the relationship between authority and power. See Barnes, "On Authority and Its Relationship to Power"; and Friedman, "On the Concept of Authority."

33. Michael Barnett and Raymond Duvall, eds., *Power in Global Governance* (New York: Cambridge University Press, 2004).

34. Actors, of course, can possess power without authority. We would not "speak of an armed robber 'exerting his authority.'" David Bell, *Power, Influence, and Authority* (New York: Oxford University Press, 1975), 15.

35. For various statements to this effect, see Weber, *From Max Weber,* 232–35; see also Barry Barnes, *The Elements of Social Theory* (Princeton: Princeton University Press, 1995), chap. 8.

36. Keohane, *After Hegemony;* Keohane and Martin, "Promise of Institutionalist Theory"; Helen Milner, *Interests, Institutions, and Information: Domestic Politics and International Relations* (Princeton: Princeton University Press, 1997); and Martin and Simmons, "Theories and Empirical Studies of International Institutions."

37. As Burkhart Holzner summarized, "'knowledge' can only mean the 'mapping' of experienced reality by some observer. It cannot mean the 'grasping' of reality itself. . . . More strictly speaking, we are compelled to define 'knowledge' as the communicable mapping of some aspect of experienced reality by an observer in symbolic terms." *Reality Construction in Society* (Cambridge, Mass.: Schenkman, 1968), 20. Cited in Holzner and Marx, *Knowledge Application,* 92. As Peter Berger and Thomas Luckmann put it, "the social construction of knowledge is concerned with the social construction of reality." *The Social Construction of Reality: A Treatise in the Sociology of Knowledge* (Boston: Anchor, 1967), 3. Also see Peter Burke, *A Social History of Knowledge: From Gutenberg to Diderot* (Malden, Mass.: Polity Press, 2000), 11.

38. Ferguson, *Anti-politics Machine;* Geoffrey C. Bowker and Susan Leigh Star, *Sorting Things Out: Classification and Its Consequences* (Cambridge: MIT Press, 1999); Paul Starr, "Social Categories and Claims in the Liberal State," in Mary Douglas and David Hull, eds., *How Classification Works: Nelson Goodman among the Social Sciences* (Edinburgh: Edinburgh University Press, 1992), 154–79; Susan Wright, "'Culture' in Anthropology and Organizational Studies," in Susan Wright, ed., *Anthropology of Organizations* (New York: Routledge, 1994), 1–31.

39. Weick, *Sensemaking in Organizations;* Manning, "Organizations as Sense-Making Contexts."

40. A good introduction to this distinction can be found in John Searle, *The Construction of Social Reality* (New York: Free Press, 1995), 27–28. In our view, while the distinction between regulative and constitutive effects makes sense analytically, in practice the two frequently blur.

41. Ann Florini, *The Third Force: The Rise of Transnational Civil Society* (Washington, D.C.: Carnegie Endowment for International Peace, 2000).

42. For a taxonomy of tools of persuasion, see Martha Finnemore, *The Purpose of Intervention: Changing Beliefs about the Use of Force* (Ithaca: Cornell University Press, 2003), chap. 5.

43. Clarissa Hayward has discussed this in terms of "fields of action" that facilitate and constrain activity and that determine how the possible and the impossible become defined, what is considered normal and natural, what are the categories of action that are desirable and represent the aspirations of the collective, what are the best means to achieve those aspirations, and what counts as a problem that needs to be solved and who is best able to solve it. *De-Facing Power* (New York: Cambridge University Press, 2000), 30, 35.

44. See Birgit Locher and Elisabeth Prugl, "Feminism and Constructivism: Worlds Apart or Sharing the Middle Ground?" *International Studies Quarterly* 45, no. 1 (2001): 111–30; Emanuel Adler, "Constructivism and International Relations," in Walter Carlneas, Beth Simmons, and Thomas Risse, eds., *Handbook of International Relations* (Thousand Oaks, Calif.: Sage, 2002), 103; Martha Finnemore and Kathryn Sikkink, "International Norm Dynamics and Political Change," *International Organization* 52, no. 4 (1998): 887–917; Michael Barnett, *Dialogues in Arab Politics* (New York: Columbia University Press, 1998), chap. 2.

45. John Boli and George M. Thomas, *Constructing World Culture* (Stanford: Stanford University Press, 1999).

46. Don Handelman, "Commentary on Heymann," *Current Anthropology* 36 (1995): 280. See also Ian Hacking, *The Social Construction of What?* (Cambridge: Harvard University Press, 1999); Bowker and Star, *Sorting Things Out;* Starr "Social Categories and Claims in the Liberal State"; Wright, "'Culture' in Anthropology and Organizational Studies"; and Anne Schneider and Helen Ingram, "The Social Construction of Target Populations: Implications for Politics and Policy," *American Political Science Review* 87, no. 2 (1993): 334–47.

47. Murray Edelman, *Constructing the Political Spectacle* (Chicago: University of Chicago Press, 1988).

48. Joseph Raz, introduction to Raz, *Authority.* Also see Edelman, *Constructing the Political Spectacle,* 20.

49. Caroline Moorehead, "Lost in Cairo," *New York Review of Books,* June 13, 2002, 28–31.

50. Michael C. Williams, "Hobbes and International Relations: A Reconsideration," *International Organization* 50, no. 2 (1996): 213–36; Stewart R. Clegg, "Weber and Foucault: Social Theory for the Study of Organizations," *Organization* 1 (1993): 149–78; Pierre Bourdieu, "Social Space and Symbolic Power," in his *Language and Symbolic Power* (Chicago: University of Chicago Press, 1994); Edward H. Carr, *The Twenty Years' Crisis* (1939; New York: Harper Torchbooks, 1964); James Keeley, "Toward a Foucauldian Analysis of International Regimes," *International Organization* 44, no. 1 (1990): 83–105; and Lisa Wedeen, "Conceptualizing Culture: Possibilities for Political Science," *American Political Science Review* 96, no. 4 (2002): 713–28.

51. Herbert Blumer, *Symbolic Interactionism: Perspective and Method* (Engelwood Cliffs, N.J.: Prentice Hall, 1969); Edelman, *Constructing the Political Spectacle;* and Erving Goffman, *Behavior in Public Places: Notes on the Social Organization of Gatherings* (New York: Free Press, 1963).

52. Amartya Sen, *Development as Freedom* (New York: Knopf, 1999); Akhil Gupta, *Postcolonial Developments: Agriculture in the Making of Modern India* (Durham: Duke University Press, 1998); Arturo Escobar, *Encountering Development: The Making and Unmaking of the Third World* (Princeton: Princeton University Press, 1995); Frederick Cooper and Randy Packard, eds., *International Development and the Social Sciences* (Berkeley: University of California Press, 1998); Guy Gran, "Beyond African Famines: Whose Knowledge Matters?" *Alternatives* 11 (1986): 275–96; Fergu-

son, *Anti-politics Machine;* Robert Wade, "Japan, the World Bank, and the Art of Paradigm Maintenance: The East Asian Miracle in Political Perspective," *New Left Review* 217 (1996): 3–36.

53. Jessica Tuchman Matthews, "Redefining Security," *Foreign Affairs* 68 (Spring 1989): 162–77; Keith Krause and Michael Williams, "Broadening the Agenda of Security Studies: Politics and Methods," *Mershon International Studies Review* 40, no. 2 (1996): 229–54; United Nations Development Program, *Human Development Report 1994* (New York: Oxford University Press, 1994); Boutros Boutros-Ghali, *Agenda for Peace,* 2nd ed. (New York: United Nations, 1995).

54. Mayer N. Zald, "Culture, Ideology, and Strategic Framing," in Doug McAdam, John D. McCarthy, and Mayer N. Zald, eds., *Comparative Perspectives on Social Movements: Political Opportunities, Mobilizing Structures, and Cultural Framing* (New York: Cambridge University Press, 1996), 262. See also Erving Goffman, *Frame Analysis: An Essay on the Organization of Experience* (Cambridge: Harvard University Press, 1974), 21; David Snow, E. Burke Rochford, Steven K. Worden, and Robert D. Benford, "Frame Alignment Processes, Micromobilization, and Movement Participation," *American Sociological Review* 51, no. 4 (1986): 464.

55. Richard Price, "Reversing the Gun Sights: Transnational Civil Society Targets Land Mines," *International Organization* 52, no. 3: 613–44.

56. Katzenstein, *Culture of National Security;* Finnemore, *National Interests in International Society;* Jeffrey W. Legro, "Which Norms Matter? Revisiting the 'Failure' of Internationalism," *International Organization* 51, no. 1 (1997): 31–64.

57. Roland Paris, *At War's End: Building Peace after Civil Conflict* (New York: Cambridge University Press, 2004); Allen Lens, "From Peacekeeping to Peace-Building: The United Nations and the Challenge of Intrastate War," in Mark W. Zacher and Richard M. Price, eds., *The United Nations and Global Security* (New York: Palgrave Macmillan, 2004).

58. March and Olsen, *Rediscovering Institutions,* chap. 5.

59. Joseph Nye, "Nuclear Learning and U.S.-Soviet Security Regimes," *International Organization* 41, no. 3 (1987): 371–402; Haas, *When Knowledge Is Power;* Ernst Haas and Peter Haas, "Learning to Learn: Some Thoughts on Improving International Governance of the Global Problematique," in Commission on Global Governance, ed., *Issues in Global Governance* (Boston: Clair Law International, 1995); Scott Sagan, *The Limits of Safety: Organizations, Accidents, and Nuclear Weapons* (Princeton: Princeton University Press, 1993).

60. Two exceptions are Gallarotti, "Limits of International Organization," and Snidal, "Political Economy and International Institutions."

61. Snidal, "Political Economy and International Institutions."

62. See Diane Vaughan, "The Dark Side of Organizations," *Annual Review of Sociology* 25 (1999): 283–84, for a similar discussion concerning the difficulty in determining what constitutes a "mistake" and the need to take into account the organization's perspective.

63. This is consistent with what anthropologists call a multisited analysis. See George Marcus, "Ethnography in/of the World System: The Emergence of Multi-Sited Ethnography," in his *Ethnography through Thick and Thin* (Princeton: Princeton University Press, 1998), 79–104; Shore and Wright, "Policy," 14; Michael Burawoy et al., eds., *Global Ethnography: Forces, Connections, and Imaginations in a Postmodern World* (Berkeley: University of California Press, 2000).

64. Graham Allison and Phillip Zelikow, *Essence of Decision: Explaining the Cuban Missile Crisis,* 2nd ed. (New York: Longman, 1999); Haas, *When Knowledge Is Power;* Cox, Jacobson, et al., *Anatomy of Influence;* Cox and Jacobson, "Decision Making."

65. Graham Allison, *Essence of Decision: Explaining the Cuban Missile Crisis* (Boston: Little, Brown, 1971), 144; Jonathan Bendor and Thomas Hammond, "Rethinking Allison's Models," *American Political Science Review* 82, no. 2 (1992): 301–22; Edmund Beard, *Developing the ICBM: A Study in Bureaucratic Politics* (New York: Columbia University Press, 1976).

66. We use these distinctions between external and internal culture and between material and cultural arguments as analytic tools only. As others have argued, organizations can be permeated by their environments, making the two difficult to distinguish, and culture is not separable from the material world.

67. John Meyer and Brian Rowan, "Institutionalized Organizations: Formal Structure as Myth and Ceremony," *American Journal of Sociology* 83 (1977): 340–63; Martha Finnemore, "Norms, Culture, and World Politics: Insights from Sociology's Institutionalism," *International Organization* 50, no. 2 (1996): 325–47.

68. Connie McNeely, *Constructing the Nation-State: International Organization and Prescriptive Action* (Westport, Conn.: Greenwood Press, 1995).

69. The term *pathologies* to describe organizational behavior has been used elsewhere, most extensively in W. Richard Scott, *Organizations: Rational, Natural, and Open Systems,* 3rd ed. (Englewood Cliffs: Prentice-Hall, 1992), chap. 12. Scott's concerns are not international, and he focuses mostly on individual-level causes of pathological behavior. Karl Deutsch also used the concept of pathology in *The Nerves of Government: Models of Political Communication and Control* (Glencoe: Free Press, 1963), 170. We thank Hayward Alker for drawing our attention to Deutsch's similar usage of the concept.

70. Vaughan, *Challenger Launch Decision;* Lipartito, "Culture and the Practice of Business History."

71. March and Olsen, *Rediscovering Institutions,* 21–27; Meyer and Rowan, "Institutionalized Organizations."

72. March and Olsen, *Rediscovering Institutions,* 26–27.

73. Paul DiMaggio and Walter Powell, "The Iron Cage Revisited: Institutional Isomorphism and Collective Rationality in Organizational Fields," *American Sociological Review* 48, no. 2 (1983): 147–60; Schein, "Culture."

74. Vaughan, *Challenger Launch Decision,* 64.

75. Starr, "Social Categories and Claims in the Liberal State," 160; Mary Douglas, *How Institutions Think* (Syracuse: Syracuse University Press, 1986); Berger and Luckmann, *Social Construction of Reality,* chap. 1.

76. Campbell, "Institutional Analysis and the Role of Ideas in Political Economy," 378; Immergut, "Theoretical Core of the New Institutionalism," 14–19.

77. In "The Politics, Power, and Pathologies of International Organizations," we provide brief illustrations of pathologies associated with these mechanisms.

78. David Beetham, *Max Weber and the Theory of Modern Politics* (New York: Polity, 1985), 76.

79. Josiah McC. Heyman, "Putting Power in the Anthropology of Bureaucracy," *Current Anthropology* 36 (1995): 262.

80. Haas, *When Knowledge Is Power,* chap. 3.

81. Vaughan, *Challenger Launch Decision.*

82. Berger and Luckmann, *Social Construction of Reality,* chap. 1; Douglas, *How Institutions Think;* March and Olsen, *Rediscovering Institutions;* Starr, "Social Categories and Claims in the Liberal State."

83. March and Olsen, *Rediscovering Institutions,* chap. 5.

84. Stewart Clegg, "Power and Institutions in the Theory of Organizations," in John Hassard and Martin Parker, eds., *Toward a New Theory of Organizations* (New York: Routledge, 1994), 30; Vaughan, *Challenger Launch Decision,* 64; Martin, *Cultures in Organizations.*

85. Haas, *When Knowledge Is Power,* 188.

86. Philip Selznick, *Leadership in Administration: A Sociological Interpretation* (Evanston: Peterson, 1957); Charles Perrow, *Complex Organizations: A Critical Essay* (New York: Random House, 1986).

87. Pfeffer and Salancik, *External Control of Organizations.*

88. Morton Halperin, *Bureaucratic Politics and Foreign Policy* (Washington, D.C.: Brookings Institution, 1974).

89. G. John Ikenberry, *After Victory: Institutions, Strategic Restraint, and the Rebuilding of Order after Major Wars* (Princeton: Princeton University Press, 2001).

90. Keohane, *After Hegemony.*

91. Thatcher and Sweet, "Theory and Practice of Delegation to Non-majoritarian Institutions."

92. Howard Alford, *Organizations Evolving* (Thousand Oaks, Calif.: Sage, 2000), 49.

93. W. Richard Scott, "The Adolescence of Institutional Theory," *Administrative Science Quarterly* 32, no. 4 (1987): 493–511.

94. Weick, *Sensemaking in Organizations.*

95. These observations also are well established in the literature on organizational theory and bureaucratic change. See March, "Footnotes to Organizational Change," in his *Decisions and Organizations,* 167–87; and James G. March, "The Evolution of Evolution," in his *Pursuit of Organizational Intelligence* (Malden, Mass.: Blackwell, 1999), 100–113.

96. Raymond Miles and Charles Snow, *Organizational Strategy, Structure, and Process* (Stanford: Stanford Business Books, 2003), xv–xxv; D. Levinthal and J. March, "A Model of Adaptive Organizational Search," in March, *Decisions and Organizations,* 187–218.

97. Shanks, Jacobson, and Kaplan, "Inertia and Change in the Constellation of International

Governmental Organizations"; Jon Pevehouse, "Tracing the Dynamics of International Organizations," manuscript, University of Wisconsin–Madison, 2002.

CHAPTER 3. EXPERTISE AND POWER AT THE INTERNATIONAL MONETARY FUND

1. Although those adopting principal-agent analyses provide sophisticated explanations for the source of the IMF's autonomy, they are less interested in how staff use that autonomy, what policies they want to pursue, and why. See for example Lisa Martin, "Distribution, Information, and Delegation in International Organizations: The Case of IMF Conditionality," manuscript, August 2002.

2. Moisés Naím discusses goal congestion and its effect on the World Bank in "The World Bank: Its Role, Governance, and Organizational Culture," in Bretton Woods Commission, *Bretton Woods: Looking to the Future* (Washington, D.C.: Bretton Woods Commission, 1994), C273–87.

3. For full text see article 1 of the Articles of Agreement.

4. Margaret Garritsen de Vries, *Balance of Payments Adjustment, 1945–1986: The IMF Experience* (Washington, D.C.: International Monetary Fund, 1987), 1.

5. For a complete list of executive directors and countries they represent, see http://www.imf.org/external/np/sec/memdir/eds.htm. Interestingly, the executive board rarely votes on most matters. Instead, the managing director simply concludes the discussions with a statement about "the sense of the meeting," which constitutes the board's decision. There is a strong norm of consensus decision making in the board. Of course, "consensus" in these cases does not necessarily mean that all EDs agree; but it does mean that they all recognize how a vote would come out if one were taken and they prefer not to oppose the inevitable publicly. This modus operandi seems a bit anomalous since state representatives in other large public bureaucracies seem perfectly willing to stake out opposed positions. See discussion in Kenneth W. Stiles, *Negotiating Debt: The IMF Lending Process* (Boulder: Westview Press, 1981), 37–40; also R. S. Eckaus, "How the IMF Lives with Its Conditionality," *Policy Sciences* 19 (1986): 237–52.

6. After the messy selection of Horst Köhler in March 2000, the Fund began revising its selection procedures for the managing director's position. For current details, see the Fund website at http://www.imf.org. The tradition of European managing directors came about largely by accident. The Americans had originally wanted Harry Dexter White to be the first managing director, but he was knocked out of the running for political reasons, and a Belgian, Camille Gutt, was chosen. The Americans then claimed the Bank leadership, and this division has persisted ever since. See Harold James, *International Monetary Cooperation since Bretton Woods* (New York: Oxford University Press, 1996), 72.

7. Because of their direct connection to voting rights, quota increases are highly political. The February 2001 decision to increase China's quota only to the exact level of the smallest G-7 country (Canada) was widely perceived by developing countries as a clear signal that no developing country would be allowed more votes than a G-7 member. Saudi Arabia is the exception. It holds 3.23 percent of the votes in the Fund, but its huge foreign exchange earnings from oil exports give it a unique place in monetary politics. For a complete and current listing of percent votes held by members, see the posting at the Fund's website: http://www.imf.org/external/np/sec/memdir/members.htm#total. Totals quoted here are as of March 2004. For more on quota assessments see http://www.imf.org/external/pubs/ft/exrp/what.htm#2.

8. Note, however, that the Fund does have the authority to raise money on private sources even though it has never used it. See Jonathan E. Sanford, "IMF and World Bank: US Contributions and Agency Budgets," *Congressional Research Service Report for Congress RS20413*, December 9, 1999. Available at http://www.cnie.org/nle/inter-51.html. Further, the Fund does often broker arrangements between state borrowers and private banks, arrangements that have functional similarities to private market resources, but the similarities are limited. Under these packages, members borrow from the banks directly, and banks oversee these loans, not the Fund. The recent debt relief initiative for heavily indebted poor countries (HIPC) also suggests some branching out into voluntary contributions as a source of funding. HIPC funds are essentially voluntary contributions by wealthy states for the purpose of debt relief among the poorest states. They are administered by the Fund and the Bank within the Poverty Reduction and Growth Facility but are treated as a separate pot of money that complements regular Fund lending. Since these are entirely state monies, there is no obvious reason why they would constitute

a source of autonomy for the Fund. For more on HIPC see http://www.imf.org/external/np/hipc/hipc.htm.

9. For more on where the IMF gets its money see Sanford, "IMF and World Bank"; also see the Fund's own account at http://www.imf.org/external/np/tre/ffo/2001/fin.htm.

10. Note that this autonomy for staff was also not anticipated by states when they created the Fund. In its earliest years, EDs were much more directly involved in the Fund's work than they are today. For example, in the late 1940s, EDs still approved the staff composition of every mission to member states and often participated in missions themselves. These practices ended in the late 1940s and 1950s, and both scholars and participants in these changes agree that the substantial degree of staff autonomy that currently exists at the Fund was consolidated in this period. See M. G. de Vries and J. K. Horsefield, *Analysis*, vol. 2 of *The International Monetary Fund, 1945–1965: Twenty Years of International Monetary Cooperation*, ed. J. Keith Horsefield (Washington, D.C.: International Monetary Fund, 1969), 10–12; J. K. Horsefield, *Chronicle*, vol. 1 of *The International Monetary Fund, 1945–1965*, 470–73; Frank A. Southard, *The Evolution of the International Monetary Fund* (Princeton, N.J.: International Finance Section, Dept. of Economics, Princeton University, 1979), 3; Martin "Distribution, Information, and Delegation in International Organizations."

11. Staff interviews with Finnemore; Stanley Fischer, "Applied Economics in Action: IMF Programs," AEA Papers and Proceedings, *American Economic Review* 87, no. 2 (1997): 23–27. Note, too, that members cannot go directly to the board with a program and ask for resources. Argentina tried this once in 1984 and was rejected. They must work through the staff. Similarly, the United Kingdom invited the managing director to London for direct negotiations in 1967, bypassing the usual staff mission. The invitation was "indignantly" declined. See Stiles, *Negotiating Debt*, 174 and 30.

12. For a more detailed analysis of Fund staffing and personnel recruitment, see Peter Evans and Martha Finnemore, "Expanding the Voice of the South at the International Monetary Fund," G-24 Discussion Paper Series no. 15 (New York: UNCTAD, December 2001), available at http://www.unctad.org/en/docs//pogdsmdpbg24d15.en.pdf

13. For a more detailed discussion of the internal workings of the Fund, including missions, see Stiles, *Negotiating Debt*, chap. 2; and Richard H. R. Harper, *Inside the IMF: An Ethnography of Documents, Technology, and Organizational Action* (New York: Academic Press, 1998).

14. Continuity among staff is relatively high at the Fund, certainly higher than on the executive board, many of whose members rotate and stay only a few years. De Vries and Horsefield, among others, argue that this experience has increased deference to staff. De Vries and Horsefield, *Analysis*, 11–12.

15. De Vries's treatment of this history is excellent and very readable. See De Vries, *Balance of Payments Adjustment*, chap. 1. See also Edward Bernstein's firsthand account in "The Early Years of the International Monetary Fund," in Jacob A. Frenkel and Morris Goldstein, eds., *International Financial Policy: Essays in Honor of Jacques J. Polak* (Washington, D.C.: International Monetary Fund, 1991), 58–63. Bernstein was the first director of the Fund's research department. For a more contemporary analysis see Ngaire Woods, "The IMF, the World Bank, and International Relations," manuscript, 2004, esp. chap. 3.

16. Logistics for the system had to be provided by some loose coordination among central bankers under Bank of England leadership, but there was certainly no formal arrangement of international policy coordination. Beth A. Simmons, "Legalization of International Monetary Affairs," *International Organization* 54. no. 3 (2000): 575.

17. Kenneth W. Dam, *The Rules of the Game: Reform and Evolution of the International Monetary System* (Chicago: University of Chicago Press, 1982), chaps. 2–3; De Vries, *Balance of Payments Adjustment*, chap. 1. Louis Pauly gives an excellent and detailed account of the intertwined evolution of intellectual and normative understandings in this period in *Who Elected the Bankers? Surveillance and Control in the World Economy* (Ithaca: Cornell University Press, 1997), esp. chaps. 3–4.

18. Bernstein, "Early Years of the International Monetary Fund," 58–63; Jacques J. Polak, "The IMF Monetary Model: A Hardy Perennial," *Finance and Development* 34 (December 1997): 16–19; De Vries, *Balance of Payments Adjustment*, chap. 1. Bernstein was the first director of the IMF's research department; Polak was his deputy and later succeeded him.

19. De Vries, *Balance of Payments Adjustment*; James, *International Monetary Cooperation since Bretton Woods*, esp. 82–83.

20. Jacques J. Polak, "International Trade Theory—Discussion," American Economic Asso-

ciation Annual Meetings, December 1951, *American Economic Review, Papers and Proceedings* 42 (May 1952): 179–81, as cited in Jacob A. Frenkel, Morris Goldstein, and Mohsin S. Khan, "Major Themes in the Writings of Jacques J. Polak," in Frenkel and Goldstein, eds., *International Financial Policy*, 8–9.

21. Jacques J. Polak, "Depreciation to Meet a Situation of Overinvestment," September 10, 1948. The paper was eventually published in a volume of essays written in Polak's honor. See Frenkel and Goldstein, eds., *International Financial Policy*, 46–57.

22. Sidney S. Alexander, "Effects of a Devaluation on a Trade Balance," *IMF Staff Papers* 2 (April 1952): 263–78. Note that elasticities by no means disappeared as an analytic tool, but their role was much different. See De Vries, *Balance of Payments Adjustment*, 19.

23. For discussions of the development and importance of the absorption approach, see Frenkel, Goldstein, and Kahn, "Major Themes in the Writings of Jacques J. Polak," 8–10; De Vries, *Balance of Payments Adjustment*, 16–19; James, *International Monetary Cooperation since Bretton Woods*, 82–83.

24. Jacques J. Polak, "Monetary Analysis of Income Formation and Payments Problems," *IMF Staff Papers*, no. 6 (1957): 1–50. Early versions of these ideas were introduced at the Fund by Robert Triffin in a 1946 paper and had been explored by Bernstein, head of the research department, in the early 1950s, but it was Polak's paper that pulled together several strands of thinking into the more complete model and showed its utility. See De Vries, *Balance of Payments Adjustment*, 27–30; Frenkel, Goldstein, and Kahn, "Major Themes in the Writings of Jacques J. Polak," 20–22.

25. This framework continues to be the basis for the Fund's analyses, as illustrated by its most recent staff paper on techniques of financial programming, "Theoretical Aspects of the Design of Fund-Supported Adjustment Programs," International Monetary Fund, Occasional Paper no. 55, September 1987; also see Frenkel, Goldstein, and Kahn, "Major Themes in the Writings of Jacques J. Polak," 21. For more on the content and history of this model, see Jacques J. Polak, "The IMF Monetary Model at Forty," *IMF Working Paper*, April 1997; Polak, "IMF Monetary Model: A Hardy Perennial," 16–19; Frenkel, Goldstein, and Kahn, "Major Themes in the Writings of Jacques J. Polak"; James, *International Monetary Cooperation since Bretton Woods*, chap. 5, esp. pp. 140–42; De Vries, *Balance of Payments Adjustment*, chap. 1; Stiles, *Negotiating Debt*, 4–16; Wilfred L. David, *The IMF Policy Paradigm* (New York: Praeger, 1985), chap. 3; Eckaus, "How the IMF Lives with Its Conditionality," 239–42.

26. In "Economic Missionaries," chap. 3, Woods also discusses alternative understandings of the balance-of-payments problem not adopted by the Fund.

27. There is a "scarce currency" clause in the articles that could provide the basis for some expanded authority vis-à-vis surplus states, just as the "adequate safeguard" language became the basis for the huge edifice of conditionality. We could find no evidence that this attempt had ever been made, however.

28. Polak, "IMF Monetary Model at Forty"; Polak, "IMF Monetary Model: A Hardy Perennial"; David, *IMF Policy Paradigm*, 39–40.

29. On the concept of intellectual technologies, see Peter Miller and Nikolas Rose, "Governing Economic Life," *Economy and Society* 19, no. 1 (1990): 1–31. Intellectual technologies "render aspects of existence amenable to inscription and calculation," according to Miller and Rose.

30. The articles were amended in 1969 to recognize the principle of conditionality. See Sidney Dell, *On Being Grandmotherly: The Evolution of IMF Conditionality*, Essays in International Finance 144 (Princeton, N.J.: International Finance Section, Dept. of Economics, Princeton University, 1981), 13–14.

31. Harold James, "From Grandmotherliness to Governance: The Evolution of IMF Conditionality," *Finance and Development* 35, no. 4 (1998); see online version at http://www.imf.org/external/pubs/ft/fandd/1998/12/james.htm.

32. Dell, *On Being Grandmotherly*, has a good discussion of these debates. See also James, "From Grandmotherliness to Governance."

33. Dell, *On Being Grandmotherly*, 6; Horsefield, *Chronicle*, 69.

34. On the overarching normative and political goals of the Bretton Woods institutions, see Pauly, *Who Elected the Bankers?* esp. chap. 5.

35. Horsefield, *Chronicle*, 276; Dell, *On Being Grandmotherly*, 8–9.

36. E.B. Decision no. 102-(52/11), February 13, 1952; J. Keith Horsefield and Gertrud Lovasy, "Evolution of the Fund's Policy on Drawings," in De Vries and Horsefield, *Analysis*, 402; Horsefield, *Chronicle*, 321–26; James, *International Monetary Cooperation since Bretton Woods*, 80–81.

37. Part of the reason standbys became such powerful tools of conditionality was that while there is a legal right of members to draw under the articles, there is no legal right to a standby arrangement. Hence, Fund staff discretion in these matters is high. See Dam, *Rules of the Game,* 122–27; James, *International Monetary Cooperation since Bretton Woods,* 78–83; Horsefield, *Chronicle,* 328–32.

38. In fact, subsequent evaluation by Fund staff indicated that the use of Fund reserves had been relatively unimportant in the rapid and successful stabilization of these countries through the 1950s. What had mattered much more, the Fund found, was the rediscovery of monetary policy as a tool. Monetary policy had fallen into disfavor (and disuse) after the Depression, and the founders of the Fund at Bretton Woods had not anticipated it as a useful tool. Postwar inflation and huge transfers of resources from the United States made it possible for Europe and Japan to use monetary policy to disinflate their economies with minimal impact on employment or growth. These findings bolstered their confidence in recommending uses of monetary instruments elsewhere. See J. Marcus Fleming, "Developments in the International Payments System," *IMF Staff Papers* 10 (November 1963): 461–82, and De Vries's discussion in *Balance of Payments Adjustment,* 36–59.

39. According to the managing director in 1981, "While we continue to stress the importance of appropriate demand management, we now systematically emphasize the development of the productive base of the economy and we contemplate that countries may, therefore, need our financing for longer periods." *IMF Survey,* February 9, 1981, 35.

40. IMF, "Theoretical Aspects of the Design of Fund-Supported Adjustment Programs," Occasional Paper no. 55 (Washington, D.C.: IMF, 1987).

41. For detailed tables and analysis see Devesh Kapur and Richard Webb, "Governance-Related Conditionalities of the IFIs," paper prepared for the XII Technical Group Meeting of the Intergovernmental Group of 24 for International Monetary Affairs, Lima, Peru, March 1–3, 2000. Revised May 2000.

42. James, *International Monetary Cooperation since Bretton Woods,* 133; Horsefield, *Chronicle,* 552–59.

43. Horsefield, *Chronicle,* 310–21; James, *International Monetary Cooperation since Bretton Woods,* 133–34.

44. There is an extended literature now on the sociology of statistics that investigates, among other things, the ways in which "statistics are lenses through which we form images of our society." See, for example, William Alonso and Paul Starr, eds., *The Politics of Numbers* (New York: Russell Sage Foundation, 1987); and Theodore M. Porter, *Trust in Numbers: The Pursuit of Objectivity in Science and Public Life* (Princeton: Princeton University Press, 1995). Quotation is from Alonso and Starr's introduction, p. 3.

45. For an ethnography of the Fund that includes the author's account of accompanying a mission, see Harper, *Inside the IMF.*

46. Jacques J. Polak, *The Changing Nature of IMF Conditionality,* Essays in International Finance 184 (Princeton, N.J.: International Finance Section, Dept. of Economics, Princeton University, 1991), 2.

47. Graham Bird, *IMF Lending to Developing Countries: Issues and Evidence* (New York: Routledge, 1995); Tony Killick, *IMF Programmes in Developing Countries: Design and Impact* (London: Routledge, 1995); IMF, "Theoretical Aspects of the Design of Fund-Supported Adjustment Programs," 28; Fischer, "Applied Economics in Action"; Polak, *Changing Nature of IMF Conditionality,* 41–50; Mohsin S. Khan, "Evaluating the Effects of IMF-Supported Adjustment Programs: A Survey," in Kate Phylaktis and Mahmood Pradhan, eds., *International Finance and the Less-Developed Countries* (London: Macmillan, 1990).

48. For details on governance conditionality, see Kapur and Webb, "Governance-Related Conditionalities of the IFIs."

49. Time is the major constraint on such meetings. The missions are still only a few weeks long and still entail the original core tasks of collecting and analyzing data on which to formulate a program.

50. Fund staff interviews with Finnemore. Note that this runs counter to the previous conventional wisdom. Academics and policymakers used to believe that authoritarian governments would be better able to implement economic austerity programs than democratic ones because they were not beholden to broad constituent bases hurt by austerity. Now the conventional wisdom is the opposite: only democratic governments have the legitimacy to impose aus-

terity and get it accepted by their societies. See Kurt Weyland, "The Political Fate of Market Reform in Latin America, Africa, and Eastern Europe," *International Studies Quarterly* 42, no. 4 (1998): 645–73.

51. Interviews suggest some variation in practice. Some staff take a more hands-off approach to the writing of these papers than others; some borrower governments are more interested in writing the papers themselves than others.

52. Martin, "Distribution, Information, and Delegation in International Organizations."

53. Dell, *On Being Grandmotherly*, 12–14.

54. Staff interviews with Finnemore; and Polak, *Changing Nature of IMF Conditionality*, esp. 24–41. Note that once these concerns are handed to the staff, staff begin constructing connections between the environment, military spending, and so on and their macroeconomic frameworks. As a result, the Fund's environmental concerns focus on issues most directly related to economic viability and sustainable balance of payments. For example, the Fund discourages reckless logging of tropical hardwood resources and recommends that governments adopt adequate tax and investment policies to promote sustainable management. It is also extremely interested in quantifying environmental costs since this would render knowledge about the environment objective and susceptible to action by the Fund and other IOs. (See section V of this chapter.) For a good example of the Fund's thinking on environmental issues see Ved P. Gandhi, "The IMF and the Environment" (Washington, D.C.: International Monetary Fund, 1998). Available at http://www.imf.org/external/pubs/ft/exrp/environ/index.htm#4.

55. Erica Gould, "Money Talks: Supplementary Financiers and International Monetary Fund Conditionality," *International Organization* 57, no. 3 (2003): 551–86.

56. The Fund's concern with the environment, for example, can be traced to legislation by the U.S. Congress directing the U.S. executive director at the Fund to persuade the Fund to provide systematic reviews of the impact of its policies on the environment and sustainable natural resources. The concern with poverty has diffuse roots, but both interview and written sources agree that external criticism of the effects of Fund programs by academics and NGOs was crucial to gaining the attention of managing directors Jacques de Larosière and Michel Camdessus. Staff interviews with Finnemore; and Polak, *Changing Nature of IMF Conditionality*, 24–29.

57. Staff interviews with Finnemore. This finding is consistent with previous research on mission expansion at the World Bank. William Ascher similarly found that directives that required staff to undertake tasks outside their professional expertise were neglected, even resisted, by Bank staff. Michelle Miller-Adams's study of the Bank also showed how politically driven missions coming from outside the Fund, such as good governance and participatory development, tended to be sidelined within the organizational structure rather than integrated into the heart of project planning, whereas new missions that made sense to the development economists at the Bank (such as development of the private sector in borrowing countries) tended to be more mainstreamed in the project-planning process. William Ascher, "New Development Approaches and the Adaptability of International Agencies: The Case of the World Bank," *International Organization* 37, no. 3 (1983): 415–39; Michelle Miller-Adams, *The World Bank: New Agendas in a Changing World* (New York; Routledge, 1999).

58. Staff interviews with Finnemore.

59. Friends of the Earth, World Resources Institute, and Center of Concern, among others, have published numerous critiques of IMF activities that are available at their websites: http://www.foe.org, www.wri.org, and www.igc.org/coc/rbwtext.htm.

60. Many would argue that the most important pathological behavior coming out of the Fund is the result not of goal congestion but of the core macroeconomic policy recommendations themselves. Critics have charged that Fund programs consistently favor rich financiers and hurt the poor in deficit countries, and might characterize this as pathological. Certainly these policies come from the internal shared knowledge of the Fund and in that sense fit our definition of pathology. Whether they run counter to the organization's mission, though, is a matter of perspective, as discussed in chapter 2. The Fund responds to these critics by saying that its mission is to stabilize the financial system, and doing so often has unfortunate consequences for the poor. Thus, much of that debate is less about poor performance than about the nature of the mission.

61. Dell, *On Being Grandmotherly*, 16–24.

62. See Martin Feldstein, "Refocusing the IMF," *Foreign Affairs* 77 (March/April 1998): 20–33; Steven Radelet and Jeffrey D. Sachs, "What Have We Learned, So Far, from the Asian Fi-

nancial Crisis," HIID working paper available at http://www.hiid.edu/pub/other/aea122.pdf; Paul Krugman, "The Return of Depression Economics," *Foreign Affairs* 78 (January/February 1999): 56–74.

63. For example, the IMF established a special fund in 1974 to help states deal with huge swings in the price of oil.

64. Porter offers a more generalized argument about the interrelationship of public bureaucracy and quantification. Public bureaucracies generate most of the world's statistics because counting and measuring are essential to their intervention in societies and have been since the rise of the state in the early modern era, when taxation and conscription were greatly facilitated by knowledge of where money and people resided. Statistics, in turn, legitimate exercises of bureaucratic power because they appear objective, impartial, and efficient. See Porter, *Trust in Numbers*, 3–86.

65. Ibid., 8.

66. This creates a Catch-22 situation for the Fund. The Fund, like many bureaucracies, has been heavily criticized for applying "cookie-cutter" policy prescriptions that ignore diverse local circumstances; however, this behavior flows from the need to appear objective and fair. While they cannot avoid exercising judgment and discretion and are quick to deny charges of cookie-cutter policies, staff also fear that excessive tailoring of programs may prompt charges of favoritism, of arbitrariness, or being political in their actions. Staff interviews with Finnemore. Staff are well aware that political views of other states toward a borrower can influence Fund policy (Russia in the 1990s was the example most cited in interviews), but staff tend to view insertion of geostrategic political concerns of this type as the province of the board. Offering unbiased recommendations is the staff's job; if the board chooses to modify these in view of geostrategic considerations, that is its privilege. Staff interviews with Finnemore.

67. This section draws on the arguments of Porter, *Trust in Numbers;* Harper, *Inside the IMF;* Jean Lave, "The Values of Quantification," in John Law, ed., *Power, Action, and Belief* (London: Routledge and Kegan Paul, 1986), 88–111; Peter Miller and Ted O'Leary, "Accounting and the Construction of the Governable Person," *Accounting, Organizations and Society* 12, no. 3 (1987): 235–65; and Alonso and Starr, *Politics of Numbers.*

68. Note that standardized formal mathematics is itself a social construction. People can often perform sophisticated arithmetic calculations in diverse practical situations but are unable to perform the same type of calculation with pencil and paper in formal mathematical tests. Lave, "Values of Quantification," 88–111.

69. Moreover, when scholars of epistemic communities examine the influence of technical knowledge, they usually assume that the knowledge is already out there, waiting to be applied to problems. Our examination of the Fund shows that the creation of expertise is a major task of these experts and a crucial source of their influence. See Peter M. Haas, ed., "Knowledge, Power, and International Policy Coordination," *International Organization* 47 (1992), special issue.

70. For the pre-UN history, see Anthony Endres and Grant Fleming, *International Organizations and the Analysis of Economic Policy, 1919–1950* (New York: Cambridge University Press, 2002).

71. Staff interviews with Finnemore; Harper, *Inside the IMF*, esp. chap. 8. In chapter 6 Harper provides an extended analysis of the Fund's statistics department. Staff descriptions of dealing with poor data on missions are very much in line with Harper's account.

72. Harper, *Inside the IMF*, 226.

73. Porter calls this "the creative power of statistics" (*Trust in Numbers*, 37). For an extended discussion of the ways in which bureaucratization creates statistics and statistics then re-create the world, see pp. 1–86.

74. William A. Niskanen, *Bureaucracy and Representative Government* (Chicago: Aldine, 1971).

CHAPTER 4. DEFINING REFUGEES AND VOLUNTARY REPATRIATION AT THE UNITED NATIONS HIGH COMMISSIONER FOR REFUGEES

1. See Louise Holborn, *Refugees, Problem of Our Time: The Work of the United Nations High Commissioner for Refugees*, 2 vols. (Metuchen, N.J.: Scarecrow Press, 1975), 1:109, on the lack of UNHCR autonomy because of the dependence on state authority and resources. Gil Loescher provides a succinct statement on UNHCR's autonomy in "The UNHCR and World Politics:

State Interests vs. Institutional Autonomy," *International Migration Review* 35 (Spring 2001): 33–56.

2. Pitterman, however, notes various ways in which large donors do not control outcomes. See Shelly Pitterman, "International Responses to Refugee Situations: The United Nations High Commissioner for Refugees," in Elizabeth G. Ferris, ed., *Refugees and World Politics* (New York: Praeger, 1985), 67–68, 77.

3. Sadruddin Aga Khan, "Legal Problems Relating to Refugees and Displaced Persons," paper delivered at the Hague Academy of International Law, August 4–6, 1976, 42–43; Félix Schnyder, "Les aspects juridiques actuels du problème des réfugiés," *Hague Academy of International Law, Recueil des cours,* 114 (1965): 6, 13; B. S. Chimni, "The Meaning of Words and the Role of the UNHCR in Voluntary Repatriation," *International Journal of Refugee Law* 5, no. 3 (1993): 443; Chimni, "The Geopolitics of Refugee Studies: A View from the South," *Journal of Refugee Studies* 11, no. 4 (1998): 350–74; Gil Loescher, *The UNHCR in World Politics: A Perilous Path* (New York: Oxford University Press, 2001).

4. See Barry Stein, "Durable Solutions for Developing Country Refugees," *International Migration Review* 20, no. 2 (1986): 264–82; Marjolene Zieck, *UNHCR and Voluntary Repatriation of Refugees* (Boston: Martinus Nijhoff, 1997), 434; Fred Cuny and Barry Stein, "Prospects for and Promotion of Spontaneous Repatriation," in Gil Loescher and Laila Monahan, eds., *Refugees and International Relations* (New York: Oxford University Press, 1989), 306; Guy Goodwin-Gill, "Voluntary Repatriation: Legal and Policy Issues," in ibid., 274; Jeff Crisp, "Voluntary Repatriation Programmes for African Refugees: A Critical Examination," *Refugee Issues* 1, no. 2 (1984): 1–25; Hiram Ruiz, "When Refugees Won't Go Home: The Dilemma of Chadians in Sudan," report for the U.S. Committee on Refugees, 1987; Human Rights Watch, *Uncertain Refugee: International Failures to Protect Refugees,* Human Rights Watch Report vol. 9, no. 1(G) (1997), 5–12.

5. Throughout we use Burma instead of Myanmar. In 1989 the military regime promoted the name Myanmar (a derivative of the Burmese short-form name Myanma Naingngandawas) as the conventional name for their state. Because this decision was not approved by any sitting legislature in Burma and instead was a unilateral act done by a highly authoritarian government, many states, including the United States, and many NGOs, including the ones that produced the reports that we use in this book, continue to use Burma. We follow this convention.

6. According to the *Oxford English Dictionary,* the word *refugee* in English was first applied to French Huguenots who came to England after the revocation of the Edict of Nantes in 1685.

7. See Aristide Zolberg, Astri Suhrke, and Sergio Aguayo, *Escape from Violence: Conflict and the Refugee Crisis in the Developing World* (New York: Oxford University Press, 1989), chap. 1; and Gil Loescher, *Beyond Charity: International Cooperation and the Global Refugee Crisis* (New York: Oxford University Press, 1993), 32–36, for concise overviews of refugee flows in historical perspective.

8. Diplomats and formal state representatives were the first holders of such state-authorizing travel documents in Renaissance Europe; it was not until the nineteenth and twentieth centuries that such documenting became generalized. See Garrett Mattingly, *Renaissance Diplomacy* (New York: Dover, 1988); John Torpey, *The Invention of the Passport: Surveillance, Citizenship, and the State* (New York: Cambridge University Press, 1999).

9. John Stoessinger, *The Refugee and the World Community* (Minneapolis: University of Minnesota Press, 1956).

10. Holborn, *Refugees, Problem of Our Time.*

11. Nansen's "humanitarian" instincts did not always produce outcomes that accord with contemporary human or refugee rights. In expanding HCR's role he became the principal architect of the permanent, compulsory exchange of populations between Greece and Turkey, signed at Lausanne in January 1923, which expelled and resettled nearly five hundred thousand people. Gervase Coles, "Approaching the Refugee Problem Today," in Loescher and Monahan, *Question of Refugees,* 373–410.

12. Gervase Coles, "Solutions to the Problem of Refugees and the Protection of Refugees: A Background Study," prepared for the Round Table on Durable Solutions and the Protection of Refugees, convened by the Office of the United Nations High Commissioner for Refugees in conjunction with the International Institute of Humanitarian Law, 1989, p. 43.

13. Gervase Coles, "Voluntary Repatriation: A Background Study," prepared for the Round Table on Voluntary Repatriation, convened by the Office of the United Nations High Commissioner for Refugees in conjunction with the International Institute of Humanitarian Law, San Remo, July 16–19, 1985, p. 31.

14. Coles, "Solutions to the Problem of Refugees," 60–61.

15. Holborn, *Refugees, Problem of Our Time;* Loescher, *UNHCR in World Politics*, 35–37.

16. Goran Melander, *The Two Refugee Definitions* (Lund, Sweden: Raoul Wallenberg Institute, 1987), 8.

17. Lawyers Committee for Human Rights, *UNHCR at 40: Refugee Protection at the Crossroads* (New York: LCHR, 1991), 25–26; Holborn, *Refugees, Problem of Our Time*, chap. 3.

18. Holborn, *Refugees, Problem of Our Time*, 1:63–64.

19. Ibid., 1:59–60; Loescher, *Beyond Charity*, 53.

20. Because a refugee is someone who by definition fears persecution from his national country, every time UNHCR labels an individual a refugee it invariably creates an adversarial relationship between itself and that country. Coles, "Approaching the Refugee Problem Today," 375.

21. There is a hint that the Refugee Convention omitted people displaced from armed conflicts "in part on the assumption that international rules that governed their treatment were or could be incorporated in other articles concerned with human rights of individuals in situations of conflict." Dennis Gallagher, "The Evolution of the International Refugee System," *International Migration Review* 23, no. 3 (1989): 581.

22. Holborn, *Refugees, Problem of Our Time*, 1:62.

23. Aga Khan, "Legal Problems Relating to Refugees and Displaced Persons," 45.

24. David Kennedy, "International Refugee Protection," *Human Rights Quarterly* 8 (1986): 4; also see Holborn, *Refugees, Problem of Our Time*, chap. 4; UNHCR, *State of the World's Refugees: In Search of Solutions* (New York: Oxford University Press, 1995), 83.

25. Kennedy, "International Refugee Protection," 5; also see Jerzy Sztucki, "The Conclusions on the International Protection of Refugees Adopted by the Executive Committee of the UNHCR Programme," *International Journal of Refugee Law* 1, no. 3 (1989): 290–92; Holborn, *Refugees, Problem of Our Time*, 1:156.

26. Gilbert Jaeger, "Status and the Protection of Refugees," International Institute of Human Rights, Ninth Study Session, July 1978, pp. 2 and 38–39.

27. Quoted from Coles, "Solutions to the Problem of Refugees," 81.

28. Holborn, *Refugees, Problem of Our Time*, 1:100, 135.

29. As a humanitarian and apolitical organization, UNHCR was charged with helping to coordinate the operational activities of states and NGOs and with providing legal assistance for refugees. Stated negatively, the UNHCR was not expected to be an operational agency or to address ways to eliminate refugee problems, which, by definition, were political matters. Kennedy, "International Refugee Protection," 14–15; Claudena Skran, "The International Refugee Regime: The Historical and Contemporary Context of International Responses to Asylum Problems," in Gil Loescher, ed., *Refugees and the Asylum Dilemma in the West* (University Park: Pennsylvania State University Press, 1992), 25, 28; Holborn, *Refugees, Problem of Our Time*, 1:89–90. Later the agency developed an operational arm and four key assistance programs: emergency relief operations; longer-term care and maintenance programs; local settlement programs, for those awaiting a solution to their plight and hoping to become self-sufficient in the asylum country; and repatriation and reintegration programs.

30. Holborn, *Refugees, Problem of Our Time*, 1:325–27.

31. Coles, "Approaching the Refugee Problem Today," 389–90; and "Solutions to the Problem of Refugees," 304.

32. Coles, "Solutions to the Problem of Refugees," 105.

33. Ibid., 109–10.

34. Ibid., 149.

35. UNHCR, "The Meaning of Material Assistance," *UNHCR Reports* no. 24 (May–June 1963): 1.

36. Chimni, "Geopolitics of Refugee Studies."

37. UNHCR Executive Committee, "Note on International Protection," July 23, 1985, p. 9; http://www.unhcr.ch.refworld/unhcr/notes/660.htm.

38. See Sztucki, "Conclusions on the International Protection of Refugees," 303–8, for a discussion of how UNHCR conclusions can contribute to international soft law.

39. Michael Barnett, "Humanitarianism with a Sovereign Face: UNHCR in Global Undertow," *International Migration Review* 35, no. 1 (2001): 244–76.

40. Loescher, *UNCHR in World Politics.*

41. Holborn, *Refugees, Problem of Our Time*, 1:158, 160.

42. Aga Khan, "Legal Problems Relating to Refugees and Displaced Persons," 46.

43. James Hathaway, "Reconceiving Refugee Law as Human Rights Protection," *Journal of Refugee Studies* 4, no. 2 (1991): 122.

44. Goodwin-Gill, "Voluntary Repatriation," 260; Guy Goodwin-Gill, *The Refugee in International Law,* 2nd ed. (New York: Oxford University Press, 1996), chap. 4; Skran, "International Refugee Regime," 16; Leon Gordenker, *Refugees in International Politics* (New York: Columbia University Press, 1987), 41.

45. Goodwin-Gill, "Voluntary Repatriation."

46. Loescher, *Beyond Charity,* 64–66; and Loescher, *UNHCR in World Politics.*

47. Skran, "International Refugee Regime," 16; Holborn, *Refugees, Problem of Our Time,* 1:387.

48. Importantly, these high-profile operations also made it easier for U.S. State Department officials to argue that UNHCR furthered U.S. national interests, thus easing U.S. appropriations for the organization. Loescher, *Beyond Charity,* 67.

49. Jaeger, "Status and the Protection of Refugees," 48. See Schnyder, "Les aspects juridiques," for a comparable recollection of the historical circumstances that led member states to expand UNHCR's competence to handle extreme cases, and how those deviations became normalized and institutionalized over time.

50. Res. 1006 of November 9, 1956, and 1039 of January 23, 1957. Holborn, *Refugees, Problem of Our Time,* 1:19.

51. Loescher, *UNHCR in World Politics,* 86.

52. Jaeger, "Status and the Protection of Refugees," 9.

53. Gallagher, "Evolution of the International Refugee System," 582; Holborn, *Refugees, Problem of Our Time,* chap. 16.

54. Res. 1167 (X11) of November 26, 1957.

55. Melander, *Two Refugee Definitions,* 11.

56. Schnyder, "Les aspects juridiques," 14. In 1959 and in the context of the World Refugee Year, the General Assembly asked UNHCR to use its good offices to transmit assistance and contributions to those who did not come under its competence. Gordenker, *Refugees in International Politics,* 39.

57. Schnyder, "Les aspects juridiques," 15.

58. Cited from Coles, "Solutions to the Problem of Refugees," 124.

59. Loescher, *UNHCR in World Politics,* 106

60. Res. 1673 (XVI) of December 18, 1961. Gallagher, "Evolution of the International Refugee System," 583.

61. Sadruddin Aga Khan, "The Challenge of Refugee Problems in Africa," *UNHCR Reports,* no. 27 (November 1963): 1–2. Holborn noted that the high commissioner's office typically gave three specific reasons for acting on the basis of good offices and not the statute in situations such as those in Africa: these groups needed material assistance and not international protection; refugees were so numerous that it was difficult to make an individual determination of status; and persecution was not the reason for flight, as it had been in Europe. Cited from Coles, "Solutions to the Problem of Refugees," 135. But it became clear that UNHCR omitted protection imperatives as a tactical move in order to facilitate assistance; to invoke its protection mission would be to suggest that there was a group that was being persecuted by its government. Ibid., 137–38. By the mid-1960s the high commissioner was asserting that he was seeking solutions and international protection. Aga Khan, "Challenge of Refugee Problems in Africa," 1–2.

62. Schnyder, "Les aspects juridiques," 18. Also see Aga Khan, "Legal Problems Relating to Refugees and Displaced Persons," 48.

63. Zieck, *UNHCR and Voluntary Repatriation of Refugees,* 73, and Loescher, *Beyond Charity,* 80, also note this conceptual elasticity and observe that over time this distinction and phrase disappeared from resolutions and common usage.

64. Loescher, *Beyond Charity,* 73–74. In 1967 the UN passed a protocol that dropped the geographical and temporal restrictions in the convention, though it did not tamper with the original definition. Regional organizations were formally doing so. In 1969 the Organization of African Unity adopted a convention that used the definition of a refugee established by the Refugee Convention but extended it to include those who fled "owing to external aggression, occupation, foreign domination or events seriously disturbing the public order." UNHCR was not merely gratified by an expanded definition that paralleled its own thinking—it was instrumental in shaping the views of African governments and the debate in the OAU. Gordenker, *Refugees in International Politics,* 41; also see Coles, "Approaching the Refugee Problem Today,"

378; Holborn, *Refugees, Problem of Our Time,* 1:182–94; UNHCR, "The Addis Ababa Conference," *UNHCR Reports,* no. 49 (November/December 1967–January 1968): 6–7; Loescher, *UNHCR in World Politics,* 124–26. In 1984 Central and South American states forged the Cartegena Declaration on Refugees and struck upon similar language.

65. Coles, "Approaching the Refugee Problem Today," 381.

66. Although the expanding refugee definition implied that there was no internationally recognized definition, in practice the agency was now helping "refugees" who did not meet the restrictive convention and statutory definitions, and its working definition became the focal point for most discussions and subsequent decisions. Kennedy, "International Refugee Protection," 20–21; Loescher, *Beyond Charity,* 81.

67. Gordenker, *Refugees in International Politics,* 40; Melander, *Two Refugee Definitions,* 10.

68. Aga Khan, "Legal Problems Relating to Refugees and Displaced Persons," 56. By 1961 High Commissioner Schnyder could uncontroversially observe that the prior General Assembly resolutions gave him the authority to intervene on behalf of "new" refugees. UNHCR, "The United Nations High Commissioner for Refugees Draws Attention to Refugee Problems in Africa," *UNHCR Reports,* no. 11 (December 1961): 13.

69. Schnyder "Les aspects juridiques," 7, 8, 16–17.

70. The expanding category of refugee meant that UNHCR had to develop specific decision-making guidelines to determine whether it had the competence to act. According to High Commissioner Aga Khan, "Legal Problems Relating to Refugees and Displaced Persons," 54–55, UNHCR used the following criteria: (1) the needs to be met and action to be taken were strictly humanitarian and nonpolitical; (2) the government or governments directly concerned had requested UNHCR assistance (essential since UNHCR respects the sovereignty of the member states and could operate effectively and legitimately only with their consent); and (3) the persons to be assisted were either refugees or "in a situation analogous to that of refugees." Aga Khan noted that these three criteria were not novel; rather, their novelty "lies in their application to a range of situations which are far more varied than those originally envisaged and which do not necessarily belong to the earlier narrow framework of UNHCR's activities related to persons fearing persecution." Although these criteria do exclude some groups of displaced populations, they do not exclude many.

71. Loescher, *UNHCR in World Politics,* 118.

72. Coles, "Solutions to the Problem of Refugees," 131.

73. As noted by High Commissioner Schnyder, these resolutions "allowed potentially for flexibility which was indispensable to the action of my Office. Those resolutions, together with the mandate, formed a coherent whole into which it should in future be possible to integrate divergent situations as those concerning the 'old' and new refugee problems." "Les aspects juridiques," 18.

74. Loescher, *UNHCR in World Politics,* 140.

75. Barnett interview with Pirkko Kourala, Geneva, January 24, 2000; Gordenker, *Refugees in International Politics,* 36–37; Loescher, *UNHCR in World Politics,* 140–41; Leon Gordenker, "Organizational Expansion and Limits in International Services for Refugees," *International Migration Review* 15 (1981): 81.

76. UN doc. A/AC.96/887 9, September 1997.

77. Skran, "International Refugee Regime," 8; Michael Barutciski, "Involuntary Repatriation When Refugee Protection Is No Longer Necessary," *International Journal of Refugee Law* 10, nos. 1/2 (1998): 241–42; Loescher, *UNHCR in World Politics,* 238.

78. UNHCR Executive Committee, "Note on International Protection," August 9, 1984, p. 7. Many of the subsequent "Notes on International Protection" reminded states that the concept of refugee had expanded considerably from the "classic" concept (note that reference is not made to "statutory") to include all peoples who flee violence and harm. Hathaway, "Reconceiving Refugee Law as Human Rights Protection," 115.

79. UNHCR Executive Committee, "Note on International Protection," August 27, 1990, p. 6.

80. See Nicholas Morris, "Refugees: Facing Crisis in the 1990s—A Personal View from within UNHCR," *International Journal of Refugee Law* 2 (September 1990): 46–52, for an insider's account of the financial and management crisis.

81. LCHR, *UNHCR at 40,* 87–89, 135; Loescher, *UNHCR in World Politics,* chap. 8.

82. UNHCR Executive Committee, Conclusion 18 (XXXI, 1980). Goodwin-Gill, "Voluntary Repatriation," 263–65; Barbara Hurrell-Bond, "Repatriation: Under What Conditions Is It the Most Desirable Solution for Refugees?" *African Studies Review* 32 (1989): 44–45; LCHR, *UNHCR at 40,* 61.

83. LCHR, *UNHCR at 40*, 41.

84. Ibid., 42.

85. Barnett interviews with UNHCR officials, Washington, D.C., and Geneva. The term "exilic bias" was coined by former UNHCR official Gervase Coles.

86. Hathaway, "Reconceiving Refugee Law as Human Rights Protection"; Goodwin-Gill, *Refugee in International Law.*

87. Cuny and Stein, "Prospects for and Promotion of Spontaneous Repatriation."

88. See Daniel Warner, "Voluntary Repatriation and the Meaning of Returning Home: A Critique of Liberal Mathematics," *Journal of Refugee Studies* 7, nos. 2/3 (1994): 160–74, on the discourse of "home." Also see Bill Frelick, "The Right to Return," *International Journal of Refugee Law* 2 (1990): 442–48.

89. Barnett interview with UNHCR official, Geneva, January 24, 2000.

90. LCHR, *UNHCR at 40*, 18, 117–19; Coles, "Approaching the Refugee Problem Today," 399.

91. Barnett interviews with UNHCR officials, Geneva, January 2000.

92. LCHR, *UNHCR at 40*, 62.

93. Coles, "Voluntary Repatriation"; also see Zieck, *UNHCR and Voluntary Repatriation of Refugees*, 85.

94. Cited from LCHR, *UNHCR at 40*, 138.

95. Speech by High Commissioner Sadaka Ogata, June 26, 1992. See also UNHCR, *State of the World's Refugees*, 31.

96. Barry Stein and Frederick Cuny, "Repatriation in a Civil War/Conflict Situation," paper presented at Roundtable Consultation on Voluntary Repatriation and UNHCR, Geneva, Switzerland, June 2–3, 1993, cited in Chimni, "Meaning of Words and the Role of UNHCR in Voluntary Repatriation," 448; Zieck, *UNHCR and Voluntary Repatriation of Refugees*, 438–39; Saul Takahashi, "The UNHCR Handbook on Voluntary Repatriation: The Emphasis of Return or Protection," *International Journal of Refugee Law* 9, no. 4 (1997): 594, 602; Geoff Gilbert, "Rights, Legitimate Expectations, Needs, and Responsibilities: UNHCR and the New World Order," *International Journal of Refugee Law* 10, no. 3 (1998): 379–80.

97. Zieck, *UNHCR and Voluntary Repatriation of Refugees*, 81–82, italics added.

98. Coles, "Solutions to the Problem of Refugees," 165, 192–93.

99. Barnett interviews with UNHCR officials. Also see Julie Barbero, "Refugee Protection during Conflict: A New Conventional Wisdom," *Refuge* 12, no. 8 (1993): 7–12; Goodwin-Gill, *Refugee in International Law*, 275; B. S. Chimni, "From Resettlement to Repatriation: Towards a Critical History of Durable Solutions to Refugee Problems," *New Issues in Refugee Research*, Working Paper no. 2 (Geneva: UNHCR, 1999).

100. Barnett interview with Irene Khan, UNHCR, Geneva, January 26, 2000.

101. Confidential interview, Geneva, January 28, 2000.

102. A 1992 UNHCR working group determined that protection could have many meanings, including relief and repatriation. Loescher, *UNHCR in World Politics*, 297. Also see Morris, "Refugees," for an insider's view of protection dilemmas. Zieck, *UNHCR and Voluntary Repatriation of Refugees*, 82.

103. LCHR, *UNHCR at 40*, 56–57; Hurrell-Bond, "Repatriation," 55–56.

104. See, in particular, UNHCR Executive Committee, "Note on International Protection," July 15, 1986. Note that this debate about unsafe camps began before the winding down of the Cold War and the emergence of the postconflict settings of the 1990s.

105. On prevention, see Chimni, "Meaning of Words and the Role of the UNHCR in Voluntary Repatriation," 444; and Bill Frelick, "Preventing Refugee Flows: Protection or Peril?" *World Refugee Survey* (1993), 5–13. On root causes, see Coles, "Solutions to the Problem of Refugees," 207–11; and UNHCR Executive Committee, "Note on International Protection," August 31, 1983, p. 2. On "state responsibility," see "Note on International Protection," August 27, 1990, p. 8.

106. Mark Cutts, "Politics and Humanitarianism," *Refugee Survey Quarterly* 17, no. 1 (1998): 1–15; Barnett, "Humanitarianism with a Sovereign Face."

107. UNHCR Executive Committee, "Annual Theme: The Pursuit and Implementation of Durable Solutions," August 30, 1996, A/AC.96/872, p. 2.

108. "UNHCR's Protection Role in Countries of Origin," 18 March 1996, EC/46/SC/CRP.17, p. 1.

109. Skran, "International Refugee Regime," 26.

110. In recent years UNHCR's involvement has expanded to the point that it openly wonders whether it has now become a "humanitarian trustee" in those areas of refugee return. That is, there is a sense that UNHCR is increasingly providing statelike functions in many countries,

providing everything from education to development to basic necessities. See Jeff Crisp and Erin Mooney, "Report on the Workshop on Internal Displacement in Africa, Addis Ababa, October 19–20, 1998," *International Migration Review* 33, no. 2 (1999): 468–83.

111. Frelick, "Preventing Refugee Flows"; Tom Weiss and Amir Pasic, "Reinventing UNHCR: Enterprising Humanitarians in the Former Yugoslavia, 1991–95," *Global Governance* 3 (1996): 41–58.

112. UNHCR Executive Committee, "Note on International Protection," September 9, 1991, p. 10.

113. The original acknowledgment of this concern can be found in ibid., p. 1. The attempt to reassure can be found in "Note on International Protection," August 31, 1993, p. 10.

114. UNHCR Executive Committee, "Note on International Protection," July 15, 1986, p. 3.

115. Loescher, *UNHCR in World Politics*, 249–50.

116. LCHR, *UNHCR at 40*, 56–59.

117. Ibid., 109–10; Barnett interview with Michel Moussalli, Geneva, January 25, 2000.

118. Jean-Pierre Hocke, "Beyond Humanitarianism: The Need for Political Will to Resolve Today's Refugee Problem," Inaugural Joyce Pearce Memorial Lecture, Refugee Studies Programme, QEH, Oxford, October 29, 1986. Cited in Hurrell-Bond, "Repatriation." This is a remarkable statement, Hurrell-Bond notes, for UNHCR is suggesting that the weakest members of society knowingly return to the very conditions that precipitated their flight and to countries that have no welfare systems.

119. "Note on International Protection," UN doc. A/AC.96/799 (1992), paras. 38, 39.

120. UNHCR, *State of the World's Refugees*, 107.

121. Zieck, *UNHCR and Voluntary Repatriation of Refugees;* Chimni, "Meaning of Words and the Role of the UNHCR in Voluntary Repatriation."

122. Loescher, *UNHCR in World Politics*, 363.

123. "Note on International Protection," UN doc. A/AC.96/815 (1993). Cited in Zieck, *UNHCR and Voluntary Repatriation of Refugees*, 89.

124. "Once the solution of voluntary repatriation is presented as the humane solution, it generates undue pressure to pursue it even when it is relatively inappropriate; an idealized image of the ultimate solution legitimizes a degree of coercion since it is perceived as a solution which the refugees should themselves desire most." B. S. Chimni, "Perspectives on Voluntary Repatriation: A Critical Note," *International Journal of Refugee Law* 3, no. 3 (1991): 543.

125. Human Rights Watch, *The Rohingyan Muslims: Ending a Cycle of Exodus?* Human Rights Watch Report vol.8 , no. 9(C) (1996), 19n43; confidential NGO memo.

126. Barnett interview with Irene Khan, January 26, 2000.

127. Barnett interview, Geneva, January 27, 2000.

128. This background draws from many sources, though largely from Human Rights Watch (HRW), *The Rohingyan Muslims.*

129. Tony Reid, "Repatriation of Arkanese Muslims from Bangladesh to Burma, 1978–79: The 'Arranged' Reversal of the Flow of an Ethnic Minority," paper presented at the Fourth International Research and Advisory Panel Conference, Somerville College, University of Oxford, January 1994.

130. There were five mass exoduses between 1942 and the contemporary period.

131. U.S. Committee for Refugees (USCR), *The Return of the Rohingyan Refugees to Burma: Voluntary Repatriation or Refoulement?* Washington, D.C., March 1995, p. 5.

132. C. R. Abrar, "Repatriation of Rohingya Refugees," manuscript, 1995, p. 9; USCR, *Return of the Rohingyan Refugees to Burma*, 5.

133. USCR, *Return of the Rohingyan Refugees to Burma*, 5.

134. Bangladesh has forcibly repatriated refugees on several occasions, using a variety of tactics including coercion, cutting rations, and imprisonment. HRW, *The Rohingyan Muslims*, 14; Abrar, "Repatriation of Rohingya Refugees," 10, 11; USCR, *Return of the Rohingyan Refugees to Burma*, 5.

135. For the general maltreatment at the hands of camp officials, see Asia Watch, *Bangladesh: Abuse of Burmese Refugees from Arakan*, Human Rights Watch Short Report vol. 5, no. 17 (1993). Quoted from Abrar, "Repatriation of Rohingya Refugees," 12. USCR, *Return of the Rohingyan Refugees to Burma.*

136. USCR, *Return of the Rohingyan Refugees to Burma*, 5.

137. Abrar, "Repatriation of Rohingya Refugees," 12; USCR, *Return of the Rohingyan Refugees to Burma*, 6.

138. Neither Bangladesh nor Burma is a signatory of the refugee convention or protocol, which meant that UNHCR probably had a more difficult time using normative arguments than would otherwise be the case.

139. Abrar, "Repatriation of Rohingya Refugees," 13; USCR, *Return of the Rohingyan Refugees to Burma*, 6.

140. USCR, *Return of the Rohingyan Refugees to Burma*, 6; David Petrasek, "Through Rose-Coloured Glasses: UNHCR's Role in Monitoring the Safety of the Rohningya Refugees Returning to Burma," paper, 1996, p. 6; Médicins sans Frontières—Holland, "Better Off in Burma? The Plight of the Burmese Rohingyas," November 1997, p. 21.

141. Abrar, "Repatriation of Rohingya Refugees," 14; HRW, *The Rohingyan Muslims*, 17.

142. For discussion of forced labor and UNHCR's blind spots in Burma, see Australian Council for Overseas Aid, "Repatriation of Burmese Refugees from Thailand and Bangladesh," Deakin, Australia, March 1996. Abrar, "Repatriation of Rohingya Refugees," p. 14; confidential NGO memo.

143. Abrar, "Repatriation of Rohingya Refugees," 13; HRW, *The Rohingyan Muslims*, 17.

144. Confidential NGO memo.

145. HRW, *The Rohingyan Muslims*, 17.

146. Ibid., 17; confidential NGO memo.

147. HRW, *The Rohingyan Muslims*, 18–19.

148. This figure was consistent with a similar survey conducted in April. Dhaka officials were hardly overjoyed by the news, and on April 25 the Bangladesh government told UNHCR that it would not be renewing the MoU that was due to expire on May 12, but would be extending the agreement for an additional month. USCR, *Return of the Rohingyan Refugees to Burma*, 6; Abrar, "Repatriation of Rohingya Refugees," 15; HRW, *The Rohingyan Muslims*, 17, 18.

149. HRW, *The Rohingyan Muslims*, 18.

150. Refugees International filed a series of reports that those returning to Burma were sending back messages to refugees not to return, that they had not been contacted by UNHCR officials inside Burma, and that repression continued. They also reported coercion. "Some families who dared to say 'no' at the UNHCR interview in the transit camp were sent back to their original camp where, under the eyes of UNHCR staff, they were deprived of food and water and forced to stand on one leg and beaten until they fell repeatedly." As a consequence, refugees mistrusted UNHCR, fearing that it was little better than the local governments. Yvette Pierpaoli, "Rohingya Refugees in Bangladesh," *Refugees International Bulletin*, June 6, 1994. HRW, *The Rohingyan Muslims*, 18.

151. This conclusion draws from various NGO reports.

152. Abrar, "Repatriation of Rohingya Refugees," 15; HRW, *The Rohingyan Muslims*, 19.

153. USCR, *Return of the Rohingyan Refugees to Burma*, 9–15; confidential NGO memos.

154. USCR, *Return of the Rohingyan Refugees to Burma*, 5.

155. In an internal and confidential review of the Arakan situation, UNHCR concluded that "monitoring would be delicate as complaisance could compromise our credibility with zealous orthodoxy, could spoil UNHCR's chances of remaining involved in Arakan." Cited from HRW, *The Rohingyan Muslims*, 21. USCR, *Return of the Rohingyan Refugees to Burma*, 8–9.

156. USCR, *Return of the Rohingyan Refugees to Burma*, 21.

157. Abrar, "Repatriation of Rohingya Refugees," 17–18; Barnett interviews with UNHCR officials, Geneva, January 2000.

158. However, one UNHCR official interviewed estimated that about 50 percent of all those repatriated were forced. USCR, *Return of the Rohingyan Refugees to Burma*, 6.

159. Also see the supporting evidence in ibid.

160. See Médicins sans Frontières—Holland, "Awareness Survey of Rohingyan Refugee Camps," March 15, 1995, and "MSF's Concerns on the Repatriation of Rohingyan Refugees from Bangladesh to Burma," May 1, 1995. Referring to this survey, one field officer doubted that the refugees adequately understood what was being asked of them (though the same could be said about UNHCR's original survey). Confidential NGO memo; Barnett interviews with personnel from NGOs.

161. Cited in HRW, *The Rohingyan Muslims*, 16, italics added. UNHCR responded to a USCR site visit report that was critical of the agency's repatriation activities in the following way: "In the absence of a better alternative . . . [UNHCR] decided to become actively involved in the repatriation in order to ensure its voluntary character in the country of asylum and . . . that the

repatriates can safely return to their respective villages. Whilst not denying that this voluntary repatriation program, *unique in its many facets,* remains a challenge to UNHCR, our presence has made a difference on a number of issues . . . and a general improvement of the living conditions in the area." Cited from USCR, "USCR Site Visit to Bangladesh, June 20–July 1," issue brief, 1996, p. 10; italics added. Also see HRW, *The Rohingyan Muslims,* 16.

162. Chimni, "From Resettlement to Repatriation."

163. However, the repatriation exercises in 1992–93 and 1996 did occur under physical duress.

164. Barnett interview with protection officer, Geneva, January 28, 2000.

165. Ibid.

166. Abrar, "Repatriation of Rohingya Refugees," 19.

167. Ibid., 17–18.

168. Petrasek, "Through Rose-Coloured Glasses," 8.

169. HRW, *The Rohingyan Muslims,* 15, 19–21.

170. Karin Landgren, "The Future of Refugee Protection," *Journal of Refugee Studies* 11, no. 4 (1998): 427.

171. HRW, *The Rohingyan Muslims,* 15; Barnett interviews with UNHCR officials, Geneva, January 2000.

172. HRW, *The Rohingyan Muslims,* 15; USCR, *Return of the Rohingyan Refugees to Burma,* 12–13.

173. Médicins sans Frontières—Holland, "Better Off in Burma?" 11.

174. Petrasek, "Through Rose-Coloured Glasses"; confidential NGO memo; Barnett interviews with UNHCR officials, Geneva, January 21–28, 2000.

175. USCR, "USCR Site Visit to Bangladesh, June 20–July 1," 3, 7; Amnesty International, "Rohingyas: The Search for Safety," 1997; Petrasek, "Through Rose-Coloured Glasses," 1; Médicins sans Frontières—Holland, "Better Off in Burma?" 5–6.

176. USCR, "USCR Site Visit to Bangladesh, June 20–July 1," 7; Médicins sans Frontières—Holland, "Better Off in Burma?" 10; Human Rights Watch, *Rohingya Refugees in Bangladesh: The Search for a Lasting Solution* Human Rights Watch Report vol. 9, no. 7(C) (1997), 9.

177. Petrasek, "Through Rose-Coloured Glasses," 10; Médicins sans Frontières—Holland, "Better Off in Burma?" 8.

178. Petrasek, "Through Rose-Coloured Glasses," 11.

179. Médicins sans Frontières—Holland, "Better Off in Burma?" 5.

180. HRW, *The Rohingyan Muslims,* 15, 19–21; confidential NGO memos.

181. Barnett interview with UNHCR protection officer, Geneva, January 28, 2000.

182. Petrasek, "Through Rose-Coloured Glasses," 8; Médicins sans Frontières—Holland, "Better Off in Burma?" 21; confidential NGO memos.

183. Petrasek, "Through Rose-Coloured Glasses."

184. Ibid., 12; also see Médicins sans Frontières—Holland, "Better Off in Burma?" 23.

185. Barnett in possession of cable.

186. Petrasek, "Through Rose-Coloured Glasses," identified a slightly larger number of UNHCR staff in Burma, roughly forty local staff, the majority of whom were in Arakan. USCR, *Return of the Rohingyan Refugees to Burma,* 1–2, 14–15.

187. Petrasek, "Through Rose-Coloured Glasses," 8; Médicins sans Frontières—Holland, "Better Off in Burma?" 21; HRW, *The Rohingyan Muslims,* 21–22; Barnett interview with UNHCR official, Geneva, January 25, 2000.

188. This relates to whether UNHCR is becoming involved in a strategy of containment. See Julie Mertus, "The State and the Post–Cold War Refugee Regime: New Models, New Questions," *International Journal of Refugee Law* 10, no. 3 (1998): 340; Michael Barutciski, "The Reinforcement of Non-Admission Policies and the Subversion of UNHCR: Displacement and Internal Assistance in Bosnia-Herzegovina," *International Journal of Refugee Law* 8, no. 1 (1996): 49–110; and Andrew Shacknove, "From Asylum to Containment," *International Journal of Refugee Law* 5, no. 4 (1993): 516–33.

189. This pragmatic approach, argues Petrasek, can be defended on one of two grounds. The first is that there is evidence that this policy does improve the situation for the Rohingyas. According to Petrasek, however, there is no evidence of this. The second is that this position did not compromise what UNHCR consistently noted was its primary mission: to safeguard refugee rights, to preserve their right to flee persecution, and to defend the principle of nonrefoulement. Petrasek, "Through Rose-Coloured Glasses," 5.

CHAPTER 5. GENOCIDE AND THE PEACEKEEPING CULTURE AT THE UNITED NATIONS

1. *Shake Hands with the Devil: The Failure of Humanity in Rwanda* (Toronto: Random House Canada, 2003), Roméo Dallaire's firsthand account, provides no evidence that the Secretariat privately wanted an intervention but felt constrained by the Security Council. Nor have any of the many investigations turned up this evidence, though most have looked. Human Rights Watch, *Leave None to Tell the Story: Genocide in Rwanda* (New York: HRW, 1999); Alain Destexhe, *Rwanda and Genocide in the Twentieth Century* (New York: NYU Press, 1995); Carol Off, *The Lion, the Fox, and the Eagle: A Story of Generals and Justice in Rwanda and Yugoslavia* (Toronto: Random House Canada, 2001); Arthur Jay Klinghoffer, *The International Dimension of Genocide in Rwanda* (New York: NYU Press, 1998); United Nations, *The United Nations and Rwanda, 1993–1996* (New York: Dept. of Public Information, UN, 1996); Joint Evaluation of Emergency Assistance to Rwanda, *The International Response to Conflict and Genocide: Lessons from the Rwanda Experience* (Copenhagen: Joint Evaluation of Emergency Assistance to Rwanda, 1996); UN DPKO, *Comprehensive Report on Lessons Learned from United Nations Assistance Mission for Rwanda (UNAMIR)* (New York: UN, 1996); United Nations, *Final Report of the International Commission of Inquiry (Rwanda)* (New York: UN, 1999); Belgium, Senate, *Parliamentary Commission of Inquiry concerning Rwanda,* December 1997; Howard Adelman and Astri Suhrke, eds., *The Path of a Genocide: The Rwanda Crisis from Uganda to Zaire* (New Brunswick, N.J.: Transaction, 1999); Organization of African Unity, *Report on the UN and Genocide in Rwanda* (Addis Ababa: Organization of African Unity, 2000); and Michael Barnett, *Eyewitness to a Genocide: The United Nations and Rwanda* (Ithaca: Cornell University Press, 2002), chap. 4.

2. This distinction was first introduced by John MacKinley and Jarat Chopra, "Second Generation Multinational Operations," *Washington Quarterly* (Summer 1992), 113–31. The peacekeeping literature has exploded over the past decade. See Alan James, *Peacekeeping in International Politics* (New York: St. Martin's Press, 1990); A. B. Fetherston, *Towards a Theory of United Nations Peacekeeping* (New York: St. Martin's Press, 1994); Paul Diehl, *International Peacekeeping* (Baltimore: Johns Hopkins University Press, 1993); Paul Durch, ed., *The Evolution of UN Peacekeeping* (New York: St. Martin's Press, 1993); Michael Doyle et al., eds., *Keeping the Peace: Multidimensional UN Operations in Cambodia and El Salvador* (New York: Cambridge University Press, 1997); and Thomas Weiss, ed., *The United Nations and Civil Wars* (Boulder: Lynne Rienner, 1995). For a reflective statement from a former UN official, see Marrack Goulding, *Peacemonger* (Baltimore: Johns Hopkins University Press, 2003). For the factual side, see United Nations, "United Nations Peacekeeping Information Notes" (New York: United Nations Press, 1995); and *Blue Helmets: A Review of UN Peace-Keeping,* 3rd ed. (New York: United Nations, Department of Public Information, 1996).

3. United Nations, General Assembly, "Report of the Secretary-General Pursuant to General Assembly Resolution 53/35: The Fall of Srebrenica," November 15, 1999, A/54/549, p. 111.

4. See Brian Urquhart, "In the Name of Humanity," *New York Review of Books* 47 (April 27, 2000): 19–22, for a good summary of the deliberately designed institutional checks on the Office of the Secretary-General.

5. For overviews of the Suez War, see W. Roger Louis and Roger Owen, eds., *Suez 1956: The Crisis and Its Consequences* (New York: Oxford University Press, 1989).

6. "Regulations for the United Nations Emergency Force" (February 20, 1957) and "Second and Final Report of the Secretary-General on the Plan for an Emergency International United Nations Force," November 6, 1956 (UN doc. A/3302), reprinted in R. C. R. Siekmann, *Basic Documents on United Nations and Related Peacekeeping Forces,* 2nd enlarged ed. (Dordrecht: Martinus Nijhoff, 1989), 40 and 4. Cited from Paris, *At War's End,* 14.

7. As Brian Urquhart writes, "The setting up of the first UN Emergency Force (UNEF) was a major development in international relations. The employment of armed troops instead of unarmed individual observers required new principles and rules, as well as command, staff, and logistical arrangements. [Ralph] Bunche, who had set up and directed the pioneering truce-observation operation in the Middle East in 1948 and had written the basic principles, procedures, and rules of conduct for that operation, was the obvious choice to supervise this new type of international military adventure." *Ralph Bunche: An American Life* (New York: Norton, 1993), 266. Also see James, *Peacekeeping in International Politics,* for a discussion of the pre-peacekeeping monitoring institutions.

8. For a brief overview of the development of these principles, see Rod Paschall, "U.N. Peacekeeping Tactics: The Impartial Buffer," in Barbara Benton, ed., *Soldiers for Peace* (New York:

Facts on File, 1996), 50–55; Indar Jit Rikhye, Michael Harbottle, and Bjørn Egge, *The Thin Blue Line: International Peacekeeping and Its Future* (New Haven: Yale University Press, 1974), chap. 2; Marrack Goulding, "The Evolution of United Nations Peacekeeping," *International Affairs* 69, no. 3 (1993): 453–55; Cedric Thornberry, "Civil Affairs in the Development of UN Peacekeeping," *International Peacekeeping* 1, no. 4 (1994): 479; and Donald C. F. Daniel and Bradd C. Hayes with Chantal de Jonge Oudraat, *Coercive Inducement and the Containment of International Crises* (Washington, D.C.: United States Institute of Peace Press, 1999).

9. "Report of the Secretary-General on the Implementation of Security Council Resolution 425," March 19, 1978 (UN doc. S/12611), reprinted in Siekmann, *Basic Documents on United Nations and Related Peacekeeping Forces*, 216. Cited from Paris, *At War's End*.

10. For these various arguments, see Martha Finnemore, "Constructing Norms of Humanitarian Intervention," in Peter Katzenstein, ed., *The Culture of National Security* (New York: Columbia University Press, 1996), 153–85; Michael Barnett, "Bringing in the New World Order: Legitimacy, Liberalism, and the United Nations," *World Politics* 49, no. 4 (1997): 526–51; Gene Lyons and Michael Mastanduno, "Introduction: International Intervention, State Sovereignty, and the Future of International Society," in G. Lyons and M. Mastanduno, eds., *Beyond Westphalia? State Sovereignty and International Intervention* (Baltimore: Johns Hopkins University Press, 1995), 12.

11. Hans Kelsen, *The Law of the United Nations: A Critical Analysis of Its Fundamental Problems* (New York: Praeger, 1951), 727; and Rosalyn Higgins, *The Development of International Law through the Organs of the United Nations* (New York: Oxford University Press, 1963), 266.

12. Michael Howard, "The Historical Development of the UN's Role in International Security," in Adam Roberts and Benedict Kingsbury, ed., *United Nations, Divided World: The UN's Roles in International Relations* (New York: Oxford University Press, 1993), 69–70; N. D. White, *Keeping the Peace* (Manchester: Manchester University Press, 1993), chap. 2.

13. Michael Barnett, "The New U.N. Politics of Peace: From Juridical Sovereignty to Empirical Sovereignty," *Global Governance* 1, no. 1 (1995): 79–97; Gerald Helman and Steven Ratner, "Saving Failed States," *Foreign Policy* 89 (Winter 1992/93), 3–20; Steven Ratner, *The New UN Peacekeeping* (New York: St. Martin's Press, 1996).

14. Adam Roberts and Benedict Kingsbury, "Introduction: The UN's Roles in International Society since 1945," in Roberts and Kingsbury, *United Nations, Divided World*, 50–52; and Tom Farer and Felice Gaer, "The UN and Human Rights: At the End of the Beginning," in Roberts and Kingsbury, *United Nations, Divided World*, 240–96.

15. Boutros Boutros-Ghali, *An Agenda for Peace* (New York: United Nations, 1992).

16. Boutros Boutros-Ghali, *Unvanquished: A U.S.-UN Saga* (New York: Random House, 1999).

17. Inis Claude, "Collective Legitimization as a Political Function of the United Nations," *International Organization* 20, no. 3 (1966): 367–79; Michael Barnett, "The UN Security Council, Indifference, and Genocide in Rwanda," *Cultural Anthropology* 12, no. 4 (1997): 551–78; and Hurd, "Legitimacy and Authority in International Politics."

18. Also see Boutros Boutros-Ghali, "An Agenda for Peace: One Year Later," *Orbis* 37 (Summer 1993): 329; idem, "Democracy: A Newly Recognized Imperative," *Global Governance* 1, no. 1 (1995), 3–11; idem, *An Agenda for Democratization* (New York: United Nations, Department of Public Information, 1996); idem, "Global Leadership after the Cold War," *Foreign Affairs* 75 (March/April 1996): 86–98.

19. Paris, *At War's End;* and Lens, "From Peacekeeping to Peace-Building."

20. Barnett, "New U.N. Politics of Peace."

21. Ronald Paris, "International Peacebuilding and the 'Mission Civilisatrice,'" *Review of International Studies* 28, no. 4 (2002): 637–56; Barnett, "Bringing in the New World Order"; Lens, "From Peacekeeping to Peace-Building."

22. Many IOs and regional organizations now have "rule of law" programs, and these programs demonstrate a degree of diversity within unity—a diversity that is generated by the different mandates of these institutions but a semblance of unity that derives from a general notion of what the rule of law is (but still demonstrates tremendous operational divergence). See Rama Mani, "Conflict Resolution, Justice, and the Law: Rebuilding the Rule of Law in the Aftermath of Complex Political Emergencies," *International Peacekeeping* 5, no. 3 (1998): 1–25.

23. On the question of interagency coordination, see James Whitman, *Peacekeeping and UN Agencies* (New York: Frank Cass, 1999).

24. Sashi Tharoor, "The Changing Face of Peacekeeping," in Barbara Benton, ed., *Soldiers for Peace* (New York: Facts on File, 1996), 215.

25. U.S. Assistant Secretary of State for International Organizations Douglas Bennet remarked, "Call it lessons learned. What's been happening is a pretty steep learning curve on which we have discovered some of the strengths and weaknesses of collective peacekeeping." Jon Stewart, "U.N. Learns Hard Lessons on Peacekeeping," *San Francisco Chronicle,* March 28, 1995, A1. Thornberry, "Civil Affairs in the Development of UN Peacekeeping," 481–83.

26. On the shadow of Somalia and its influence on the UN's operation in Rwanda, see Joint Evaluation of Emergency Assistance to Rwanda, *International Response to Conflict and Genocide.*

27. "United Nations Peacekeeping: Trotting to the Rescue," *Economist,* June 25, 1994, pp. 19–22; Richard Bernstein, "Sniping Is Growing at U.N.'s Weakness as a Peacekeeper," *New York Times,* June 21, 1993, A1, A8.

28. Gillian Tett, "Red Tape Tangles Up UN Troops in Bosnia," *Financial Times,* January 21, 1994, p. 6; Julia Preston, "Supply Office at U.N. Hamstrung by Probe," *Washington Post,* August 20, 1994, A1, A14.

29. *The Clinton Administration's Policy on Reforming Multilateral Peace Operations,* PDD-25, Department of State Publication 10161, Washington, D.C., May 1994. For commentary, see "Peacekeeping Guidelines," editorial, *Washington Post,* May 8, 1994, C6.

30. Stanley Meisler, "Kofi Annan: The Soft-Spoken Economist Who Runs U.N. Peacekeeping Forces," *Los Angeles Times,* June 19, 1994, M3.

31. Barbara Crossette, "U.N. Falters in Post-Cold-War Peacekeeping, but Sees Role as Essential," *New York Times,* December 5, 1994, A12. Also see "United Nations Peacekeeping: Trotting to the Rescue," 22.

32. Julia Preston, "U.N. Officials Scale Back Peacemaking Ambitions; Planned U.S. Withdrawal from Somalia Demonstrates Limitations," *Washington Post,* October 28, 1993, A40.

33. Paul Lewis, "Five Key Nations Urge Prudence in Setting Peacekeeping Goal," *New York Times,* October 1, 1993, A2. Also see James Bone, "Hurd Puts Limit on Peacekeeping," *London Times,* September 29, 1993.

34. United Nations, *Statement on the Conditions for the Deployment and Renewal of Peacekeeping Operations,* Security Council Presidential Statement (S/PRST/1994/22), May 3, 1994. This proposal was seen as a natural follow-on to previous resolutions, including that of May 28, 1993 (S/25859).

35. John Ruggie, "The U.N.: Wandering into the Void," *Foreign Affairs* 72 (November/December 1993): 26–31.

36. See Simon Duke, "The United Nations and Intra-State Conflict," *International Peacekeeping* 1, no. 4 (1994): 375–93.

37. Barbara Crossette, "U.N. Chief Ponders Future of Peacekeepers," *New York Times,* March 3, 1995, A3; Meisler, "Kofi Annan," M3. For a good analysis of the dangers of enforcement, see Mats Berdal, *Whither UN Peacekeeping?* (London: International Institute for Strategic Studies, 1993); and Edward Mortimer, "Peace Role in Process," *Financial Times,* November 17, 1993, p. 14.

38. Tharoor, "Changing Face of Peacekeeping," 215.

39. Julia Preston, "Vision of a More Aggressive UN Now Dims," *Washington Post,* January 5, 1994, p. 24. Also see Georgie Anne Geyer, "The World as Viewed from the U.N. Helm," *Washington Times,* April 3, 1994, B4; Barbara Crossette, "U.N. Leader to Call for Changes in Peacekeeping," *New York Times,* January 3, 1995, A3.

40. Preston, "U.N. Officials Scale Back Peacemaking Ambitions."

41. Geyer, "World as Viewed from the U.N. Helm."

42. United Nations, "Report of the Commission of Inquiry Established Pursuant to Security Council Resolution 885 (1993) to Investigate Armed Attacks on UNOSOM II Personnel Which Led to Casualties among Them," February 24, 1994, internal memo.

43. Sashi Tharoor similarly concluded that "multidimensional peacekeeping" still rests on the principles of consent and impartiality. See Tharoor, "Changing Face of Peacekeeping," 213.

44. Meisler, "Kofi Annnan: The Soft-Spoken Economist Who Runs U.N. Peacekeeping Forces."

45. Preston, "Vision of a More Aggressive UN Now Dims."

46. Stewart, "U.N. Learns Hard Lessons on Peacekeeping."

47. The Security Council's decision not to authorize a peacekeeping operation in Burundi in late October 1993, when nearly one hundred thousand persons died in ethnic violence, was driven in part by these considerations. Alan Ferguson, "U.N. to Reject Burundi's Plea for Peacekeepers," *Toronto Star,* November 3, 1993, A17. Also see Julia Preston, "No Mission to Burundi, U.N. Says; Peace Deployments Apparently on Hold," *Washington Post,* November 2, 1993, A10.

48. This section is informed by Mahmood Mamdani, *When Victims Become Killers: Colonialism, Nativism, and the Genocide in Rwanda* (Princeton: Princeton University Press, 2001); Human Rights Watch, *Leave None to Tell the Story;* Chris Taylor, *Sacrifice as Terror: The Rwandan Genocide of 1994* (New York: Berg, 1999); Gerard Prunier, *The Rwanda Crisis: History of a Genocide*, 2nd ed. (New York: Columbia University Press, 1999); Rakiya Omaar and Alex de Waal, *Rwanda: Death, Despair, and Defiance* (London: African Rights, 1995); Destexhe, *Rwanda and Genocide in the Twentieth Century;* Catharine Newbury, *The Cohesion of Oppression: Clientship and Ethnicity in Rwanda, 1860–1960* (New York : Columbia University Press, 1988); and René Lemarchand, *Rwanda and Burundi* (New York: Praeger Press, 1970).

49. For an excellent discussion of the Arusha Accords and the UN's involvement during this phase, see Bruce Jones, *Peacemaking in Rwanda: The Dynamics of Failure* (Boulder: Lynne Rienner, 2001). For a UN perspective on these developments, see Dallaire, *Shake Hands with the Devil.* Also see United Nations, *United Nations and Rwanda;* and Gilbert Khadiagala, "Implementing the Arusha Agreement on Rwanda," in Stephen Stedman, Donald Rothchild, and Elizabeth Cousens, eds., *Ending Civil War: The Implementation of Peace Agreements* (Boulder: Lynne Rienner, 2002), 421–62.

50. Barnett interview with member of the U.S. Mission, May 14, 2000.

51. Astri Suhrke, "Dilemmas of Protection: The Log of the Kigali Battalion," in Adelman and Suhrke, *Path of a Genocide,* 257.

52. Philip Gourevitch, "The Genocide Fax," *New Yorker,* May 11, 1998, pp. 42–46; Linda Melvern, *A People Betrayed: The Role of the West in Rwanda's Genocide* (New York: Zed Books, 2000).

53. Dallaire, *Shake Hands with the Devil,* chaps. 5–6.

54. Col. Luc Marchal, *Frontline* interview, http://www.pbs.org/wgbh/pages/frontline/shows/evil/interviews/marchal.html.

55. Barnett telephone interview with Dallaire, December 5, 2000. For Dallaire's account of the telegram and DPKO's reaction, see *Shake Hands with the Devil,* 142–50.

56. Barnett interview with Dallaire, December 5, 2000.

57. Iqbal Riza, *Frontline* interview, http://www.pbs.org/wgbh/pages/frontline/shows/evil/interviews/riza.html; Gourevitch, "Genocide Fax"; Organization of African Unity, *Report on the UN and Genocide in Rwanda.*

58. Riza, *Frontline* interview.

59. Ibid.

60. The telegram was shared with the other members of the contact group, France, the United States, and Belgium, but it did not widely circulate and did not cause either France or the United States to reassess the UN's approach to Rwanda.

61. Cf. Turid Laegrid, "U.N. Peacekeeping in Rwanda," in Adelman and Suhrke, *Paths of a Genocide,* 234.

62. Dallaire, *Shake Hands with the Devil,* 147.

63. Riza, *Frontline* interview.

64. Consistent with this passive profile was the Secretariat's insistence on a narrow definition of what the mandate permitted regarding the rules of engagement (RoE). The RoE, and in particular paragraph 17 (which allowed peacekeepers to use force to halt "ethnically or politically motivated criminal acts" and specified that it would "take the necessary action to prevent any crime against humanity") gave UNAMIR tremendous flexibility in the field, but beginning in January UNHQ began insisting on a much more narrow interpretation that permitted the discharge of weapons only when peacekeepers were directly attacked or threatened. As a consequence, Dallaire repeatedly ordered his troops to negotiate with the parties and to seek their consent at all times. Human Rights Watch, *Leave None to Tell the Story,* 596; and Dallaire, *Shake Hands with the Devil,* 180–81. For a more detailed discussion of the RoEs, see Suhrke, "Dilemmas of Protection," 255.

65. Stephen Stedman, "The Perils of Peace Processes: Spoiler Problems in Peace Processes," *International Security* 22, no. 2 (1997): 5–53.

66. United Nations, "Second Progress Report of the Secretary-General on the United Nations Assistance Mission for Rwanda," S/1994/360, March 30, 1994.

67. Human Rights Watch, *Leave None to Tell the Story.*

68. Gourevitch, "Genocide Fax"; Melvern, *A People Betrayed.*

69. United Nations, *United Nations and Rwanda,* 31.

70. Riza, *Frontline* interview.

71. United Nations, *United Nations and Rwanda,* 32.

72. Cables in Barnett's possession.

73. Laegrid, "U.N. Peacekeeping in Rwanda," 234; Joint Evaluation of Emergency Assistance to Rwanda, *International Response to Conflict and Genocide,* chap. 3, p. 5.

74. Dallaire, *Shake Hands with the Devil,* 166–67, 180–81. Also see the secretary-seneral's report to the Security Council of March 30, 1994, which linked the parties' failure to establish the transitional government with a deteriorating security situation. United Nations, "Second Progress Report of the Secretary-General," para. 27.

75. For analyses of the Security Council's decision, see Melvern, *A People Betrayed;* United Nations, *Final Report of the International Commission of Inquiry;* Belgium, Senate, *Parliamentary Commission of Inquiry Concerning Rwanda;* Organization of African Unity, *Report on the UN and Genocide in Rwanda;* and Barnett, "UN Security Council, Indifference, and Genocide in Rwanda."

76. Barnett interview with Dallaire, December 5, 2000.

77. Cable in Barnett's possession. UNDP is the UN Development Program.

78. Barnett interview with Dallaire, December 5, 2000. Also see Dallaire, *Shake Hands with the Devil,* chaps. 10 and 11.

79. Melvern, *A People Betrayed;* Barnett interview with Dallaire, December 5, 2000; Dallaire, *Shake Hands with the Devil,* chaps. 10 and 11.

80. Human Rights Watch, *Leave None to Tell the Story,* 598, x.

81. Dallaire, *Shake Hands with the Devil,* chaps. 10 and 11.

82. Barnett, "The UN Security Council, Indifference, and Genocide in Rwanda"; Bjørn Willum, "Legitimizing Inaction towards Genocide in Rwanda: Matter of Misperception?" *International Peacekeeping* 6, no. 3 (1999): 11–30.

83. Dallaire, *Shake Hands with the Devil,* chap. 11.

84. Riza, *Frontline* interview. Also see Sylvana Faor, UN press briefing, November 27, 1996, cited in Willum, "Legitimizing Inaction towards Genocide in Rwanda," 13.

85. The failure is reminiscent the failure to catch the Japanese surprise attack at Pearl Harbor: "it is much easier *after* the event to sort the relevant from the irrelevant signals"; information from the field arrives cluttered and "embedded in an atmosphere of noise." Roberta Wolhstetter, *Pearl Harbor: Warning and Decision* (Stanford: Stanford University Press, 1962), 387; italics in original.

86. Richard Ned Lebow, *Between Peace and War* (Baltimore: Johns Hopkins University Press, 1981), 104; Weick, *Sensemaking in Organizations,* 56–61; Chun Wei Choo, *The Knowing Organization: How Organizations Use Information to Construct Meaning, Create Knowledge, and Make Decisions* (New York: Oxford University Press, 1998), chap. 3.

87. D. Kahneman and A. Tversky, "Prospect Theory: An Analysis of Decision under Risk," *Econometrica* 47 (1979): 263–91. Also see A. Tversky and D. Kahneman, "Judgment under Uncertainty: Heuristics and Biases," *Science* 185 (1974): 1124–31.

88. See Edelman, *Constructing the Political Spectacle;* Goffman, *Frame Analysis.*

89. Willum, "Legitimizing Inaction towards Genocide in Rwanda"; Joint Evaluation of Emergency Assistance to Rwanda, *International Response to Conflict and Genocide.*

90. Riza, *Frontline* interview; italics added.

91. See Schutz, *On Phenomenology and Social Relations.*

92. Riza, *Frontline* interview.

93. Ibid.

94. Willum, "Legitimizing Inaction towards Genocide in Rwanda."

95. Dallaire, *Shake Hands with the Devil,* 265.

96. Interview with Barnett, December 5, 2000.

97. Dallaire, *Shake Hands with the Devil,* chap. 11.

98. As the Secretariat marched through April, though, it did exhibit a desire to find a way to protect civilians as well as possible. Although it never advocated an intervention, neither did it ever advocate a complete withdrawal. Indeed, DPKO worked closely with New Zealand ambassador Colin Keating, the president of the Security Council during the month of April 1994, to oppose the U.S. desire to withdraw the operation completely in favor of a token presence. Melvern, *A People Betrayed;* Barnett, telephone interview with Keating, September 25, 2000.

99. Dallaire, *Shake Hands with the Devil,* 306.

100. Ibid., 320.

101. Ibid., 290.

102. Cables in Barnett's possession.

103. Laegreid, "U.N. Peacekeeping in Rwanda," 239.

104. Human Rights Watch, *Leave None to Tell the Story,* 597.

105. Suhrke, "Dilemmas of Protection," 264, 269.

106. Dallaire, *Shake Hands with the Devil,* p. 299.

107. Ibid., 295.

108. Ibid., 312. At one point Dallaire attempted to make the case for protecting civilians by posing an argument for withdrawal as an alternative, expecting that DPKO would rank protection over withdrawal. Instead, to his shock he found that DPKO jumped on the withdrawal option. According to Dallaire, the DPKO cable stated: "Your plans to start sharp reduction of UNAMIR personnel is approved. This also will demonstrate imminence of withdrawal of UNAMIR if cease-fire is not achieved." Ibid., 308.

109. Joint Evaluation of Emergency Assistance to Rwanda, *International Response to Conflict and Genocide,* chap. 4, p. 2.

110. Ibid., chap. 4, 8.

111. The Secretariat also believed that by remaining impartial, even after it became understood that this was a genocide, it could preserve its source of influence over the génocidaires. Ibid.

112. For a general argument regarding the secretary-general's persuasive abilities, see Ian Johnstone, "The Role of the UN Secretary-General: The Power of Persuasion Based on Law," *Global Governance* 9 (2003): 441–58.

113. See Joint Evaluation of Emergency Assistance to Rwanda, *International Response to Conflict and Genocide,* chap. 4, p. 1; and United Nations, *Final Report of the International Commission of Inquiry.*

114. Telephone interview with Barnett, July 3, 2000.

115. United Nations, General Assembly, "Fall of Srebrenica," 111.

116. Kofi Annan, "Two Concepts of Sovereignty," *Economist,* September 18, 1999.

CHAPTER 6. THE LEGITIMACY OF AN EXPANDING GLOBAL BUREAUCRACY

1. Barbara Koremenos, Charles Lipson, and Duncan Snidal, eds., *The Rational Design of International Institutions,* special issue of *International Organization* 55, no. 4 (2001): 761–99; Robert Keohane and Lisa Martin, "The Promise of Institutionalist Theory," *International Security* 20, no. 1 (1995): 39–51; Martin and Simmons, "Theories and Empirical Studies of International Institutions." This research agenda has even led to a neglect of the question of whether IOs are effective at their assigned tasks.

2. The exact mechanisms that drive this tendency toward efficiency are never specified or even investigated.

3. Thatcher and Sweet, "Theory and Practice of Delegation to Non-majoritarian Institutions."

4. Catherine Weaver and Ralf Leiteritz, "Organizational Culture and Change at the World Bank," manuscript, University of Kansas, Lawrence, 2002.

5. For a review of principal-agent applications to IOs, see Mark Pollack, "Learning from the Americanists (Again): Theory and Method in the Study of Delegation," *West European Politics* 25, no. 1 (2002): 200–219. Many scholars of principal-agent analysis have decided to simply assume that agents have some degree of autonomy and have concentrated their energies on other facets of the principal-agent logic. John Huber and Charles Shipan, *Deliberate Discretion? The Institutional Foundations of Bureaucratic Autonomy* (New York: Cambridge University Press, 2003).

6. For other statements regarding the conservative orientation of bureaucracies, see Douglas, *How Institutions Think;* Levinthal and March, "Model of Adaptive Organizational Search."

7. For an analogous argument about the World Bank, see Ferguson, *Anti-politics Machine,* conclusion.

8. Jeff Crisp, "Mind the Gap! UNHCR, Humanitarian Assistance, and the Development Process," *New Issues in Refugee Research,* Working Paper no. 43, United Nations High Commissioner for Refugees, May 2001.

9. Miles and Snow, *Organizational Strategy, Structure, and Process,* xv–xxv; Levinthal and March, "Model of Adaptive Organizational Search"; James G. March, "Footnotes to Organizational Change," in his *Decisions and Organizations,* 167–87; and March, "The Evolution of Evolution," in his *Pursuit of Organizational Intelligence,* 100–113.

10. For interesting statements regarding the relationship between agency and creative transformation, see Hans Joas, *The Creativity of Action* (New York: Polity Press, 1996); Mustafa Emirbayer and Anne Mische, "What Is Agency?" *American Journal of Sociology* 103, no. 4 (1998): 962–1023; Mustafa Emirbayer, "Manifesto for a Relational Sociology," *American Journal of Sociology* 103, no. 2 (1997): 281–317; and William Sewell, "A Theory of Structure: Duality, Agency, and Transformation," *American Journal of Sociology* 98, no. 1 (1992): 1–29.

11. We draw this argument from Swidler, "Culture in Action."

12. Emirbayer and Mische, "What Is Agency?" 970.

13. Weick, *Sensemaking in Organizations.*

14. Carpenter, *Forging of Bureaucratic Autonomy,* 355; Noll and Weingast, "Rational Actor Theory"; Robert Cox, "The Executive Head: An Essay on Leadership in International Organization," in his *Approaches to World Order* (New York: Cambridge University Press, 1996).

15. For some, this is equivalent to learning, but others reserve learning for those moments when organizations change not only their rules but also their ends. See Haas, *When Knowledge Is Power.*

16. Barnett, "Humanitarianism with a Sovereign Face." For a good discussion of the tensions between different parts of UNHCR's mandate, see Michael Barutciski, "A Critical View on UNHCR's Mandate Dilemmas," *International Journal of Refugee Law* 14, nos. 2/3 (2002): 365–81.

17. United Nations, General Assembly, "Fall of Srebrenica," 111.

18. Barry Barnes discusses this as a broad distinction between "power to" and "power over." See *The Nature of Power* (Cambridge: Polity, 1988).

19. Some argue that it is because of this sort of work that IOs are able to build an international community and are pluralizing world politics in ways that give more groups and peoples more of a voice. Akira Iriye, *Global Community: The Role of International Organizations in the Making of the Contemporary World* (Berkeley: University of California Press, 2002).

20. Charles Call and Susan Cook, "On Democratization and Peacebuilding," *Global Governance* 9, no. 2 (2003): 233–46.

21. See Finnemore, *National Interests in International Society,* for this argument.

22. Loescher, *UNHCR in World Politics.*

23. B. S. Chimni, "International Organizations Today: An Old Fashioned View from the Third World," Vienna Symposium: The International Legal Order, November 2002; John Judis, "History Lesson: What Woodrow Wilson Can Teach Today's Imperialists," *New Republic,* June 9, 2003, p. 21.

24. Paris, *At War's End.*

25. Frank Schimmelfennig, *The EU, NATO, and the Integration of Europe: Rules and Rhetoric* (New York: Cambridge University Press, 2003).

26. Hannah Arendt, *On Violence* (New York: Harcourt Brace Jovanovich, 1970), 38.

27. This does not mean that authority is zero-sum. See Barnett, "Authority, Intervention, and the Outer Limits of International Relations Theory," on this point.

28. Zygmunt Bauman, *Modernity and the Holocaust* (Ithaca: Cornell University Press, 2000), 196.

29. Sen, *Development as Freedom.*

30. For other discussions of UNHCR and power over refugees, see Barbara Hurrell-Bond, "Can Humanitarian Work with Refugees Be Humane?" *Human Rights Quarterly* 24 (2002): 51–85; and Michael Alexander, "Refugee Status Determination Conducted by UNHCR," *International Journal of Refugee Law* 11, no. 2 (1999): 251–89.

31. Boli and Thomas, *Constructing World Culture.*

32. Michael Barnett and Martha Finnemore, "The Power of Liberal International Organizations," in Michael Barnett and Raymond Duvall, eds., *Power in Global Governance* (New York: Cambridge University Press, 2004).

33. For a good collection of essays on the issue of IO legitimacy, see Jean-Marc Coicaud and Veijo Heiskanen, eds., *The Legitimacy of International Organizations* (New York: United Nations University Press, 2001).

34. See Lloyd Gruber, *Ruling the World: Power Politics and the Rise of Supranational Institutions* (Princeton: Princeton University Press, 2000) on voluntaristic decisions to join an international organization.

35. Mark Suchman, "Managing Legitimacy: Strategic and Institutional Approaches," *Academy of Management Review* 20, no. 3 (1995): 579.

36. Boli and Thomas, *Constructing World Culture;* Gili Drori, John Meyer, Francisco Ramirez, and Evan Shofer, *Science in the Modern World Polity: Institutionalization and Globalization* (Stanford: Stanford University Press, 2003).

37. Suchman, "Managing Legitimacy," 580.

38. Meyer and Rowan, "Institutionalized Organizations."

39. For various statements on the relationship between the procedural legitimacy organizations and accountability of international organizations, see Michael Camdessus, "The IMF at the Beginning of the Twenty-First Century: Can We Establish a Humanized Globalization?" *Global Governance* 7, no. 4 (2001): 363–70; Ngaire Woods and Amrita Narlikar, "Governance and the Limits of Accountability: The WTO, the IMF and the World Bank," *International Social Science Journal* 170 (November 2001): 569–83; August Reinisch, "Securing the Accountability of International Organizations," *Global Governance* 7, no. 2 (2001): 131–50; Coicard and Heiskanen, *Legitimacy of International Organizations;* and Ngaire Woods, "Accountability, Governance, and the Reform of the IMF," in David Vines and Christopher L. Gilbert, eds., *The IMF and Its Critics: Reform of Global Financial Architecture* (New York: Cambridge University Press, 2003), 396–416.

40. Robert O. Keohane, "Governance in a Partially Globalized World," in David Held and Anthony McGrew, eds., *Governing Globalization: Power, Authority, and Global Governance* (New York: Polity Press, 2002), 325–47.

41. Ibid.

42. Robert Dahl, "Can International Organizations Be Democratic? A Skeptic's View," in David Held and Anthony McGrew, eds., *The Global Transformations Reader* (Boston: Polity Press, 2003), 530–41; and Karel Wellens, *Remedies against International Organisations* (New York: Cambridge University Press, 2002).

43. Robert E. Goodin, *Protecting the Vulnerable: A Re-analysis of Our Social Responsibilities* (Chicago: University of Chicago Press, 1985), 114.

44. Roderick Kiewert and Matthew D. McCubbins, *The Logic of Delegation: Congressional Parties and the Appropriations Process* (Chicago: University of Chicago Press, 1991).

45. Sanjeev Khagram, "Restructuring the Global Politics of Development: The Case of India's Narmada Valley Dams," in S. Khagram, James Riker, and Kathryn Sikkink, eds., *Restructuring World Politics: Transnational Social Movements* (Minneapolis: University of Minnesota Press, 2002), 206–31.

46. Robert O. Keohane, "The Concept of Accountability in World Politics and the Use of Force," *Michigan Journal of International Law* 24 (Fall 2003): 1121–41

47. Fareed Zakaria, *The Future of Freedom: Illiberal Democracy at Home and Abroad* (New York: Norton, 2003). Just as we transpose the elements of Zakaria's phrase "illiberal democracy," so too do we reverse our policy concerns. At the national level, he worries about too much democracy (relative to liberalism); at the international level, we worry about too little. Note that the undemocratic character of contemporary global governance and international organizations is an increasingly prominent theme in academic and policy debates. See David Held, *Democracy and the Global Order* (New York: Polity Press, 1995); Daniele Archibugi and David Held, *Cosmopolitan Democracy* (New York: Polity Press, 1995).

BIBLIOGRAPHY

Abbott, Kenneth, and Duncan Snidal. 1988. "Why States Act through Formal International Organizations." *Journal of Conflict Resolution* 42:3–32.

Abrar, C. R. 1995. "Repatriation of Rohingya Refugees." Manuscript.

Adelman, Howard, and Astri Suhrke, eds. 1999. *The Paths of a Genocide: The Rwanda Crisis from Uganda to Zaire.* New Brunswick, N.J.: Transaction.

Adler, Emanuel. 2002. "Constructivism and International Relations." In *Handbook of International Relations,* ed. W. Carlneas, B. Simmons, and T. Risse. Thousand Oaks, Calif.: Sage Press.

Aga Khan, Sadruddin. 1963. "The Challenge of Refugee Problems in Africa." *UNHCR Reports,* no. 27 (November): 5–6.

———. 1976. "Legal Problems Relating to Refugees and Displaced Persons." Paper delivered at the Hague Academy of International Law, August 4–6.

Agnew, John. 1994. "The Territorial Trap: The Geographic Assumptions of International Relations Theory." *Review of International Political Economy* 1, no. 1: 53–80.

Albrow, Martin. 1970. *Bureaucracy.* London: Pall Mall Press.

Alexander, Michael. 1999. "Refugee Status Determination Conducted by UNHCR." *International Journal of Refugee Law* 11, no. 2: 251–89.

Alexander, Sidney S. 1952. "Effects of a Devaluation on a Trade Balance." *IMF Staff Papers* 2 (April): 263–78.

Alford, Howard. 2000. *Organizations Evolving.* Thousand Oaks, Calif.: Sage Press.

Allison, Graham. 1971. *Essence of Decision: Explaining the Cuban Missile Crisis.* Boston: Little, Brown.

Allison, Graham, and Phillip Zelikow. 1999. *Essence of Decision: Explaining the Cuban Missile Crisis.* 2nd ed. New York: Longman.

Alonso, William, and Paul Starr, eds. 1987. *The Politics of Numbers.* New York: Russell Sage Foundation.

Alvesson, Mats. 1993. *Cultural Perspectives on Organizations.* New York: Cambridge University Press.

Archer, Clive. 2001. *International Organizations.* 3rd ed. New York: Routledge.

Archibugi, Daniele, and David Held. 1995. *Cosmopolitan Democracy.* New York: Polity Press.

Arend, Anthony Clark. 1999. *Legal Rules and International Society.* New York: Oxford University Press.

Arendt, Hannah. 1968. *Between Past and Future.* New York: Viking Press.

———. 1970. *On Violence.* New York: Harcourt Brace Jovanovich.

Ascher, William. 1983. "New Development Approaches and the Adaptability of International Agencies: The Case of the World Bank." *International Organization* 37:415–39.
Ashley, Richard. 1984. "The Poverty of Neorealism." In *Neorealism and Its Critics*, ed. R. Keohane, 255–300. New York: Columbia University Press.
Asia Watch. 1993. *Bangladesh: Abuse of Burmese Refugees from Arakan*. Human Rights Watch Short Report vol. 5, no. 17.
Australian Council for Overseas Aid. 1996. "Repatriation of Burmese Refugees from Thailand and Bangladesh." Deakin, Australia. March.
Baldwin, David A., ed. 1993. *Neorealism and Neoliberalism*. New York: Columbia University Press.
Barbero, Julie. 1993. "Refugee Protection during Conflict: A New Conventional Wisdom." *Refuge* 12, no. 8: 7–12.
Barnard, Chester. 1940. *The Functions of the Executive*. Cambridge: Harvard University Press.
Barnes, Barry. 1986. "On Authority and Its Relationship to Power." In *Power, Action, and Belief: A New Sociology of Knowledge*, ed. J. Law, 180–95. New York: Routledge.
——. 1988. *The Nature of Power*. Cambridge: Polity Press.
Barnett, Michael. 1995. "The New U.N. Politics of Peace: From Juridical Sovereignty to Empirical Sovereignty." *Global Governance* 1, no. 1: 79–97.
——. 1997. "Bringing in the New World Order: Legitimacy, Liberalism, and the United Nations." *World Politics* 49, no. 4: 526–51.
——. 1997. "The UN Security Council, Indifference, and Genocide in Rwanda." *Cultural Anthropology* 12, no. 4: 551–78.
——. 1998. *Dialogues in Arab Politics*. New York: Columbia University Press.
——. 2001. "Humanitarianism with a Sovereign Face: UNHCR in Global Undertow." *International Migration Review* 35, no. 1: 244–76.
——. 2002. "Authority, Intervention, and the Outer Limits of International Relations Theory." In *Authorities and Interventions in World Politics*, ed. T. Callaghy, R. Latham, and R. Kassimer. New York: Cambridge University Press.
——. 2002. *Eyewitness to a Genocide: The United Nations and Rwanda*. Ithaca: Cornell University Press.
Barnett, Michael, and Raymond Duvall, eds., 2004. *Power in Global Governance*. New York: Cambridge University Press.
Barnett, Michael N., and Martha Finnemore. 1999. "The Politics, Power, and Pathologies of International Organizations." *International Organization* 53, no. 4: 699–732.
——. "The Power of Liberal International Organizations." 2004. In *Power in Global Governance*, ed. M. Barnett and R. Duvall. New York: Cambridge University Press.
Barutciski, Michael. 1996. "The Reinforcement of Non-admission Policies and the Subversion of UNHCR: Displacement and Internal Assistance in Bosnia-Herzegovina." *International Journal of Refugee Law* 8:49–110.
——. 1998. "Involuntary Repatriation When Refugee Protection Is No Longer Necessary." *International Journal of Refugee Law* 10, nos. 1/2: 236–55.
——. 2002. "A Critical View on UNHCR's Mandate Dilemmas." *International Journal of Refugee Law* 14, nos. 2/3: 365–81.
Bauman, Zygmunt. 2000. *Modernity and the Holocaust*. Ithaca: Cornell University Press.
Beard, Edmund. 1976. *Developing the ICBM: A Study in Bureaucratic Politics*. New York: Columbia University Press.
Beetham, David. 1996. *Bureaucracy*. 2nd ed. Minneapolis: University of Minnesota Press.
Belgium. Senate. 1997. *Parliamentary Commission of Inquiry Concerning Rwanda*. December.
Bell, David. 1975. *Power, Influence, and Authority*. New York: Oxford University Press.
Bendix, Reinhard. 1972. *Max Weber: An Intellectual Portrait*. Berkeley: University of California Press.
Bendor, Jonathan, Amihai Glazer, and Thomas Hammond. 2001. "Theories of Delegation." *Annual Review of Political Science* 4:235–69.
Bendor, Jonathan, and Thomas Hammond. 1992. "Rethinking Allison's Models." *American Political Science Review* 82, no. 2: 301–22.
Benton, Barbara, ed. 1996. *Soldiers for Peace: Fifty Years of UN Peacekeeping*. New York: Facts on File.
Berdal, Mats R. 1993. *Whither UN Peacekeeping?* London: Brassey's for the International Institute for Strategic Studies.
Berger, Peter, and Thomas Luckmann. 1967. *The Social Construction of Reality: A Treatise in the Sociology of Knowledge*. Boston: Anchor.

Bernstein, Edward. 1991. "The Early Years of the International Monetary Fund." In *International Financial Policy: Essays in Honor of Jacques J. Polak*, ed. Jacob A. Frenkel and Morris Goldstein, 58–63. Washington, D.C.: International Monetary Fund.

Bernstein, Richard. 1993. "Sniping Is Growing at U.N.'s Weakness as a Peacekeeper." *New York Times*, June 21, A1, A8.

Bird, Graham. 1995. *IMF Lending to Developing Countries: Issues and Evidence.* New York: Routledge.

Blau, Peter. 1963. "Critical Remarks on Weber's Theory of Authority." *American Political Science Review* 57:305–16.

Blumer, Herbert. 1969. *Symbolic Interactionism: Perspective and Method.* Englewood Cliffs, N.J.: Prentice Hall.

Boli, John, and George M. Thomas. 1999. *Constructing World Culture.* Stanford: Stanford University Press.

Bone, James. 1993. "Hurd Puts Limit on Peacekeeping." *London Times*, September 29.

Bourdieu, Pierre. 1977. *Outline of a Theory of Practice.* New York: Cambridge University Press.

——. 1994. *Language and Symbolic Power.* Chicago: University of Chicago Press.

Boutros-Ghali, Boutros. 1993. "An Agenda for Peace: One Year Later." *Orbis* 37 (Summer): 323–32.

——. 1995. *An Agenda for Peace.* 2nd ed. New York: United Nations.

——. 1996. *An Agenda for Democratization.* New York: United Nations, Department of Public Information.

——. 1996. "Global Leadership after the Cold War." *Foreign Affairs* 75 (March/April): 86–98.

——. 1999. *Unvanquished: A U.S.-UN Saga.* New York: Random House.

Bowker, Geoffrey C., and Susan Leigh Star. 1999. *Sorting Things Out: Classification and Its Consequences.* Cambridge: MIT Press.

Brint, Steven. 1994. *In an Age of Experts: The Changing Role of Professionals in Politics and Public Life.* Princeton: Princeton University Press.

Bruner, Jerome. 1990. *Acts of Meaning.* Cambridge: Harvard University Press.

Burawoy, Michael, et al., eds. 2000. *Global Ethnography: Forces, Connections, and Imaginations in a Postmodern World.* Berkeley: University of California Press.

Burke, Peter. 2000. *A Social History of Knowledge: From Gutenberg to Diderot.* Malden, Mass.: Polity Press.

Burley, Anne-Marie, and Walter Mattli. 1993. "Europe before the Court: A Political Theory of Integration." *International Organization* 47:41–76.

Call, Charles, and Susan Cook. 2003. "On Democratization and Peacebuilding." *Global Governance* 9, no. 2: 233–46.

Camdessus, Michael. 2001. "The IMF at the Beginning of the Twenty-First Century: Can We Establish a Humanized Globalization?" *Global Governance* 7, no. 4: 363–70.

Campbell, John L. 1998. "Institutional Analysis and the Role of Ideas in Political Economy." *Theory and Society* 27:377–409.

Carpenter, Daniel. 2001. *The Forging of Bureaucratic Autonomy: Reputations, Networks, and Policy Innovation in Executive Agencies, 1862–1928.* Princeton: Princeton University Press.

Carr, Edward H. 1964. *The Twenty Years' Crisis.* 1939; New York: Torchbooks.

Chimni, B. S. 1991. "Perspectives on Voluntary Repatriation: A Critical Note." *International Journal of Refugee Law* 3, no. 3: 541–46.

——. 1993. "The Meaning of Words and the Role of the UNHCR in Voluntary Repatriation." *International Journal of Refugee Law* 5, no. 3: 442–60.

——. 1998. "The Geopolitics of Refugee Studies: A View from the South." *Journal of Refugee Studies* 11, no. 4: 350–74.

——. 1999. "From Resettlement to Repatriation: Towards a Critical History of Durable Solutions to Refugee Problems." *New Issues in Refugee Research.* Working Paper no. 2. Geneva: UNHCR.

Choo, Chun Wei. 1998. *The Knowing Organization: How Organizations Use Information to Construct Meaning, Create Knowledge and Make Decisions.* New York: Oxford University Press.

Claude, Inis. 1966. "Collective Legitimization as a Political Function of the United Nations." *International Organization* 20:367–79.

——. 1971. *Swords into Ploughshares.* 4th ed. New York: Random House.

Clegg, Stewart R. 1993. "Weber and Foucault: Social Theory for the Study of Organizations." *Organization* 1:149–78.

——. 1994. "Power and Institutions in the Theory of Organizations." In *Toward a New Theory of Organization*, ed. J. Hassard and M. Parker. New York: Routledge.

The Clinton Administration's Policy on Reforming Multilateral Peace Operations. 1994. PDD-25. Department of State Publication 10161. Washington, D.C. May.

Coicaud, Jean-Marc, and Veijo Heiskanen, eds. 2001. *The Legitimacy of International Organizations.* New York: United Nations University Press.

Coles, Gervase. 1985. "Voluntary Repatriation: A Background Study." Prepared for the Round Table on Voluntary Repatriation, convened by the Office of the United Nations High Commissioner for Refugees in conjunction with the International Institute of Humanitarian Law, San Remo, July 16–19.

——. 1989. "Approaching the Refugee Problem Today." In *Refugees and International Relations,* ed. G. Loescher and L. Monahan, 373–410. New York: Oxford University Press.

Coles, Gervase. 1989. "Solutions to the Problem of Refugees and the Protection of Refugees: A Background Study." Prepared for the Round Table on Durable Solutions and the Protection of Refugees, convened by the Office of the United Nations High Commissioner for Refugees in conjunction with the International Institute of Humanitarian Law.

Cooper, Frederick, and Randy Packard, eds. 1998. *International Development and the Social Sciences.* Berkeley: University of California Press.

Cox, Robert W. 1996. *Approaches to World Order.* New York: Cambridge University Press.

Cox, Robert W., and Harold K. Jacobson. 1977. "Decision Making." *International Social Science Journal* 29:115–35.

Cox, Robert W., Harold K. Jacobson, et al. 1974. *The Anatomy of Influence: Decision Making in International Organizations.* New Haven: Yale University Press.

Crisp, Jeff. 1984. "Voluntary Repatriation Programmes for African Refugees: A Critical Examination." *Refugee Issues* 1, no. 2: 1–25.

——. 2001. "Mind the Gap! UNHCR, Humanitarian Assistance, and the Development Process." *New Issues in Refugee Research.* Working Paper no. 43. United Nations High Commissioner for Refugees. May.

Crisp, Jeff, and Erin Mooney. 1999. "Report on the Workshop on Internal Displacement in Africa, Addis Ababa, October 19–20, 1998." *International Migration Review* 33, no. 2: 468–83.

Crossette, Barbara. 1994. "U.N. Falters in Post-Cold-War Peacekeeping, but Sees Role as Essential." *New York Times,* December 5, A12.

——. 1995. "U.N. Chief Ponders Future of Peacekeepers." *New York Times,* March 3, A3.

——. 1995. "U.N. Leader to Call for Changes in Peacekeeping." *New York Times,* January 3, A3.

Cuny, Fred, and Barry Stein. 1989. "Prospects for and Promotion of Spontaneous Repatriation." In *Refugees and International Relations,* ed. G. Loescher and L. Monahan, 293–312. New York: Oxford University Press.

Cupitt, Richard, Rodney Whitlock, and Lynne Whitlock. 1997. "The (Im)morality of International Governmental Organizations." In *The Politics of Global Governance: International Organizations in an Interdependent World,* ed. P. Diehl, 7–23. Boulder: Lynne Rienner.

Cutler, A. Claire. 1999. "Locating 'Authority' in the Global Political Economy." *International Studies Quarterly* 43, no. 1: 59–83.

Cutler, A. Claire, Virginia Haufler, and Tony Porter, eds. 1999. *Private Authority and International Affairs.* Albany: State University of New York Press.

Cutts, Mark. 1998. "Politics and Humanitarianism." *Refugee Survey Quarterly* 17, no. 1: 1–15.

Dahl, Robert. 2003. "Can International Organizations Be Democratic? A Skeptic's View." In *The Global Transformations Reader,* ed. D. Held and A. McGrew, 530–41. Boston: Polity Press.

——. 2003. *Shake Hands with the Devil: The Failure of Humanity in Rwanda.* Toronto: Random House Canada.

Dam, Kenneth W. 1982. *The Rules of the Game: Reform and Evolution of the International Monetary System.* Chicago: University of Chicago Press.

Daniel, Donald C. F., and Bradd C. Hayes, with Chantal de Jonge Oudraat. 1999. *Coercive Inducement and the Containment of International Crises.* Washington, D.C.: United States Institute of Peace Press.

David, Wilfred L. 1985. *The IMF Policy Paradigm.* New York: Praeger.

Dell, Sidney. 1981. *On Being Grandmotherly: The Evolution of IMF Conditionality.* Essays in International Finance 144. Princeton, N.J.: International Finance Section, Dept. of Economics, Princeton University.

Destexhe, Alain. 1996. *Rwanda and Genocide in the Twentieth Century.* New York: New York University Press.

Deutsch, Karl. 1963. *The Nerves of Government: Models of Political Communication and Control.* Glencoe: Free Press.

De Vries, Margaret Garritsen. 1987. *Balance of Payments Adjustment, 1945–1986: The IMF Experience.* Washington, D.C.: International Monetary Fund.

De Vries, M. G., and J. K. Horsefield. 1969. *Analysis.* Vol. 2 of *The International Monetary Fund, 1945–1965,* ed. J. Keith Horsefield. Washington, D.C.: International Monetary Fund.

Diehl, Paul. 1993. *International Peacekeeping.* Baltimore: Johns Hopkins University Press.

DiMaggio, Paul, and Walter Powell. 1983. "The Iron Cage Revisited: Institutional Isomorphism and Collective Rationality in Organizational Fields." *American Sociological Review* 48:147–60.

Douglas, Mary. 1986. *How Institutions Think.* Syracuse: Syracuse University Press.

Doyle, Michael, et al., eds. 1997. *Keeping the Peace: Multidimensional UN Operations in Cambodia and El Salvador.* New York: Cambridge University Press.

Drori, Gili, John Meyer, Francisco Ramirez, and Evan Shofer. 2003. *Science in the Modern World Polity: Institutionalization and Globalization.* Stanford: Stanford University Press.

Duke, Simon. 1994. "The United Nations and Intra-State Conflict." *International Peacekeeping* 1, no. 4: 375–93.

Durch, Paul, ed. 1993. *The Evolution of UN Peacekeeping.* New York: St. Martin's Press.

Eckaus, R. S. 1986. "How the IMF Lives with Its Conditionality." *Policy Sciences* 19:237–52.

Edelman, Murray. 1988. *Constructing the Political Spectacle.* Chicago: University of Chicago Press.

Emirbayer, Mustafa. 1997. "Manifesto for a Relational Sociology." *American Journal of Sociology* 103, no. 2: 281–317.

Emirbayer, Mustafa, and Anne Mische. 1998. "What Is Agency?" *American Journal of Sociology* 103, no. 4: 962–1023.

Endres, A. M., and Grant A. Fleming. 2002. *International Organizations and the Analysis of Economic Policy, 1919–1950.* New York: Cambridge University Press.

Escobar, Arturo. 1995. *Encountering Development: The Making and Unmaking of the Third World.* Princeton: Princeton University Press.

Farer, Tom, and Felice Gaer. 1993. "The UN and Human Rights: At the End of the Beginning." In *United Nations, Divided World: The UN's Roles in International Relations,* ed. Adam Roberts and Benedict Kingsbury, 240–96. New York: Oxford University Press.

Feld, Werner J., and Robert S. Jordan, with Leon Hurwitz. 1988. *International Organizations: A Comparative Approach.* 2nd ed. New York: Praeger.

Feldstein, Martin. 1998. "Refocusing the IMF." *Foreign Affairs* 77 (March/April): 20–33.

Ferguson, Alan. 1993. "U.N. to Reject Burundi's Plea for Peacekeepers." *Toronto Star,* November 3, A17.

Ferguson, James. 1990. *The Anti-politics Machine: "Development," Depoliticization, and Bureaucratic Domination in Lesotho.* New York: Cambridge University Press.

Ferguson, Yale H., and Richard W. Mansbach. 1996. *Polities: Authority, Identities, and Change.* Columbia: University of South Carolina Press.

Fetherston, A. B. 1994. *Towards a Theory of United Nations Peacekeeping.* New York: St. Martin's Press.

Finnemore, Martha. 1996. "Constructing Norms of Humanitarian Intervention." In *The Culture of National Security: Identity and Norms in World Politics,* ed. Peter Katzenstein, 153–85. New York: Columbia University Press.

——. 1996. *National Interests in International Society.* Ithaca: Cornell University Press.

——. 1996. "Norms, Culture, and World Politics: Insights from Sociology's Institutionalism." *International Organization* 50:325–47.

——. 2003. *The Purpose of Intervention: Changing Beliefs about the Use of Force.* Ithaca: Cornell University Press.

Finnemore, Martha, and Kathryn Sikkink. 1998. "International Norm Dynamics and Political Change." *International Organization* 52:887–917.

Fischer, Stanley. 1997. "Applied Economics in Action: IMF Programs." *American Economic Review* 87, no. 2: 23–27.

Fisher, William. 1997. "Doing Good? The Politics and Antipolitics of NGO Practices." *Annual Review of Anthropology* 26:439–64.

Flathman, Richard. 1980. *The Practice of Political Authority.* Chicago: University of Chicago Press.

Fleming, J. Marcus. 1963. "Developments in the International Payments System." *IMF Staff Papers* 10 (November): 461–82.

Forsythe, David. 2001. "UNHCR's Mandate: The Politics of Being Non-political." *New Issues in Refugee Research.* Working Paper no. 33. United Nations High Commissioner for Refugees. March.

Franck, Thomas M. 1995. *Fairness in International Law and Institutions.* New York: Oxford University Press.

Frelick, Bill. 1990. "The Right to Return." *International Journal of Refugee Law* 2:442–48.
——. 1993. "Preventing Refugee Flows: Protection or Peril?" *World Refugee Survey*, 5–13.
Frenkel, Jacob A., Morris Goldstein, and Mohsin S. Kahn. 1991. "Major Themes in the Writings of Jacques J. Polak." In *International Financial Policy: Essays in Honor of Jacques J. Polak*, ed. J. Frenkel and M. Goldstein. Washington, D.C.: International Monetary Fund.
Friedman, Richard B. 1990. "On the Concept of Authority in Political Philosophy." In *Authority*, ed. Joseph Raz, 56–91. New York: New York University Press.
Gallagher, Dennis. 1989. "The Evolution of the International Refugee System." *International Migration Review* 23, no. 3: 579–98.
Gallarotti, Giulio. 1991. "The Limits of International Organization." *International Organization* 45:183–220.
Gandhi, Ved P. 1998. "The IMF and the Environment." Washington, D.C.: International Monetary Fund. http://www.imf.org/external/pubs/ft/exrp/environ/index.htm#4.
George, Alexander. 1979. "Case Studies and Theory Development: The Method of Structured, Focused Comparison." In *Diplomacy: New Approaches in History, Theory, and Policy*, ed. Paul G. Lauren, 43–68. New York: Free Press.
Geyer, Georgie Anne. 1994. "The World as Viewed from the U.N. Helm." *Washington Times*, April 3, B4.
Gilbert, Geoff. 1998. "Rights, Legitimate Expectations, Needs, and Responsibilities: UNHCR and the New World Order." *International Journal of Refugee Law* 10, no. 3: 349–88.
Goffman, Erving. 1963. *Behavior in Public Places: Notes on the Social Organization of Gatherings*. New York: Free Press.
——. 1974. *Frame Analysis: An Essay on the Organization of Experience*. Cambridge: Harvard University Press.
Goodin, Robert E. 1985. *Protecting the Vulnerable: A Re-analysis of Our Social Responsibilities*. Chicago: University of Chicago Press.
Goodwin-Gill, Guy. 1989. "Voluntary Repatriation: Legal and Policy Issues." In *Refugees and International Relations*, ed. G. Loescher and L. Monahan, 255–91. New York: Oxford University Press.
——. 1996. *The Refugee in International Law*. 2nd ed. New York: Oxford University Press.
Gordenker, Leon. 1981. "Organizational Expansion and Limits in International Services for Refugees." *International Migration Review* 15:74–87.
——. 1987. *Refugees in International Politics*. New York: Columbia University Press.
Gould, Erica. 2003. "Money Talks: Supplementary Financiers and International Monetary Fund Conditionality." *International Organization* 57 (Summer): 551–86.
Goulding, Marrack. 1993. "The Evolution of United Nations Peacekeeping." *International Affairs* 69, no. 3: 453–55.
——. 2003. *Peacemonger*. Baltimore: Johns Hopkins University Press.
Gourevitch, Philip. 1998. "The Genocide Fax." *New Yorker*, May 11, pp. 42–46.
Gran, Guy. 1986. "Beyond African Famines: Whose Knowledge Matters?" *Alternatives* 11:275–96.
Gruber, Lloyd. 2000. *Ruling the World: Power Politics and the Rise of Supranational Institutions*. Princeton: Princeton University Press.
Gupta, Akhil. 1998. *Postcolonial Developments: Agriculture in the Making of Modern India*. Durham: Duke University Press.
Guzzini, Stefano. 2000. "A Reconstruction of Constructivism in International Relations." *European Journal of International Relations* 6, no. 2: 147–82.
Haas, Ernst B. 1964. *Beyond the Nation-State: Functionalism and International Organization*. Stanford: Stanford University Press.
——. 1990. *When Knowledge Is Power: Three Models of Change in International Organizations*. Berkeley: University of California Press.
Haas, Ernst, and Peter Haas. 1995. "Learning to Learn: Some Thoughts on Improving International Governance of the Global Problematique." In *Issues in Global Governance*, ed. Commission on Global Governance. Boston: Clair Law International.
Hacking, Ian. 1999. *The Social Construction of What?* Cambridge: Harvard University Press.
Hall, Rodney Bruce. 1997. "Moral Authority as a Power Resource." *International Organization* 51, no. 4: 591–622.
Hall, Rodney Bruce, and Thomas Biersteker, eds. 2002. *The Emergence of Private Authority in Global Governance*. New York: Cambridge University Press.

Halperin, Morton. 1974. *Bureaucratic Politics and Foreign Policy.* Washington, D.C.: Brookings Institution.

Handelman, Don. 1995. "Commentary on Heyman." *Current Anthropology* 36: 280–81.

Handler, Richard. 1988. *Nationalism and the Politics of Culture in Quebec.* Madison: University of Wisconsin Press.

Harper, Richard H. R. 1998. *Inside the IMF: An Ethnography of Documents, Technology, and Organizational Action.* New York: Academic Press.

Hatch, Mary Jo. 1993. "The Dynamics of Organizational Culture." *Academy of Management Review* 18, no. 4: 657–93.

Hathaway, James. 1991. "Reconceiving Refugee Law as Human Rights Protection." *Journal of Refugee Studies* 4, no. 2: 113–31.

Hayward, Clarissa. 2000. *De-Facing Power.* New York: Cambridge University Press.

Held, David. 1995. *Democracy and the Global Order.* New York: Polity Press.

Helman, Gerald, and Steven Ratner. 1992–93. "Saving Failed States." *Foreign Policy* 89 (Winter): 3–20.

Herzfeld, Michael. 1993. *The Social Production of Indifference: Exploring the Symbolic Roots of Western Bureaucracy.* Chicago: University of Chicago Press.

Hewson, Martin, and Tim Sinclair, eds. 1999. *Approaches to Global Governance Theory.* Albany: State University of New York Press.

Heyman, Josiah McC. 1995. "Putting Power in the Anthropology of Bureaucracy." *Current Anthropology* 36:261–88.

Higgens, Rosalyn. 1963. *The Development of International Law through the Organs of the United Nations.* New York: Oxford University Press.

Higgott, Richard A., Geoffrey R. D. Underhill, and Andreas Bieler, eds. 2000. *Non-state Actors and Authority in the Global System.* New York: Routledge.

Holborn, Louise. 1975. *Refugees, Problem of Our Time: The Work of the United Nations High Commissioner for Refugees.* 2 vols. Metuchen, N.J.: Scarecrow Press.

Holzner, Burkhart. 1968. *Reality Construction in Society.* Cambridge, Mass.: Schenkman.

Holzner, Burkhart, and John Marx. 1979. *Knowledge Application: The Knowledge System in Society.* Boston: Allyn and Bacon.

Horsefield, J. Keith. 1969. *Chronicle.* Vol. 1 of *The International Monetary Fund, 1945–1965,* ed. J. Keith Horsefield. Washington, D.C.: International Monetary Fund.

Howard, Michael. 1993. "The Historical Development of the UN's Role in International Security." In *United Nations, Divided World: The UN's Roles in International Relations,* ed. Adam Roberts and Benedict Kingsbury. New York: Oxford University Press.

Huber, John, and Charles Shipan. 2003. *Deliberate Discretion? The Institutional Foundations of Bureaucratic Autonomy.* New York: Cambridge University Press.

Human Rights Watch. 1996. *The Rohingyan Muslims: Ending a Cycle of Exodus?* Human Rights Watch Report vol. 8, no. 9(C).

——. 1997. *Rohingya Refugees in Bangladesh: The Search for a Lasting Solution.* Human Rights Watch Report vol. 9, no. 7(C).

——. 1997. *Uncertain Refugee: International Failures to Protect Refugees.* Human Rights Watch Report vol. 9, no. 1(G).

——. 1999. *Leave None to Tell the Story: Genocide in Rwanda.* New York: Human Rights Watch.

Hurd, Ian. 1999. "Legitimacy and Authority in International Politics." *International Organization* 53, no. 2: 379–408.

Hurrell-Bond, Barbara. 1989. "Repatriation: Under What Conditions Is It the Most Desirable Solution for Refugees?" *African Studies Review* 32:41–69.

——. 2002. "Can Humanitarian Work with Refugees Be Humane?" *Human Rights Quarterly* 24:51–85.

Ikenberry, G. John. 2001. *After Victory: Institutions, Strategic Restraint, and the Rebuilding of Order after Major Wars.* Princeton: Princeton University Press.

IMF Survey. 1981. February 9.

Immergut, Ellen. 1998. "The Theoretical Core of the New Institutionalism." *Politics and Society* 26, no. 1: 14–19.

International Monetary Fund. 1987. "Theoretical Aspects of the Design of Fund-Supported Adjustment Programs." Occasional Paper no. 55. Washington, D.C.: IMF.

Iriye, Akira. 2002. *Global Community: The Role of International Organizations in the Making of the Contemporary World.* Berkeley: University of California Press.

Jacobson, Harold. 1979. *Networks of Interdependence: International Organizations and the Global Political System.* New York: Knopf.

Jaeger, Gertrude, and Philip Selznick. 1964. "A Normative Theory of Culture." *American Sociological Review* 29, no. 5: 653–69.

Jaeger, Gilbert. 1978. "Status and the Protection of Refugees." International Institute of Human Rights. Ninth Study Session.

James, Alan. 1990. *Peacekeeping in International Politics.* New York: St. Martin's Press.

James, Harold. 1996. *International Monetary Cooperation since Bretton Woods.* New York: Oxford University Press.

——. 1998. "From Grandmotherliness to Governance: The Evolution of IMF Conditionality." *Finance and Development* 35, no. 4: 44–47.

Janowitz, Morris. 1964. *The Military in the Political Development of New Nations.* Chicago: University of Chicago Press.

Joas, Hans. 1996. *The Creativity of Action.* New York: Polity Press.

Johnson, John J., ed. 1962. *The Role of the Military in Underdeveloped Countries.* Princeton: Princeton University Press.

Johnstone, Ian. 2003. "The Role of the UN Secretary-General: The Power of Persuasion Based on Law." *Global Governance* 9:441–58.

Joint Evaluation of Emergency Assistance to Rwanda. 1996. *The International Response to Conflict and Genocide: Lessons from the Rwanda Experience.* Copenhagen: Steering Committee of the Joint Evaluation of Emergency Assistance to Rwanda.

Jones, Bruce. 2001. *Peacemaking in Rwanda: The Dynamics of Failure.* Boulder: Lynne Rienner.

Jordan, Robert S. 1988. "'Truly' International Bureaucracies: Real or Imagined?" In *Politics in the United Nations System,* ed. L. Finkelstein, 424–45. Durham: Duke University Press.

Judis, John. 2003. "History Lesson: What Woodrow Wilson Can Teach Today's Imperialists." *New Republic,* June 9, pp. 19–23.

Kahneman, D., and A. Tversky. 1979. "Prospect Theory: An Analysis of Decision under Risk." *Econometrica* 47:263–91.

Kapur, Devesh, and Richard Webb. 2000. "Governance-Related Conditionalities of the IFIs." Paper prepared for the XII Technical Group Meeting of the Intergovernmental Group of 24 for International Monetary Affairs, Lima, Peru, March 1–3. Revised May 2000.

Katzenstein, Peter, ed. 1996. *The Culture of National Security: Identity and Norms in World Politics.* New York: Columbia University Press.

Keeley, James. 1990. "Toward a Foucauldian Analysis of International Regimes." *International Organization* 44:83–105.

Kelsen, Hans. 1951. *The Law of the United Nations: A Critical Analysis of Its Fundamental Problems.* New York: Praeger.

Kennedy, David. 1986. "International Refugee Protection." *Human Rights Quarterly* 8:1–69.

Keohane, Robert O. 1984. *After Hegemony.* Princeton: Princeton University Press.

——. 2002. "Governance in a Partially Globalized World." In *Governing Globalization: Power, Authority, and Global Governance,* ed. David Held and Anthony McGrew, 325–47. New York: Polity Press.

——. 2003. "The Concept of Accountability in World Politics and the Use of Force." *Michigan Journal of International Law* 24 (Fall): 1121–41.

Keohane, Robert, and Lisa Martin. 1995. "The Promise of Institutionalist Theory." *International Security* 20, no. 1: 39–51.

Keohane, Robert, and Joseph Nye. 2001. Introduction to *Governance in a Globalizing World,* ed. J. Nye and J. Donahue, 1–43. Washington, D.C.: Brookings Institution Press.

Khadiagala, Gilbert. 2002. "Implementing the Arusha Agreement on Rwanda." In *Ending Civil War: The Implementation of Peace Agreements,* ed. Stephen Stedman, Donald Rothchild, and Elizabeth Cousens, 421–62. Boulder: Lynne Rienner.

Khagram, Sanjeev. 2002. "Restructuring the Global Politics of Development: The Case of India's Narmada Valley Dams." In *Restructuring World Politics: Transnational Social Movements,* ed. S. Khagram, J. Riker, and K. Sikkink, 206–31. Minneapolis: University of Minnesota Press.

Khagram, Sanjeev, James Riker, and Kathryn Sikkink, eds. 2002. *Restructuring World Politics: Transnational Social Movements.* Minneapolis: University of Minnesota Press.

Khan, Mohsin. 1990. "Evaluating the Effects of IMF-Supported Adjustment Programs: A Survey." In *International Finance and the Less-Developed Countries,* ed. Kate Phylaktis and Mahmood Pradhan. London: Macmillan.

Kier, Elizabeth. 1996. "Culture and French Military Doctrine before World War II." In *The Culture of National Security: Identity and Norms in World Politics*, ed. Peter Katzenstein, 186–215. New York: Columbia University Press.

Kiewert, Roderick, and Matthew D. McCubbins. 1991. *The Logic of Delegation: Congressional Parties and the Appropriations Process*. Chicago: University of Chicago Press.

Killick, Tony. 1995. *IMF Programmes in Developing Countries: Design and Impact*. London: Routledge.

Klinghoffer, Arthur Jay. 1998. *The International Dimension of Genocide in Rwanda*. New York: New York University Press.

Koremenos, Barbara, Charles Lipson, and Duncan Snidal, eds. 2001. "The Rational Design of International Institutions." Special Issue of *International Organization* 55, no. 4 (Autumn).

Krasner, Stephen D., ed. 1983. *International Regimes*. Ithaca: Cornell University Press.

Krause, Keith, and Michael Williams. 1996. "Broadening the Agenda of Security Studies: Politics and Methods." *Mershon International Studies Review* 40, no. 2: 229–54.

Krugman, Paul. 1999. "The Return of Depression Economics." *Foreign Affairs* 78 (January/February): 56–74.

Kuper, Adam. 1999. *Culture: The Anthropologists' Account*. Cambridge: Harvard University Press.

Laegreid, Turid. 1999. "U.N. Peacekeeping in Rwanda." In *The Path of a Genocide: The Rwanda Crisis from Uganda to Zaire*, ed. Howard Adelman and Astri Suhrke, 231–51. New Brunswick, N.J.: Transaction Press.

Landgren, Karin. 1998. "The Future of Refugee Protection." *Journal of Refugee Studies* 11, no. 4: 416–32.

Lave, Jean. 1986. "The Values of Quantification." In *Power, Action, and Belief*, ed. John Law, 88–111. London: Routledge and Kegan Paul.

Lawyers Committee for Human Rights. 1991. *UNHCR at 40: Refugee Protection at the Crossroads*. New York: LCHR.

Lebow, Richard Ned. 1981. *Between Peace and War*. Baltimore: Johns Hopkins University Press.

Legro, Jeffrey W. 1995. *Cooperation under Fire: Anglo-German Restraint during World War II*. Ithaca: Cornell University Press.

——. 1997. "Which Norms Matter? Revisiting the 'Failure' of Internationalism." *International Organization* 51, no. 1: 31–64.

Lemarchand, René. 1970. *Rwanda and Burundi*. New York: Praeger.

Lens, Allen. 2004. "From Peacekeeping to Peace-Building: The United Nations and the Challenge of Intrastate War." In *The United Nations and Global Security*, ed. Mark W. Zacher and Richard M. Price. New York: Palgrave Macmillan.

Levinthal, D., and J. March. 1988. "A Model of Adaptive Organizational Search." In *Decisions and Organizations*, ed. J. March, 187–218. New York: Blackwell.

Lewis, Paul. 1993. "Five Key Nations Urge Prudence in Setting Peacekeeping Goal." *New York Times*, October 1, A2.

Lincoln, Bruce. 1994. *Authority*. Chicago: University of Chicago Press.

Lipartito, Kenneth. 1995. "Culture and the Practice of Business History." *Business and Economic History* 24, no. 2: 1–41.

Locher, Birgit, and Elisabeth Prugl. 2001. "Feminism and Constructivism: Worlds Apart or Sharing the Middle Ground?" *International Studies Quarterly* 45, no. 1 : 111–30.

Loescher, Gil. 1993. *Beyond Charity: International Cooperation and the Global Refugee Crisis*. New York: Oxford University Press.

——. 2001. "The UNHCR and World Politics: State Interests vs. Institutional Autonomy." *International Migration Review* 35 (Spring): 33–56.

——. 2001. *The UNHCR in World Politics: A Perilous Path*. New York: Oxford University Press.

Louis, W. Roger, and Roger Owen, eds. 1989. *Suez 1956: The Crisis and Its Consequences*. New York: Oxford University Press.

Lyons, Gene, and Michael Mastanduno. 1995. "Introduction: International Intervention, State Sovereignty, and the Future of International Society." In *Beyond Westphalia? State Sovereignty and International Intervention*, ed. G. Lyons and M. Mastanduno. Baltimore: Johns Hopkins University Press.

MacKinley, John, and Jarat Chopra. 1992. "Second Generation Multinational Operations." *Washington Quarterly* (Summer): 113–31.

Mamdani, Mahmood. 2001. *When Victims Become Killers: Colonialism, Nativism, and the Genocide in Rwanda*. Princeton: Princeton University Press.

Mani, Rama. 1998. "Conflict Resolution, Justice, and the Law: Rebuilding the Rule of Law in the Aftermath of Complex Political Emergencies." *International Peacekeeping* 5, no. 3: 1–25.
Manning, Peter. 1997. "Organizations as Sense-Making Contexts." *Theory, Culture, and Society* 14, no. 2: 139–50.
March, James G. 1988. *Decisions and Organizations.* New York: Basil Blackwell.
——. 1997. "Understanding How Decisions Happen in Organizations." In *Organizational Decision Making,* ed. Z. Shapira, 9–33. New York: Cambridge University Press.
——. 1999. *The Pursuit of Organizational Intelligence.* Malden, Mass.: Blackwell.
March, James G., and Johan P. Olsen. 1989. *Rediscovering Institutions: The Organizational Basis of Politics.* New York: Free Press.
March, James G., Martin Schulz, and Xueguang Zhou. 2000. *The Dynamics of Rules: Change in Written Organizational Codes.* Stanford: Stanford University Press.
Marcus, George. 1998. *Ethnography through Thick and Thin.* Princeton: Princeton University Press.
Marrus, Michael. 1985. *The Unwanted: European Refugees in the Twentieth Century.* New York: Oxford University Press.
Martin, Joanne. 1992. *Cultures in Organizations: Three Perspectives.* New York: Oxford University Press.
Martin, Lisa, and Beth Simmons. 1998. "Theories and Empirical Studies of International Institutions." *International Organization* 52, no. 4 (1998): 729–53.
Matthews, Jennifer Tuchman. 1989. "Redefining Security." *Foreign Affairs* 68, no. 2: 162–77.
Mattingly, Garrett. 1988. *Renaissance Diplomacy.* New York: Dover.
McAdam, Douglas, John D. McCarthy, and Mayer N. Zald. 1996. *Comparative Perspectives on Social Movements: Political Opportunities, Mobilizing Structures, and Cultural Framing.* New York: Cambridge University Press.
McNeely, Connie. 1995. *Constructing the Nation-State: International Organization and Prescriptive Action.* Westport, Conn.: Greenwood Press.
Mearsheimer, John. 1994–95. "The False Promise of International Institutions." *International Security* 19, no. 3: 5–49.
Médicins sans Frontières–Holland. 1995. "Awareness Survey of Rohingyan Refugee Camps." March 15.
——. 1995. "MSF's Concerns on the Repatriation of Rohingyan Refugees from Bangladesh to Burma." May 1.
——. 1997. "Better Off in Burma? The Plight of the Burmese Rohingyas." November.
Meisler, Stanley. 1994. "Kofi Annan: The Soft-Spoken Economist Who Runs U.N. Peacekeeping Forces." *Los Angeles Times,* June 19, M3.
Melander, Goran. 1987. *The Two Refugee Definitions.* Lund: Raoul Wallenberg Institute.
Melvern, Linda. 2000. *A People Betrayed: The Role of the West in Rwanda's Genocide.* New York: Zed Books.
Mertus, Julie. 1998. "The State and the Post–Cold War Refugee Regime: New Models, New Questions." *International Journal of Refugee Law* 10, no. 3: 320–47.
Meyer, John, and Brian Rowan. 1977. "Institutionalized Organizations: Formal Structure as Myth and Ceremony." *American Journal of Sociology* 83:340–63.
Miles, Raymond, and Charles Snow. 2003. *Organizational Strategy, Structure, and Process.* Stanford: Stanford Business Books.
Miller, Peter, and Ted O'Leary. 1987. "Accounting and the Construction of the Governable Person." *Accounting, Organizations and Society* 12, no. 3: 235–65.
Miller, Peter, and Nikolas Rose. 1990. "Governing Economic Life." *Economy and Society* 19, no. 1: 1–31.
Miller-Adams, Michelle. 1999. *The World Bank: New Agendas in a Changing World.* New York: Routledge.
Moe, Terry. 1990. "The Politics of Structural Choice: Toward a Theory of Public Bureaucracy." In *Organization Theory from Chester Barnard to the Present and Beyond,* ed. O. Williamson, 116–53. New York: Oxford University Press.
Monroe, Kristen, ed. 1991. *Economic Approaches to Politics.* New York: Harper Collins.
Moorehead, Caroline. 2002. "Lost in Cairo." *New York Review of Books,* June 13, 28–31.
Moravcsik, Andrew. 1999. "A New Statecraft? Supranational Entrepreneurs and International Cooperation." *International Organization* 53, no. 2: 267–306.
Morris, Nicholas. 1990. "Refugees: Facing Crisis in the 1990s—A Personal View from within UNHCR." *International Journal of Refugee Law* 2 (September): 38–57.

Mortimer, Edward. 1993. "Peace Role in Process." *Financial Times*, November 17, p. 14.

Mouzelis, Nicos. 1967. *Organization and Bureaucracy*. Chicago: Aldine.

Naím, Moisés. 1994. "The World Bank: Its Role, Governance, and Organizational Culture." In *Bretton Woods: Looking to the Future*, C273–87. Washington, D.C.: Bretton Woods Commission.

Ness, Gayl, and Steven Brechin. 1988. "Bridging the Gap: International Organizations as Organizations." *International Organization* 42:245–73.

Newbury, Catharine. 1988. *The Cohesion of Oppression: Clientship and Ethnicity in Rwanda, 1860–1960*. New York: Columbia University Press.

Niskanen, William A. 1971. *Bureaucracy and Representative Government*. Chicago: Aldine.

Noll, Roger, and Barry Weingast. 1991. "Rational Actor Theory, Social Norms, and Policy Implementation: Applications to Administrative Processes and Bureaucratic Culture." In *Economic Approaches to Politics*, ed. Kristen Monroe, 237–58. New York: Harper Collins.

Nye, Joseph. 1987. "Nuclear Learning and U.S.-Soviet Security Regimes." *International Organization* 41, no. 3: 371–402.

Off, Carol. 2001. *The Lion, the Fox, and the Eagle: A Story of Generals and Justice in Rwanda and Yugoslavia*. Toronto: Random House Canada.

Omaar, Rakiya, and Alex de Waal. 1995. *Rwanda: Death, Despair, and Defiance*. London: African Rights.

Onuf, Nicholas, and Frank F. Klink. 1989. "Anarchy, Authority and Rule." *International Studies Quarterly* 33: 149–73.

Organization of African Unity. 2000. *Report on the UN and Genocide in Rwanda*. Addis Ababa: Organization of African Unity. May.

Paris, Roland. 2002. "International Peacebuilding and the 'Mission Civilisatrice.'" *Review of International Studies* 28, no. 4: 637–56.

——. 2004. *At War's End: Building Peace after Civil Conflict*. New York: Cambridge University Press.

Paschall, Rod. 1996. "U.N. Peacekeeping Tactics: The Impartial Buffer." In *Soldiers for Peace: Fifty Years of UN Peacekeeping*, ed. B. Benton, 50–55. New York: Facts on File.

Pauly, Louis. 1997. *Who Elected the Bankers? Surveillance and Control in the World Economy*. Ithaca: Cornell University Press.

——. 1999. "Good Governance and Bad Policy: The Perils of International Organizational Overextension." *Review of International Political Economy* 6:401–24.

"Peacekeeping Guidelines." 1994. Editorial. *Washington Post*, May 8, C6.

Perrow, Charles. 1986. *Complex Organizations: A Critical Essay*. New York: Random House.

Petrasek, David. 1996. "Through Rose-Coloured Glasses: UNHCR's Role in Monitoring the Safety of the Rohingya Refugees Returning to Burma." Paper.

Pevehouse, Jon. 2002. "Tracing the Dynamics of International Organizations." Manuscript, University of Wisconsin–Madison.

Pfeffer, Jeffrey, and Gerald Salancik. 1978. *The External Control of Organizations*. New York: Harper and Row.

Pierpaoli, Yvette. 1994. "Rohingya Refugees in Bangladesh." *Refugees International Bulletin*, June 6.

Pitterman, Shelly. 1985. "International Responses to Refugee Situations: The United Nations High Commissioner for Refugees." In *Refugees and World Politics*, ed. Elizabeth G. Ferris, 43–81. New York: Praeger.

Polak, Jacques J. 1952. "International Trade Theory—Discussion." *American Economic Review, Papers and Proceedings* 42 (May): 179–81.

——. 1957. "Monetary Analysis of Income Formation and Payments Problems." *IMF Staff Papers*, no. 6.

——. 1991. *The Changing Nature of IMF Conditionality*. Essays in International Finance 184. Princeton, N.J.: International Finance Section, Dept. of Economics, Princeton University.

——. 1991. "Depreciation to Meet a Situation of Overinvestment." In *International Financial Policy: Essays in Honor of Jacques J. Polak*, ed. Jacob A. Frenkel and Morris Goldstein, 46–57. Washington, D.C.: International Monetary Fund.

——. 1997. "The IMF Monetary Model: A Hardy Perennial." *Finance and Development* 34 (December): 16–19.

——. 1997. "The IMF Monetary Model at Forty." *IMF Working Paper*. April.

Pollack, Mark. 2002. "Learning from the Americanists (Again): Theory and Method in the Study of Delegation." *West European Politics* 25, no. 1: 200–219.

——. 2003. *The Engines of Integration? Delegation, Agency, and Agenda Setting in the European Union.* New York: Oxford University Press.

Porter, Theodore M. 1995. *Trust in Numbers: The Pursuit of Objectivity in Science and Public Life.* Princeton: Princeton University Press.

Preston, Julia. 1993. "No Mission to Burundi, U.N. Says; Peace Deployments Apparently on Hold." *Washington Post,* November 2, A10.

——. 1993. "U.N. Officials Scale Back Peacemaking Ambitions; Planned U.S. Withdrawal from Somalia Demonstrates Limitations." *Washington Post,* October 28, A40.

——. 1994."Supply Office at U.N. Hamstrung by Probe." *Washington Post,* August 20, A1, A14.

——. 1994. "Vision of a More Aggressive UN Now Dims." *Washington Post,* January 5, p. 24.

Price, Richard. 1998. "Reversing the Gunsights: Transnational Civil Society Targets Land Mines." *International Organization* 52 (Summer): 613–44.

Prunier, Gerard. 1999. *The Rwanda Crisis: History of a Genocide.* 2nd ed. New York: Columbia University Press.

Radelet, Steven, and Jeffrey D. Sachs. 1999. "What Have We Learned, So Far, from the Asian Financial Crisis." HIID Working Paper. http://www.hiid.edu/pub/other/aea122.pdf

Ratner, Steven. 1996. *The New UN Peacekeeping.* New York: St. Martin's Press.

Raz, Joseph, ed. 1990. *Authority.* New York: Cambridge University Press.

Reid, Tony. 1994. "Repatriation of Arkanese Muslims from Bangladesh to Burma, 1978–79: The 'Arranged' Reversal of the Flow of an Ethnic Minority." Paper presented at the Fourth International Research and Advisory Panel Conference, Somerville College, University of Oxford. January.

Reinisch, August. 2001. "Securing the Accountability of International Organizations." *Global Governance* 7, no. 2: 131–50.

Rikhye, I., M. Harbottle, and B. Egge. 1974. *The Thin Blue Line: International Peacekeeping and Its Future.* New Haven: Yale University Press.

Ringer, Fritz. 1997. *Max Weber's Methodology: The Unification of the Cultural and Social Sciences.* Cambridge: Harvard University Press.

Roberts, Adam, and Benedict Kingsbury. 1993. "Introduction: The UN's Roles in International Society since 1945." In *United Nations, Divided World: The UN's Roles in International Relations,* ed. A. Roberts and B. Kingsbury. New York: Oxford University Press.

——, eds. 1993. *United Nations, Divided World: The UN's Roles in International Relations.* New York: Oxford University Press.

Roberts, Clayton. 1996. *The Logic of Historical Explanation.* University Park: Pennsylvania State University Press.

Roe, Emery. 1994. *Narrative Policy Analysis: Theory and Practice.* Durham: Duke University Press.

Ruggie, John. 1993. "The U.N.: Wandering into the Void." *Foreign Affairs* 72 (November/December): 26–31.

——. 1998. *Constructing the World Polity.* New York: Routledge.

——. 1998. "What Makes the World Hang Together." *International Organization* 52, no. 3: 855–86.

Ruiz, Hiram. 1987. "When Refuges Won't Go Home: The Dilemma of Chadians in Sudan." Unpublished report for the U.S. Committee on Refugees.

Sagan, Scott. 1993. *The Limits of Safety: Organizations, Accidents, and Nuclear Weapons.* Princeton: Princeton University Press.

Sanford, Jonathan E. 1999. "IMF and World Bank: US Contributions and Agency Budgets." *Congressional Research Service Report for Congress RS20413.* http://www.cnie.org/nle/inter-51.html.

Sarooshi, Danesh. 1999. *The United Nations and the Development of Collective Security: The Delegation by the UN Security Council of Its Chapter VII Powers.* New York: Oxford University Press.

Schein, Edgar. 1992. *Organizational Culture and Leadership.* 2nd ed. San Francisco: Jossey Bass.

——. 1996. "Culture: The Missing Concept in Organization Studies." *Administrative Studies Quarterly* 41:229–40.

Schimmelfenig, Frank. 2003. *The EU, NATO and the Integration of Europe: Rules and Rhetoric.* New York: Cambridge University Press.

Schneider, Anne, and Helen Ingram. 1993. "The Social Construction of Target Populations: Implications for Politics and Policy." *American Political Science Review* 87, no. 2: 334–47.

Schnyder, Félix. 1965. "Les aspects juridiques actuels du problème des réfugiés." *Hague Academy of International Law, Recueil des cours,* 114.

Schutz, Alfred. 1970. *On Phenomenology and Social Relations.* Chicago: University of Chicago Press.

Scott, James C. 1998. *Seeing Like a State: How Certain Schemes to Improve the Human Condition Have Failed.* New Haven: Yale University Press.

Scott, John. *Power.* 2001. Cambridge: Polity Press.

Scott, W. Richard. 1987. "The Adolescence of Institutional Theory." *Administrative Studies Quarterly* 32, no. 4: 493–511.

——. 1992. *Organizations: Rational, Natural, and Open Systems.* 3rd ed. Englewood Cliffs, N.J.: Prentice Hall.

Searle, John. 1995. *The Construction of Social Reality.* New York: Free Press.

Selznick, Philip. 1943. "An Approach to a Theory of Bureaucracy." *American Sociological Review* 8, no. 1: 47–54.

——. 1953. *TVA and the Grass Roots: A Study in the Sociology of Formal Organization.* Berkeley: University of California Press.

——. 1957. *Leadership in Administration: A Sociological Interpretation.* Evanston: Peterson.

Sen, Amartya. 1999. *Development as Freedom.* New York: Knopf.

Sewell, William. "A Theory of Structure: Duality, Agency, and Transformation." *American Journal of Sociology* 98, no. 1 (1992): 1–29.

Shacknove, Andrew. 1993. "From Asylum to Containment." *International Journal of Refugee Law* 5, no. 4 (1993): 516–33.

Shanks, Cheryl, Harold K. Jacobson, and Jeffrey H. Kaplan. 1996. "Inertia and Change in the Constellation of International Governmental Organizations, 1981–1992." *International Organization* 50, no. 4: 593–627.

Shore, Cris, and Susan Wright, eds. 1997. *Anthropology of Policy: Critical Perspectives on Governance and Power.* New York: Routledge.

Siekmann, R. C. R. 1989. *Basic Documents on United Nations and Related Peacekeeping Forces.* 2nd enlarged ed. Dordrecht: Martinus Nijhoff.

Simmons, Beth A. 2000. "Legalization of International Monetary Affairs." *International Organization* 54, no. 3: 573–602.

Skran, Claudena. 1992. "The International Refugee Regime: The Historical and Contemporary Context of International Responses to Asylum Problems." In *Refugees and the Asylum Dilemma in the West,* ed. G. Loescher, 8–34. University Park: Pennsylvania State University Press.

Smith, Roger, and Brian Wynne, eds. 1989. *Expert Evidence: Interpreting Science in the Law.* New York: Routledge.

Snidal, Duncan. 1996. "Political Economy and International Institutions." *International Review of Law and Economics* 16:121–37.

Snow, David, E. Burke Rochford, Steven K. Worden, and Robert D. Benford. 1986. "Frame Alignment Processes, Micromobilization, and Movement Participation." *American Sociological Review* 51 (August): 464–81.

Starr, Paul. 1992. "Social Categories and Claims in the Liberal State." In *How Classification Works: Nelson Goodman among the Social Sciences,* ed. Mary Douglas and David Hull, 154–79. Edinburgh: Edinburgh University Press.

Stedman, Stephen. 1997. "The Perils of Peace Processes: Spoiler Problems in Peace Processes." *International Security* 22, no. 2: 5–53.

Stedman, Stephen John, Donald Rothchild, and Elizabeth Cousens, ed. 2002. *Ending Civil War: The Implementation of Peace Agreements.* Boulder: Lynne Rienner.

Stein, Barry. 1986. "Durable Solutions for Developing Country Refugees." *International Migration Review* 20, no. 2: 264–82.

Stein, Barry, and Frederick Cuny. 1993. "Repatriation in a Civil War/Conflict Situation." Paper presented at Roundtable Consultation on Voluntary Repatriation and UNHCR, Geneva, Switzerland. June 2–3.

Stewart, Jon. 1995. "U.N. Learns Hard Lessons on Peacekeeping." *San Francisco Chronicle,* March 28, A1.

Stiles, Kenneth W. 1981. *Negotiating Debt: The IMF Lending Process.* Boulder: Westview Press.

Stoessinger, John George. 1956. *The Refugee and the World Community.* Minneapolis: University of Minnesota Press.

Suchman, Mark. 1995. "Managing Legitimacy: Strategic and Institutional Approaches." *Academy of Management Review* 20, no. 3: 571–610.

Suhrke, Astri. 1999. "Dilemmas of Protection: The Log of the Kigali Battalion." In *The Path of a*

Genocide: The Rwanda Crisis from Uganda to Zaire, ed. H. Adelman and A. Suhrke, 253–70. New Brunswick, N.J.: Transaction Press.

Swidler, Ann. 1986. "Culture in Action: Symbols in Strategies." *American Sociological Review* 51, no. 2 (1986): 273–86.

Sztucki, Jerzy. 1989. "The Conclusions on the International Protection of Refugees Adopted by the Executive Committee of the UNHCR Programme." *International Journal of Refugee Law* 1, no. 3: 285–318.

Takahashi, Saul. 1997. "The UNHCR Handbook on Voluntary Repatriation: The Emphasis of Return or Protection." *International Journal of Refugee Law* 9, no. 4: 592–612.

Taylor, Chris. 1999. *Sacrifice as Terror: The Rwandan Genocide of 1994*. New York: Berg.

Tett, Gillian. 1994. "Red Tape Tangles Up UN Troops in Bosnia." *Financial Times*, January 21.

Tharoor, Shashi. 1996."The Changing Face of Peacekeeping." In *Soldiers for Peace: Fifty Years of UN Peacekeeping*, ed. B. Benton. New York: Facts on File.

Thatcher, Mark, and Alec Stone Sweet. 2002. "Theory and Practice of Delegation to Non-majoritarian Institutions." *West European Politics* 25, no. 1: 1–22.

Thornberry, Cedric. 1994. "Civil Affairs in the Development of UN Peacekeeping." *International Peacekeeping* 1, no. 4: 471–84.

Tversky, A., and D. Kahneman. 1974. "Judgment under Uncertainty: Heuristics and Biases." *Science* 185:453–59.

Union of International Associations, ed. 2003. *Yearbook of International Organizations, 2003–2004*. 40th ed. Vol. 1B. Munich: K. G. Saur.

United Nations. 1956. "Second and Final Report of the Secretary-General on the Plan for an Emergency International United Nations Force." UN doc. A/3302. November 6.

——. 1957. "Regulations for the United Nations Emergency Force." February 20.

——. 1978. "Report of the Secretary-General on the Implementation of Security Council Resolution 425." UN doc. S/12611. March 19.

——. 1992. "Note on International Protection." UN doc. A/AC.96/799.

——. 1993. "Note on International Protection." UN doc. A/AC.96/815.

——. 1994. "Report of the Commission of Inquiry Established Pursuant to Security Council Resolution 885 (1993) to Investigate Armed Attacks on UNOSOM II Personnel Which Led to Casualties among Them." Internal Memo. February 24.

——. 1994. "Second Progress Report of the Secretary-General on the United Nations Assistance Mission for Rwanda." S/1994/360. March 30.

——. 1994. *Statement on the Conditions for the Deployment and Renewal of Peacekeeping Operations*. Security Council Presidential Statement. S/PRST/1994/22.

——. 1995. "United Nations Peacekeeping Information Notes." New York: UN Press.

——. 1996. *The Blue Helmets: A Review of UN Peace-Keeping*. 3rd edition. New York: United Nations, Department of Public Information.

——. 1996. *The United Nations and Rwanda, 1993–1996*. New York: United Nations, Department of Public Information.

——. 1999. *Final Report of the International Commission of Inquiry* (Rwanda). New York: United Nations.

United Nations. General Assembly. 1999. "Report of the Secretary-General Pursuant to General Assembly Resolution 53/35: The Fall of Srebrenica." A/54/549. November 15.

United Nations Department of Peacekeeping Operations. 1996. *Comprehensive Report on Lessons Learned from United Nations Assistance Mission for Rwanda* (UNAMIR). New York: United Nations.

United Nations Development Program. 1994. *Human Development Report 1994*. New York: Oxford University Press.

United Nations High Commissioner for Refugees. 1956. Resolution 1006. November 9.

——. 1957. Resolution 1039. January 23.

——. 1957. Resolution 1167 (X11). November 26.

——. 1961. Resolution 1673 (XVI). December 18.

——. 1961. "The United Nations High Commissioner for Refugees Draws Attention to Refugee Problems in Africa." *UNHCR Reports*, no. 11 (December): 12–13.

——. 1963. "The Meaning of Material Assistance." *UNHCR Reports*, no. 24 (May–June): 1–10.

——. 1967. "The Addis Ababa Conference." *UNHCR Reports*, no. 49 (Nov./Dec. 1967–Jan. 1968): 6–7.

——. 1995. *State of the World's Refugees: In Search of Solutions*. New York: Oxford University Press.

United Nations High Commissioner for Refugees Executive Committee. 1996. "Annual Theme: The Pursuit and Implementation of Durable Solutions." A/AC.96/872.
——. Various years. "Conclusions."
——. Various years. "Note on International Protection."
——. "UNHCR's Protection Role in Countries of Origin." 1996. EC/46/SC/CRP.17. March 18.
"United Nations Peacekeeping: Trotting to the Rescue." 1994. *Economist*, June 25, pp. 19–22.
United States Committee for Refugees. 1995. *The Return of the Rohingyan Refugees to Burma: Voluntary Repatriation or Refoulement?* Washington, D.C. March.
——. 1996. "USCR Site Visit to Bangladesh, June 20–July 1." Issue Brief.
Urquhart, Brian. 1993. *Ralph Bunche: An American Life*. New York: Norton.
——. 2000. "In the Name of Humanity." *New York Review of Books* 47:19–22.
Vaughan, Diane. 1996. *The Challenger Launch Decision: Risky Technology, Culture, and Deviance at NASA*. Chicago: University of Chicago Press.
——. 1999. "The Dark Side of Organizations." *Annual Review of Sociology* 25:271–305.
Vines, David, and Christopher L. Gilbert. 2003. *The IMF and Its Critics: Reform of Global Financial Architecture*. New York: Cambridge University Press.
Wade, Robert. 1996. "Japan, the World Bank, and the Art of Paradigm Maintenance: The East Asian Miracle in Political Perspective." *New Left Review* 217:3–36.
Wallace, Michael, and J. David Singer. 1970. "Intergovernmental Organizations in the Global System, 1815–1964: A Quantitative Analysis." *International Organization* 24:239–87.
Warner, Daniel. 1994. "Voluntary Repatriation and the Meaning of Returning Home: A Critique of Liberal Mathematics." *Journal of Refugee Studies* 7, nos. 2/3: 160–74.
Waters, Tony. 2001. *Bureaucratizing the Good Samaritan: The Limitations of Humanitarian Relief Operations*. Boulder: Westview Press.
Weaver, Catherine, and Ralf Leiteritz. 2002. "Organizational Culture and Change at the World Bank." Manuscript, University of Kansas, Lawrence.
Weber, Max. 1947. *Theory of Social and Economic Organization*. New York: Oxford University Press.
——. 1978. *Economy and Society*. Berkeley: University of California Press.
——. 1978. *From Max Weber: Essays in Sociology*. Ed. and trans. H. H. Gerth and C. Wright Mills. New York: Oxford University Press.
Wedeen, Lisa. 2002. "Conceptualizing Culture: Possibilities for Political Science." *American Political Science Review* 96 (December): 713–28.
Weick, Karl E. 1995. *Sensemaking in Organizations*. Thousand Oaks, Calif.: Sage.
Weiss, Thomas, ed. 1995. *The United Nations and Civil Wars*. Boulder: Lynne Rienner.
Weiss, Thomas, and Amir Pasic. 1996. "Reinventing UNHCR: Enterprising Humanitarians in the Former Yugoslavia, 1991–95." *Global Governance* 3:41–58.
Wellens, Karel. 2002. *Remedies against International Organisations*. New York: Cambridge University Press.
Wendt, Alexander. 1998. "Constitution and Causation in International Relations." *Review of International Studies* 24:101–18.
Weyland, Kurt. 1998. "The Political Fate of Market Reform in Latin America, Africa, and Eastern Europe." *International Studies Quarterly* 42:645–73.
White, N. D. 1993. *Keeping the Peace*. Manchester: Manchester University Press.
Whitman, James. 1999. *Peacekeeping and UN Agencies*. New York: Frank Cass.
Williams, Michael C. 1996. "Hobbes and International Relations: A Reconsideration." *International Organization* 50:213–36.
Williamson, Oliver, ed. 1990. *Organization Theory from Chester Barnard to the Present and Beyond*. New York: Oxford University Press.
Willum, Bjørn. 1999. "Legitimizing Inaction towards Genocide in Rwanda: A Matter of Misperception?" *International Peacekeeping* 6, no. 3: 11–30.
Winch, Peter. 1967. "Authority." In *Political Philosophy*, ed. Anthony Quinton. New York: Oxford University Press.
Wohlstetter, Roberta. 1962. *Pearl Harbor: Warning and Decision*. Stanford: Stanford University Press.
Woods, Ngaire. 2003. "Accountability, Governance, and the Reform of the IMF." In *The IMF and Its Critics: Reform of Global Financial Architecture*, ed. D. Vines and C. L. Gilbert, 396–416. New York: Cambridge University Press.
Woods, Ngaire. 2004. "The IMF, the World Bank, and International Relations." Manuscript.
Woods, Ngaire, and Amrita Narlikar. 2001. "Governance and the Limits of Accountability: The

WTO, the IMF and the World Bank." *International Social Science Journal* 53 (November): 569–83.

Wright, Susan, ed. 1994. *Anthropology of Organizations*. New York: Routledge.

Zacher, Mark W., and Richard M. Price, eds. 2004. *The United Nations and Global Security*. New York: Palgrave Macmillan.

Zakaria, Fareed. 2003. *The Future of Freedom: Illiberal Democracy at Home and Abroad*. New York: Norton.

Zald, Mayer N. 1996. "Culture, Ideology, and Strategic Framing." In *Comparative Perspectives on Social Movements: Political Opportunities, Mobilizing Structures, and Cultural Framing*, ed. D. McAdam, J. McCarthy, and M. Zald. New York: Cambriuge University Press.

Zegart, Amy. 1999. *Flawed by Design: The Evolution of the CIA, JCS, and NSC*. Stanford: University of Stanford Press.

Zieck, Marjolene. 1997. *UNHCR and Voluntary Repatriation of Refugees*. Boston: Martinus Nijhoff.

Zolberg, Aristide, Astri Suhrke, and Sergio Aguayo. 1989. *Escape from Violence: Conflict and the Refugee Crisis in the Developing World*. New York: Oxford University Press.

INDEX